EASY WEEKEND GETAWAYS FROM

Washington, DC

Short Breaks in Delaware, Maryland, Virginia, and Beyond

Jess Moss

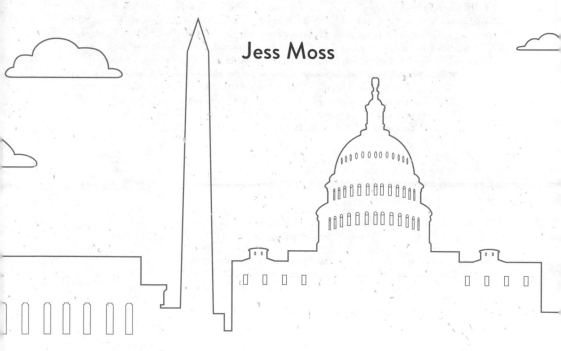

The Countryman Press
A division of W. W. Norton & Company
Independent Publishers Since 1923

We would appreciate any comments or corrections. Please write to:
Countryman Weekenders Editor
The Countryman Press
A division of W. W. Norton & Company
500 Fifth Avenue
New York, NY 10110

Manufacturing by Versa Press
Series book design by Faceout Studio, Amanda Kreutzer
Production manager: Devon Zahn

The Countryman Press
www.countrymanpress.com

A division of W. W. Norton & Company, Inc.
500 Fifth Avenue, New York, NY 10110
www.wwnorton.com

978-1-68268-386-6

10 9 8 7 6 5 4 3 2 1

For my friends and family

Contents

Welcome

As you may be aware, the location of Washington, DC, is one of the most underrated things about the city: we're within striking distance of all types of adventure. You can read by the ocean one weekend and hike mountains in Shenandoah National Park or visit a Civil War battlefield the next. Add a booming local wine and beer scene and there are now more reasons to get out of town than ever before.

This book is meant to be an idea generator for ways to weekend outside the city. It's a curated menu of trips, from wine-tasting escapes to stress-bashing hikes to lake-house trips with your crew.

You can use this guide as a checklist of cool DC getaways to cross off, or play weekend roulette—just close your eyes, flip the pages, and pick an adventure.

// View of Harpers Ferry from the
Maryland Heights trail

To write this book, I drew a roughly 3-hour radius around DC and then spent the better part of a year weekending all over it. I drove over 6,000 miles, tried upwards of 250 beers and wines (rough life, I know), and got hundreds of tips from locals about what makes their towns so special.

The following chapters are the result: an all-star lineup of my favorite weekend getaways from DC.

How to Use This Book

We are making a few assumptions in this guide:

1. You live in or near DC. Totally fine if you don't, but you may see some comparisons or nods to Washington stuff that doesn't translate if you're not from the area.
2. You have a smartphone. We'll include basic info such as names and websites for any places in this guide. We're guessing, however, that you're going to Google or Yelp most places before going. For that reason, we're saving trees and not printing out all the opening hours, addresses, etc. Please look stuff up before you show up somewhere—hours and prices change, and this book can't keep up with the Internet for those things.
3. You're going to map to wherever you're going (probably with your smartphone). We've got general directional info so you can know roughly where you're going, but please just use Waze or Google or whatever mapping app you like. That said, we will call out when we had trouble routing using an app, with instructions on how you can get there.

What Stuff Costs

We've gauged restaurants and hotels based on the following price ranges. It's not all that scientific. It's meant more to give you a ballpark:

RESTAURANTS: the average cost for a main entrée (or equivalent, such as a few tapas):

    $ = $1–10
    $$ = $11–30
    $$$ = $31–50
    $$$$ = $50+

HOTELS: the standard two-person room rate for a summer Saturday:

$ = $100 or less
$$ = $101–200
$$$ = $201–350
$$$$ = $350+

Some Notes on Safety

There's a lot of booze in this book. We make these recommendations with the assumption that you won't do anything stupid. Follow all the rules, don't drink where you're not supposed to, and choose a designated driver if you're doing anything that involves driving.

The same goes for hiking and all the outdoorsy fun: pay attention to all park or local regulations (they're usually posted online). We've done our best to call out safety tips throughout the guide, but it's on you to be careful—we can't be responsible for anything that happens while you're attempting the stuff in this book. Basically, weekend at your own risk!

Keep Us Posted!

Finally, just because something isn't in this book doesn't mean it sucks. Some cities are too big to be a fit for this guide (I see you, Baltimore, Philly, and New York). Others are incredible places that we simply didn't have space to include; new hotspots are emerging all the time.

We'd love to hear about what you find while checking out the stuff in this guide. You can share your tips with us via email (jess@dcweekendgetaways.com), or hashtag your adventures #EasyWeekendGetaways.

Oh, and we're still weekending too—follow along at @weekendsfromdc for new finds around the DC area.

Happy travels!
—Jess

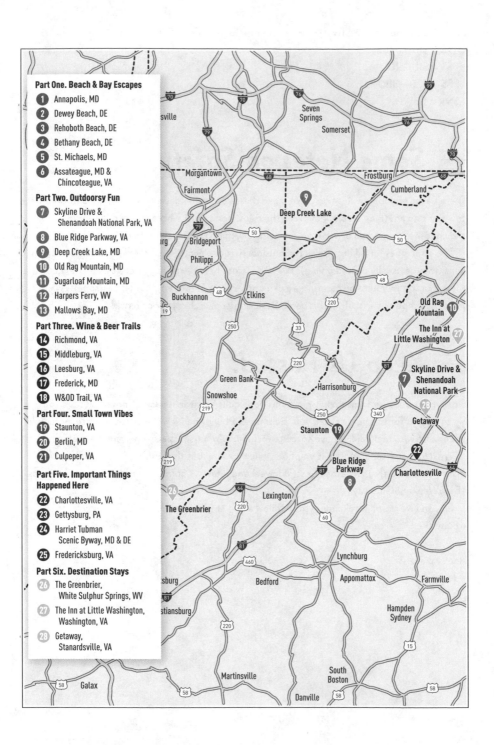

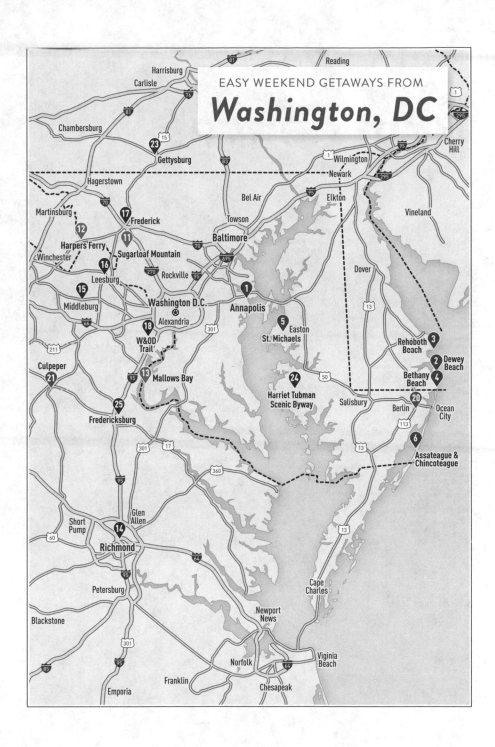

EASY WEEKEND GETAWAYS FROM

Washington, DC

Reading

Harrisburg

Carlisle

Chambersburg

23 Gettysburg

Harrisburg

Hagerstown

Martinsburg

12 **17** Frederick

Harpers Ferry

Winchester **11**

Sugarloaf Mountain

16 Rockville

Leesburg

15

Middleburg

Washington D.C. **1**

Annapolis

18 Alexandria

W&OD Trail

Culpeper

21 **13** Mallows Bay

25

Fredericksburg

Wilmington

Newark

Bel Air

Towson

Baltimore

Elkton

Cherry Hill

Vineland

Dover

5 Easton

St. Michaels

24

Harriet Tubman Scenic Byway

Salisbury

Rehoboth Beach **3**

2 Dewey Beach

Bethany Beach **4**

20 Ocean City

Berlin

6 Assateague & Chincoteague

Glen Allen

Short Pump

14

Richmond

Petersburg

Blackstone

Newport News

Cape Charles

Emporia

Franklin

Norfolk

Chesapeak

Virginia Beach

Top 10 Experiences

1 • Take in the Shenandoah views from Skyline Drive
(Chapter 7)

2 • Eat crabs straight from the bay on the Eastern Shore
(Chapter 5)

3 • Pair presidents with wine in Charlottesville
(Chapter 22)

4 • Climb Old Rag
(Chapter 10)

5 • Bike the battlefield at Gettysburg
(Chapter 23)

6 • Stay for Sunday Funday in Dewey Beach
(Chapter 2)

7 • Splurge on Michelin greatness at the Inn at Little Washington
(Chapter 27)

8 • Float down nature's lazy river near Harpers Ferry
(Chapter 12)

9 • Do a beer bar crawl in Richmond
(Chapter 14)

10 • Camp with wild ponies on Assateague
(Chapter 6)

1 Charlottesville's presidential history
2 Freshly caught blue crabs on Maryland's Eastern Shore
3 Overlook on Skyline Drive

Part One

Beach & Bay Escapes

1

Get Out on the Water

Annapolis, MD

Take a sail, eat boat-to-table, and grab a drink by the bay in the area's maritime mecca.

FROM DC: 32 MILES · 45 MINUTES
TRIP LENGTH: DAY TRIP OR OVERNIGHT

DO	EAT	DRINK	BUY
boat	blue crabs	Painkiller on the docks at Pusser's	oyster shell decor

Imagine Old Town Alexandria, but with a nautical twist. That's what you'll find in Annapolis, a.k.a. America's Sailing Capital. (It's also Maryland's state capital, but let's pause the political talk this weekend.) Set on a thumb of land etched out as creeks and the Severn River spill into the Chesapeake Bay, the city's been centered around sailing and port life for more than 300 years.

Sit by the docks and you'll see baller yachts, historic schooners, and hundreds of white-masted sailboats. Walk the red brick streets and you'll brush shoulders with midshipmen from the US Naval Academy—the midshipmen use these waters as a training ground. What's all the fuss about? Hop aboard a boat to see for yourself.

☰ *Getting to Annapolis*

Annapolis is essentially a straight shot on Route 50 east out of DC. Swing a right on Rowe Boulevard when you get here, which will lead you straight to the city's wood-domed State House and the top of Main Street. The route takes about 45 minutes with no traffic . . . but this is Washington, so expect traffic.

There are a number of parking lots and garages in the downtown shopping district—you can park and walk or use the free **Circulator** shuttle (it even has an app so you can see where the next bus is). Don't bother parking on the street; you'll have to move your car every 2 hours.

You *can* get to Annapolis without a car, but it'll double your travel time or cost. Greyhound costs around $14 but takes 2.5 hours because of a transfer in Baltimore. You can metro to New Carrollton and Uber from there, but it'll cost you about $30 for the drive alone.

>> **Photo Stop:** Swing into the National Arboretum on your way out of DC for a pic of the stately old US Capitol columns, now set up in a field.

☰ *Get Your Bearings*

Ditch your car when you get downtown; the city is incredibly walkable. A good way to get the lay of the land is to start by the State House and walk down Main Street to the water. When you hit City Dock and Ego Alley at the bottom of the hill, hang a left to visit the Naval Academy, or go right to cross the bridge into Eastport.

>> **More Info:** www.visitannapolis.org

☰ *Pick a Boat*

Take a break from solid ground and feel that fresh (read: non-Potomac) breeze in your hair. Boating is THE thing to do in Annapolis, especially from mid-April through mid-October. Watch the calendar for boat shows and regattas—they're fun times to be in town, but it can be trickier for you to actually get out on the water.

CLASSIC CRUISIN': SCHOONER *WOODWIND*

Board at Pusser's Caribbean Grille • www.schoonerwoodwind.com • Mid-April–September and late October • $46

Remember that classy sailboat from *Wedding Crashers*? You can hop aboard the very same schooner for a cruise around the bay. The 74-foot sailboat was custom-built for the Chesapeake Bay. Two-hour tours past the Naval Academy, Bay Bridge, Kent Island, and more run daily (routes depend on the wind). Go all in with a sunset sail. *Coastal Living* says this is one of the top sunset cruises in the United States. All boats are stocked with a cash bar. Buy your tickets online up to six days ahead of time.

// Schooner *Woodwind* at sunset

BOAT ON A BUDGET: *HARBOR QUEEN*

Board at City Dock • cruisesonthebay.com • Late March–September • October/November (weather permitting) • $17

Cheap, quick, and picturesque, the 40-minute *Harbor Queen* is a good bet for day-trippers. The vessel looks like an old riverboat and has lots of outdoor space, plus wine, beer and mixed drinks available to buy. You can't book this one in advance, so just head to City Dock and grab your tickets the day you want to cruise.

QUICK TRIP: WATER TAXI

Board at City Dock • cruisesonthebay.com • mid-May–September • $3 and up

If you're tight on time, you can still get on the water. Water taxis will zip you between City Dock and Eastport in a matter of minutes while still giving you that "I boated in Annapolis" cred. They'll also drop you elsewhere on demand. It's cash- or voucher-only.

PHOTO OP: THOMAS POINT LIGHTHOUSE CRUISE

Board at City Dock • cruisesonthebay.com • Late March–September, October/November (weather permitting) • $28

Cruising for the 'gram? Hop aboard the Thomas Point Lighthouse Cruise. The trip whisks you to historic Thomas Point Shoal Light, a solitary house propped up on a shoal in the middle of the bay. (If you want to actually disembark and explore the lighthouse, the Annapolis Maritime Museum runs a different cruise on select dates to do that.)

SINK OR SWIM: ANNAPOLIS SAILING SCHOOL

Marina is 2 miles from downtown • annapolissailing.com •April–October • $200 and up

Learn the difference between a tack and a jibe with a one- or two-day sailing fundamentals class. Not sure the captain's life is for you? There's a 2-hour TrySail course, where you'll learn some basics without sucking up a full day.

DIY: BOAT RENTALS

Prefer to captain your own skiff? There are a handful of boat rental outfitters in Annapolis. **GetMyBoat** (www.getmyboat.com) is like an Airbnb for boat rentals, so you can choose what size, type, and price fits your crew. (This company has boats for rent all over the area, including in DC.) **Annapolis Electric Boat Rentals** (aebrentals.com) has eco-friendly battery powered boats that seat up to 10 people, have audio hookups for your phone, and allow alcohol on board. The electric boats are basically like a golf cart on water, so, as long as you have a driver's license and are over 21, you're good to go. (Kayaking and stand-up paddle-boarding tours are also available.)

>> **Ahoy Deals:** Groupon sometimes has deals for up to 50 percent off sailing lessons or bay cruises.

≡ *While You're Here*

SHOP YOUR WAY DOWN MAIN STREET

The city's main drag is lined with colorful shops, galleries, pubs, and eateries. Don't be fooled by the tourist shops. There are some cool local boutiques in the mix. Pick up some preppy nautical styles at **The Lucky Knot** (www.theluckyknot.com) or flip through vintage maritime tomes at **Back Creek Books** (www.backcreekbooks.com). **Hobo Handbags'** (www.hobobags .com) flagship store is also here, steps from City Dock.

>> **Tip:** For more retail exercise, Maryland Avenue also has a strip of design and antiques shops up by the State House. There's a "First Sunday" arts festival here between May and November.

TOUR THE UNITED STATES NAVAL ACADEMY

www.usna.edu/Visit

Visitors can explore the gorgeous home of the US Navy and Marine Corps with free entry. You need a driver's license or government ID; it varies by what state you're from, so check online. Head to the Visitor Center, which has exhibits and a gift shop for Navy swag, and is the starting point for guided tours of the Yard (just show up; the tours run all day). You can

// View of Annapolis from the water

also explore on your own—just don't miss the Main Chapel, with its original 19th-century stained glass windows (including a Tiffany window) and crypt dedicated to John Paul Jones, the "Father of the US Navy."

YACHT WATCH IN EGO ALLEY

If you've ever dreamed of owning a yacht, here's where you can . . . see what it's like for other people. These fancy vessels parade through Ego Alley, whose name comes from the fact that captains have to steer their ships through the narrow strip of harbor while everyone at City Dock watches. It's like watching someone parallel park a very large, very expensive car.

CHECK OUT EASTPORT

This relaxed faux-breakaway republic across Spa Creek has a more neighborhood-y, less touristy vibe than downtown. (They also have their own flag.) There are a handful of places to dine with water views here, and it's an easy walk or quick ferry ride from City Dock to get here and escape the crowds.

☰ *Good Eats*

When you come to Annapolis between April and December, you've gotta get crabs. Even places that don't specialize in seafood will often have crab incorporated into the menu somehow. Beyond the blues, Annapolis has quite the foodie scene—from rustic American to Thai.

>> **Coffee stop:** If you're a **Ceremony Coffee** (ceremonycoffee.com) fan, think about detouring to the company's founding location and roastery, about 10 minutes from downtown Annapolis.

// Crabs are a must between April and December

CANTLER'S RIVERSIDE INN

4 miles north of downtown • www.cantlers.com • $$ • seafood

Cantler's is one of the city's most famous crab houses—they have watermen delivering the daily catch straight to the restaurant's docks. Because of this, you'll have to fend off crowds, and, to be honest, some say there are better crabs in Maryland, but this crab house is an institution.

MIKE'S CRAB HOUSE

6 miles southwest of downtown • www.mikescrabhouse.com • $$ • seafood

Mike's is another popular option and is often the place where people who don't like Cantler's tell you to go instead. Both spots have water views.

BOATYARD BAR & GRILL

Eastport • www.boatyardbarandgrill.com • $$ • seafood

This casual Eastport eatery is big, bustling, and serves jumbo-portion sizes. Rumor has it Michelle Obama declared the crab cakes here the best she's ever eaten.

ANNAPOLIS ICE CREAM COMPANY

Downtown • annapolisicecream.com • $ • ice cream

Prepare your stomach; the scoop sizes here are no joke. This is the best ice cream in Annapolis, and they rotate their flavors daily, so there's often something new to try. If you call in advance, they'll even make a custom flavor for you. If this place is too busy, **Kilwin's**, just down the street, is also very popular.

IRON ROOSTER

Downtown • www.ironroosterallday.com • $$ • American/comfort food

If you're a believer in all-day breakfast, Iron Rooster is your spot. It's elevated comfort food—think fried chicken and waffles, grits, and "cakes on cakes"—which is crab cakes piled on cornmeal pancakes.

CHICK & RUTH'S DELLY

Downtown • www.chickandruths.com • $$ • deli

A local fixture for over 50 years, this old-fashioned deli specializes in crab cakes, pies, and enormous milkshakes that gained fame on *Man vs. Food*. Every morning, everyone stands and pledges allegiance to the flag.

FLAMANT

West Annapolis • flamantmd.com • $$$ • European

This cozy bungalow pushes the envelope, making it one of the foodiest spots in Naptown. Helmed by former DC chef Frederik de Pue, the menu puts a Maryland spin on European fare, with dishes such as crab rolls and Bouillabaisse. It's in the becoming-cool neighborhood of West Annapolis, about a 15-minute walk from downtown.

MARKET HOUSE

City Dock • annapolismarkethouse.com • $ • market

For a more grab-and-go style meal, come to this historic food hall, which originally opened in the 1850s and was refurbished and reopened in 2018. Poke bowls, crab cakes, paninis, and kombucha are available at various stations.

LEVEL

Arts District • levelannapolis.com • $$ • tapas

Everything's about sharing at this social small-plates lounge. Most dishes put a thoughtful spin on globally inspired dishes and are powered by local ingredients. The fried Brussels sprouts are a fave.

VIN909

Eastport • vin909.com • $$ • New American

This trendy wine bar and restaurant over in Eastport serves its pizzas, burgers, and seafood dishes with a bit of playful snark. The menu changes seasonally, but you can count on locally sourced ingredients and an amazingly affordable selection of wines. Note that parking's tough if you're going to drive, and that they don't take reservations.

Time for a Drink

PUSSER'S CARIBBEAN GRILLE

pussersusa.com

Come for the views, stay for the Painkiller cocktails and rum runner–vibe at this waterfront bar at the Annapolis Waterfront Hotel. It's right on the docks and is one of the liveliest places in town.

RAMS HEAD TAVERN

www.ramsheadtavern.com

This family-run bar on Main Street serves over 100 types of beer from around the world, including some specialty house brews. They also have a good seafood menu, and live music on-site at Rams Head On Stage.

GALWAY BAY

galwaybaymd.com

This authentic Irish pub on Maryland Street has a homey atmosphere, great service, and no TVs, because they want people to actually talk to one another.

BLACKWALL HITCH

www.theblackwallhitch.com

Great cocktails come with rooftop views overlooking the harbor at this Eastport hotspot. There's live music of all genres most weekend nights, and on Sunday they do a jazz brunch.

Stay Over

Annapolis is an easy day trip from DC—you could even stay for dinner before making the trek home. But if you need more than a day's worth of water time, you'll have plenty of places to spend the night, from all the chain hotel options (some of the cheaper ones are located a little farther from downtown) to boutiques and even boats. Prices drop as you move beyond the downtown core.

ANNAPOLIS WATERFRONT HOTEL

www.annapoliswaterfront.com • $$$

Take in the harbor views from the city's only waterfront hotel. The upscale Autograph Collection Hotel is steps from City Dock—but enough steps to be out of jostling distance from summertime crowds.

STAY ON A BOAT

www.airbnb.com • prices vary

Meet **Airbnb**, Annapolis style. You can rent your own boat apartment on the site, complete with cabins, bathroom, and a kitchenette. The schooner *Woodwind* (www.schoonerwoodwind .com • $$$) also hosts overnight guests on its ship via the Boat and Breakfast package. Take the sunset sail, then settle into your bunk and get breakfast on board the next day.

RENTAL SCENE

Aside from the aforementioned boatbnbs, you'll find plenty of options here, from little bungalows to historic homes to newly renovated apartments.

≡ *When to Go*

You'll find things to do in Annapolis all year, but if boating's your goal, visit between April and October, when most tours operate. Annapolis hosts some major events throughout the year—plan ahead to join the fun, but be ready for crowds and higher hotel rates during a few big weekends.

Weekends to Plan For (or Avoid):

- **Annapolis Croquet Match (April):** A few thousand people come out each year to watch this riveting rivalry between the Naval Academy and nearby St. John's College. Spectators usually dress up Great Gatsby–style and turn it into a big lawn picnic and party.
- **Navy Commissioning Week (May):** The weeklong series of events leading up to graduation at the US Naval Academy is full of festivities. Many of the happenings are open to the public. Expect higher hotel rates.
- **Annapolis Crab Feast (August):** It's said to be the world's largest crab feast. The Rotary Club hosts the all-you-can-eat (and drink!) event every year to raise money for charity.

- **Navy Football Games (Fall):** Navy football weekends usually draw big crowds. It can be a ton of fun to cheer for the Navy blue and gold, but expect hotel prices to spike.
- **US Sailboat Show (October):** The biggest and oldest event of its kind, this is sort of like the annual Apple event, but for sailboats. New models are unveiled, and people come from all over the world to browse the boats.
- **US Powerboat Show (October):** Sailboats don't get all the love in Naptown. At this annual event, powerboats, from fishing skiffs to full-blown yachts, are front and center.

GOOD TO KNOW

- Maryland's capital. Sailing capital. Annapolis was *also* the capital of the United States for a hot second, at the end of the Revolutionary War. (The Treaty of Paris, which ended said war, was signed here in 1784.)
- The State House dome is the country's largest wood dome constructed without any nails.
- The Annapolis Rotary Club's annual all-you-can-eat crab feast is the largest crab feast in the world.

BEEN HERE, DONE THAT?

- Repeat visit! Go a bit farther afield, with a visit to Great Frogs Winery and Quiet Waters Park.
- Check out St. Michaels, a charming little waterfront town on Maryland's Eastern Shore (Chapter 5)
- Add another state capital to your travel list with a trip to Richmond, VA (Chapter 14).

2

Drink All the Orange Crushes

Dewey Beach, DE

Get after it at Delaware's biggest party beach, where it feels like college never ended.

FROM DC: 124 MILES · 3 HOURS (OR UP TO 5, DEPENDING ON TRAFFIC) | TRIP LENGTH: WEEKEND

DO	EAT	DRINK	BUY
bar hop	late-night pizza	Orange Crush	Advil

As the saying goes, Dewey Beach is "a way of life." That way of life usually includes an adult beverage . . . or many. The small Delaware beach town turns fun AF during summer, as seemingly every twenty-something from DC, Baltimore, Philly, and even New York comes here for warm beachy days and hazy dancy nights.

Most of your time will be spent bouncing between the beach and the bars, with some breaks to change clothes and eat. Wash it all down with an Orange Crush—the beach's unofficial cocktail.

☰ Getting to Dewey Beach

The most common way to get here from DC is to drive, typically caravan-style with your beach house crew.

To get here, you'll head east out of Washington on Route 50 and cross the Bay Bridge. Around Wye Mills, Route 404 branches off and takes you through Maryland towards the beaches. Near the Delaware state line you'll branch off onto Route 16, which takes you across the state to Route 1, a.k.a. the Coastal Highway. This road runs right through Dewey Beach; you don't have to turn off to get to the action. There are a few alternate routes, so check the traffic and a map app before you leave. During the summer, the best times to leave DC are Thursdays and Fridays before 10 a.m. or after 10 p.m.

As you're driving into town, keep an eye out. The elevated blood alcohol level around here causes people to dart across the street without much warning.

If you don't have a car, **BestBus** (www.bestbus.com) runs a summer bus between DC and Dewey ($40 each way).

Once you're here, you won't need (or want) a car, but be careful because parking enforcement is strict. If you're renting a house or have a hotel, ask them where to park before you get here. Kiosks around town sell parking permits. There's also a storefront near Bottle & Cork that has them.

If you're heading here for a night out from another beach town, don't drive. The legendary shore shuttle, the **Jolly Trolley** (www.jollytrolley.com), runs partiers between Rehoboth and Dewey Beach. It runs until 2 a.m. and costs $3. An Uber or taxi from Bethany Beach is only about $30.

☰ Get Your Bearings

Dewey sits in the middle of the string of beach towns that line Delaware's Atlantic coast. To the north is Rehoboth, while to the south is a stretch of undeveloped state parks, and then Bethany Beach.

DINNER ON THE WAY HOME

Cap off a weekend of partying with some Chinese take-out. Luckily, one of DC's best is directly on your route home. Tucked in a Days Inn across from the Arboretum in Northeast, **Panda Gourmet** (www.pandagourmet-dc.com) has take-out, and you can order online before you arrive.

One mile long and three blocks wide, Dewey is compact and walkable. The ocean bookends the east side of town, while the west backs up to Rehoboth Bay. The Coastal Highway (Highway 1) runs right through town, with most of the bars clustered at the central and southern ends of the strip.

>>   **More Info:** www.townofdeweybeach.com; www.visitsoutherndelaware.com

≡ *Party Dewey-Style*

One word: Pedialite.

Your shoes will stick to the bar floors. Your nights will be sweaty and hazy. There might be a fight. Or a dance-floor make-out. There'll probably be late-night pizza. There'll definitely be hangovers.

Dewey's small enough that you can bounce around and see where the night takes you. That said, there's also a certain flow to a Dewey weekend, with bars claiming days and times on the circuit. Here's what a typical weekend itinerary could look like:

// Dewey Beach bar floor

Friday Night

If you're able to sneak out of work early, head to **northbeach** (www.northbeachdewey.com) for free tacos, every Friday at around 4 p.m. (If you're a Dewey veteran, you may associate Friday with Taco Toss at **The Lighthouse** (lighthousedeweybeach.com). At this writing, that spot was closed for renovation and expected to reopen in 2019. In the meantime, northbeach has picked up the baton.)

As the night goes on, northbeach gets a bit clubbier, mixing live bands with DJs. Stick it out here or make your way to one of the other bars—just remember that bars start charging cover at a certain hour.

Come home whenever they kick you out of the bars. Chug water. Pass out.

Saturday Morning

Wake up and drag yourself out to get some coffee or brunch.

After you're caffeinated, make your way to the beach. Unlike Bethany and Rehoboth, there isn't a boardwalk at Dewey. Instead, cross-streets lead from the main drag past houses and dunes and onto the sand. It can get pretty crowded, so if you're with a group you'll want to stake out a spot early.

There's a lot going on all day on the beach—people playing football in the surf, swimming or body-surfing waves (it's not ideal to *surf*-surf here). There aren't any beach kiosks to rent equipment from, so if you want chairs, umbrellas, or boards, you've gotta bring them yourself. Same with food; you'll have to head up to the town for any eats.

Keep in mind that alcohol is illegal on the beach; you'll get a ticket if you're caught with any booze. Dogs also aren't allowed between 9:30 a.m. and 5:30 p.m. in the summer.

Saturday Afternoon

At some point, you can head back over to northbeach. No change of clothes required, this place has a sandy floor and sometimes people end up in the water off the docks.

When you're ready to ramp up the day drinking, post up at **Bottle & Cork** (www.bottleand corkdewey.com), which does an amazing Saturday afternoon jam sesh. The cover bands play songs from Tom Petty to Taylor Swift, and the music goes on all night. Watch the schedule for bands such as The Legwarmers. Cash only, FYI!

You can try to power through, but a lot of people pause around dinner time to refuel, pre-game, and get ready for the night.

Saturday Night

Saturday nights at Dewey look a little like Bourbon Street with sand. A steady flow of intoxicated twenty-somethings stumble from bar to bar along the main strip. Expect lines wherever you go, and some places have covers (so make sure those friends you're meeting are *actually* there before you go in).

The good thing about cover charges is it's usually because there are live bands playing. Dewey is known for a number of bands that return every year to perform cover jams. Do a little background research before you get here, and you'll know who's playing where—which can help you beat the lines. (Blue Label, Kristin and the Noise, and Love Seed Mama Jump are good ones to watch for.)

ORANGE CRUSH

This refreshing summer cocktail hails from Ocean City, but has become synonymous with Dewey, too. It's simultaneously delicious and dangerous. Here's how to make it at home:

- 2 ounces orange vodka
- 2 ounces triple sec
- Lemon-lime soda
- 1 juiced orange

Pour it all over a tumbler of ice cubes and bottoms up. Switch it up with other flavors (grapefruit's a fave), or go skinny and swap seltzer for the soda.

Hit up **The Rusty Rudder** (www.rustyrudderdewey.com), which has a large open-air deck overlooking the bay. Live bands play regularly and there's a huge open-air dance floor. (Expect a $10 cover charge.) **The Starboard** (thestarboard.com) is another staple. It'll be hot, it'll be crowded, and it'll be wild. Cover charges for live bands are standard here, too.

When the bars close at 1 a.m., line up at **Mama Celeste's** for a slice or a whole pizza. You've got a Sunday Funday tomorrow, so you'll need something to fight off the hangover.

Sunday

The Sunday Scaries don't really exist in Dewey—or at least they can be postponed. Drag yourself out of bed for the legendary Suicide Sundays at The Starboard. There's food. There's a huge make-your-own Bloody Mary bar. There's music and beer pong and basically it's an all-day party. Just make sure you have a designated driver if you plan on heading back to DC on Sunday night.

>> **If It Rains:** Since bars are the main attraction in Dewey, a rainy day shouldn't damper much of your weekend. It may just get more crowded in the indoor part of the bars, but hey—you're more likely to meet your next hookup that way.

≡ *While You're Here*

SUNSETGRAMS

If you time it right, you can head down to one of the docks on the bay side of town and catch a surprisingly quiet and peaceful sunset. There's a dock at the Rusty Rudder and one a little farther north. Or check out Sunset Park at the end of Dagsworthy Street.

PARASAILING

Probably not something you want to do after a few cocktails, but **Dewey Beach Parasail** (www .flydewey.com) runs tours on the bay. They have a kiosk at the Rusty Rudder.

SKIMBOARDING

One of the biggest skimboarding destinations on the East Coast is right here at Dewey Beach. (Skimboarding is that thing you've likely seen 10-year-old kids doing in the surf, where they run, throw a thin flat board into the receding water, and then jump on it and surf along the sand.)

There's actually a camp, **Alley-Oop** (alleyoopskim.com), nearby if you want to learn how, or you can go watch pros compete at the Zap Pro/Am World Championships of Skimboarding in mid-August.

STANDUP PADDLE YOGA

Put a beachy spin on your asana by doing it while floating on a paddleboard. **Delmarva Board Sport Adventures** (www.delmarvaboardsportadventures.com) partners with local instructors for classes every Saturday evening in the summer.

☰ *Good Eats*

Fine dining hasn't historically been Dewey's thing; instead, the name of the game was always "eat something to soak up all the booze." That said, there are some dining gems, in addition to plenty of cheap beach eats. Don't forget The Starboard's legendary Sunday brunch, complete with an epic Bloody Mary bar.

WOODY'S DEWEY BEACH BAR & GRILL

deweybeachbar.com • $$ • American

This casual surfer-themed grill on the main drag is said to have the best crab cakes in town. The food's all-around good, but you'll have to wait for it, sometimes up to 45 minutes. There's a solid late-night menu till 1 a.m.

MEZCALI

$$ • tacos

This California-style mezcal bar and taqueria is relatively new on the Dewey Beach scene and is a welcome departure from all the pub food. Tacos are made using fresh local ingredients and house-made wraps. The margs are nice and strong.

GROTTO PIZZA

www.grottopizza.com • $ • pizza

The Delaware beach institution has an outpost right in town. You can do lunch or dinner here (or order takeout and bring it to the beach or your house). Last call at the bars is 1 a.m., a.k.a. pizza o'clock in Dewey.

MAMA CELESTE'S PIZZERIA

$ • pizza

The slices are big and the lines are long. It's cash-only and isn't known for its customer service, but the pizza hits the spot.

DEWEY BEACH COUNTRY CLUB

$$ • American

Opened in 2018 with a Happy Gilmore vibe, DBCC has earned rave reviews for its gourmet pub food (burgers, dogs, and seafood dishes such as pan-seared tuna). Get your camera ready—the burger buns are branded and make for some cool food pics.

BAKED

www.bakedcoffeebar.com • $ • cafe

Start (or pep up) your day with an espresso and a breakfast sandwich (which are served all day). This cute cafe also has to-go burritos and salads, and you can place an order online, then come in to pick it up. Service can be slow, so be prepared to wait.

☰ *Time for a Drink*

The bars covered above are the big Dewey institutions, but there are other places to drink.

DEWEY BEER COMPANY

www.deweybeerco.com

At the north end of town, this craft beer bar provides a grown-up alternative to the beach bars hawking Bud Light specials. The vibe feels a bit more "rustic warehouse" than "beach bar," with beer-making equipment to deliver on their promise that beer won't travel more than 30 feet from production to your glass. There's also a good food menu.

38-75° BREWING

www.3875brewing.com

This small brewery makes a handful of good beers on-site. They bring in a selection of brews from other Delaware and Eastern Shore brewers, as well.

DEWEY BEACH LIQUORS

There's one main liquor store in town, right on the main drag, next to Bottle and Cork. They have craft beer, cheap beer, wine, all sorts of liquors, and a good selection of mixers.

☰ *Stay Over*

Looking for something charming or upscale? Maybe don't stay in Dewey. (If you do want all those things but still want a piece of the fun, stay in Bethany or Rehoboth and cab to Dewey.)

That's not to say that Dewey lodging is a dump—far from it. Most of the condos, hotels, and motels are clean, well-appointed, and convenient. They just err more on the side of crash pad than on the side of luxurious. (There is a fancy Hyatt Place if you want something more upscale.)

During the summer, prices downtown spike, even for the budget-style motels. Snag a place to stay as soon as you pick a weekend to go. Last-minute trips get pricey.

BEACH HOUSE DEWEY

www.beachhousedewey.com • $$$

Right on the main strip, this motel is just off the beach. There's a pool and bikes to rent. The rooms are clean and freshly designed, with pops of bright patterns and modern finishes.

BEACH RENTAL SCENE

Since beach house and condo rentals are big here, you'll find all the usual rental sites at play. You'll often see the same place listed across multiple sites, too. Check Airbnb, VRBO, Homeaway, and local rental agencies such as **Crowley Associates Realty** (www.crowleyreal estate.com).

Try to snag a house in the middle of town—Bellevue to McKinley Street is prime territory. The bars bookend the town, so if you're smack in the middle, you don't have to walk end to end to get around.

>> **House Packing List:** Most houses come with linens and bath towels, but check beforehand. Plan on bringing your own beach towel, cooler, beach games, and possibly an air mattress, if you're with a big group.

☰ *Plan Around*

Dewey's high season corresponds with good weather and summer vacation—you'll see it peak from Memorial Day to Labor Day. Come outside of that time and you'll find a calmer beach town. Come during it and you'd better be ready to party.

Weekends to Plan For (or Avoid):

- **MDW and LDW:** Start or end the season with a long-weekend blowout. Sundays are crazy enough in Dewey; add a holiday Monday to the mix and pray for your liver.
- **Beach Week (June):** College (high school, too) does the beach on this annual spring party tradition.
- **Running of the Bull (June):** Thousands of people don red Pamplona-style bandanas and chase someone in a bull costume down the beach. It's backed by a big party at Starboard.
- **Fourth of July:** Every summer weekend's wild in Dewey, but this one is peak party, with big concerts at most of the bars. You can also see the Rehoboth fireworks from the beach here.
- **Starboard Closing Party (October):** Every year in mid-October, tens of thousands of people come from far and wide for this end-of-season bar blowout.

// Running of the Bull

GOOD TO KNOW

- Hello, 1995: Many places in Dewey are still cash-only. There are ATMs, but you might want to skip the fees and take out a wad of bills before you get here.
- Probably to avoid things like drunk people swimming, there's a summer beach curfew. Cops patrol and will kick you off if you're on the sand between 1 a.m. and 5 a.m.
- There are around 300 year-round residents in Dewey Beach. On a typical summer weekend, there may be 30,000 people who come in.

BEEN HERE, DONE THAT?

- Really, do you remember all of it from last time? Or are things a little hazy? Either way, most Dewey visitors are repeat offenders, so don't be shy about making weekends here a regular thing.
- Ocean City, Maryland, is the main rival to Dewey's beach revelry. About 45 minutes down the coast, the bar/restaurant/entertainment complex Seacrets spans six acres, contains 17 bars (including one where you can float in the bay), and makes it feel like you've gone from the Mid-Atlantic to the Caribbean.
- If you've graduated from the Dewey scene but still want your beach fix, consider the more low-key neighboring Bethany Beach (Chapter 4).

3

Join the LGBTQ Beach Scene

Rehoboth Beach, DE

Can't make it up to Fire Island? Rehoboth is the best gay beach scene in the mid-Atlantic.

FROM DC: 123 MILES · 2 HOURS 45 MINUTES | TRIP LENGTH: WEEKEND

DO	EAT	DRINK	BUY
dance	oysters	flaming coffee at Back Porch Café	salt water taffy from Dolle's

Everyone's welcome in Rehoboth. The large beach town is part family-focused, part politico summer escape, and part gay beach getaway. There are over 200 LGBT-owned businesses here. Many spots aren't specifically "gay" bars—it's more that everywhere here is open to people of all orientations. That said, this is likely the best gay beach scene in the mid-Atlantic. From drag shows to beach bods to dance floors under the stars—whether you're gay or straight, prepare for a good time.

≡ *Getting to Rehoboth*

During summer, BestBus runs coach buses from Dupont Circle to Rehoboth Beach. The ride takes about 2.5 hours and costs $40 each way.

Despite the bus availability, most people get here by car. The route follows 50 East across the Bay Bridge, then straight east across Maryland and Delaware, past farmland and small towns on 404 and 16. Once you get near the beach, you'll cut down on Highway 1, which takes you right to the ocean.

Since so many people drive in, traffic is awful in the summer. Uber and Lyft are both big, so this can be a good alternative to parking.

Speaking of parking, it's not fun here. Usually your rental will only come with two to three parking passes, which work in the non-metered spots around town. You can buy passes at City Hall, or there are little carts on the side streets to the south of Rehoboth Avenue that sell them.

A Rehoboth classic is the **Jolly Trolley** (www.jollytrolley.com). This seasonal bus shuttles people between Rehoboth and Dewey Beach. It's $5 round-trip and runs till 2 a.m. Expect a wild ride.

>> **Tax-Free Shopping:** There's no sales tax in Delaware, which makes Rehoboth's Tanger Outlet (www.tangeroutlet.com) shops an even better deal.

≡ *Get Your Bearings*

At about 1.5 square miles, Rehoboth is the largest of the southern Delaware beach towns. Rehoboth Avenue is the town's main street, running west from the beach. It's lined with beachy shops, restaurants, and local businesses.

You'll find a lot of other bars, including many of the popular gay bars, along Baltimore Avenue, a block north of Rehoboth Avenue.

>> **More Info:** CAMP Rehoboth (www.camprehoboth.com) is a local LGBTQ-friendly community organization; www.cityofrehoboth.com; www.visitsoutherndelaware.com

Gay Rehoboth

The gay scene's been flourishing here since the 1960s. Some of the early institutions are still going strong, while new (or made-over) faces are constantly adding to the mix.

BEACH BOYS

During the day, **Poodle Beach** is the place to cruise. Located at Queen Street, at the south end of the Boardwalk (if you think you've gone too far, keep going), it's considered one of the best gay beaches in the country. If you want to claim a prime spot, you'll have to get here before noon to beat the crowds.

On Labor Day weekend, there's Drag Volleyball here, but every weekend brings thousands of men (and women, too) of every age and body type, so there's always something to see.

It's a bit of a hike to get here. Rather than schlepping your chair and umbrella to the beach, just pay for them there. (It's about $20 [cash only] for both.) Since you're separated from the boardwalk, usually someone operates a little grill down there, selling burgers, sandwiches, candy, and drinks.

Also, the closest bathroom facility is on the boardwalk at Laurel and Philadelphia Streets—about eight blocks away. So stop on the way to Poodle Beach to use the restroom.

LESBIAN BEACH SCENE

On the opposite side of Rehoboth from Poodle Beach, **North Shore Beach** is a popular hotspot for lesbian women. It's open to all, though—the bear community congregates here, too. Women usually cluster on the right side of the jetty, with bears and other men on the left side. It's inside Cape Henlopen State Park, so there's a $10 entrance fee. The beach is quiet; there's no boardwalk or major commercialization here, so bring what you'll need.

HOUSE PARTY

Sure, there are bars (more on those below), but a big part of the scene here is house parties. (Though in recent years, the city has started shutting these down from time to time.) Many of them are big and open to the public—keep an eye out for fliers handed out at Poodle Beach.

HAPPY HOUR: AQUA GRILL

aquagrillrehoboth.com

A go-to for Sunday brunch (yaaaas $3 mimosas and Bloodys), this Baltimore Avenue favorite has a big open patio and a welcoming attitude. Starting at happy hour, men start rolling in; if you wanna dance in the daytime, this is your spot. By night, it's packed; there'll be a line. There's live music and events such as bachelor auctions, rosé all day, and the like. Make sure to get a group house pic in the giant lifeguard chair.

LATE NIGHT: BLUE MOON

bluemoonrehoboth.com

One of the town's oldest gay bars is also one of the foodiest draws. You can come here for a romantic, fine-dining experience or for a raunchy drag show. The menu changes regularly, featuring seafood and steaks, as well as a wine list with over 100 options. If you're dining, make a reservation a few weeks in advance.

Over in the disco ball–lit bar, there's a big skylight they open up if the weather's nice, so you can dance under the stars. Friday night is Spotlight Show night, where the House Divas impersonate female icons like Cher and Celine Dion. Saturday is Legends night, with costumes, choreography, and songs from Elton John to Adele. On Sundays, it's game night, with wild Family Feud–style games. Keep an eye on the calendar for Pamela Stanley, the crowd-favorite entertainer-in-residence.

DIEGO'S HIDEAWAY

diegoshideaway.com

Come here if you're ready to dance. Opened in 2018 in the home of the old Double L, Diego's brings in a great lineup of DJs and has Rehoboth's biggest dance floor. Get here before 10 p.m. to avoid a cover charge. Stick around on Sunday to wrap up the weekend at the T-Dance. It's not all clubby here though—there's a big patio with chairs for chilling. It's also a dog-friendly spot, with a daily "yappy hour" from 3 to 7 p.m. Diego's is about a 20-minute walk west of the boardwalk.

THE PURPLE PARROT

www.ppgrill.com

The Purple Parrot looks like it came straight outta Key West: dollar bills tacked all over the walls, sand-covered patio, frozen tropical drinks. At night, it draws a mixed crowd and does a little bit of everything, from karaoke to drag shows. The main entrance is off Rehoboth Avenue, but if you come in the back, off Wilmington Avenue, you'll find a bamboo- and palm-covered beer garden.

THE POND BAR & GRILL

www.thepondrehoboth.com

This dive bar just south of Rehoboth Avenue always has something going on, whether it's trivia or karaoke or live bands. It's known as a lesbian bar, although, as with most Rehoboth faves, it's inclusive to all identities.

While You're Here

FUNLAND

www.funlandrehoboth.com

The iconic amusement park on Rehoboth's boardwalk is what you'd expect at a small-town carnival: bumper cars, a haunted house, a few rides, and some arcade games. Half of it is indoors so it's a good rainy-day option. It's open between May and September; actual hours depend on weather and crowds.

SHOPPING

No sales tax is one of Delaware's biggest selling points. Aside from the aforementioned outlets, there are a number of boutiques in town with high-quality designs and goods.

At **Spahr** (www.scottspahr.com) on Baltimore Avenue, Scott Spahr does all his own designs for men and women's fashion. Go in, pick something out, and he'll tailor it for you, and you can pick it up at the end of the weekend.

Casual men's sportswear by designers like Vince and Theory are the focus at **Rock Creek** (www.rockcreekrehoboth.com). Come here at the end of the season—you can find major deals.

For cute beach-to-city women's clothing, jewelry, and accessories, swing by **Hula Sue** (www.shopstylecrush.com), just off Rehoboth Avenue.

GET YOUR TAFFY FIX

You won't miss the big "Dolle's" sign on the heart of the boardwalk, so don't miss actually trying the beachy treat. Saltwater taffy, caramel and other popcorn, and all sorts of fudge make for great brownie points gifts for the office on Monday.

// Dolles Candyland on the boardwalk

☰ *Good Eats*

Most restaurants in Rehoboth are open year-round, but a few are seasonal, so check hours if you're here between October and April.

Rehoboth invented some of the boardwalk classics, like Grotto Pizza and Dolle's taffy and fudge, but it's not all sweet or greasy food here. Overall, Rehoboth has the best food scene of the Delaware beaches. Many of the bars mentioned above double as popular eateries.

HENLOPEN OYSTER HOUSE

www.hcoysterhouse.com • $$$ • seafood

The vibe is rustic beach-chic, and the menu is an ode to oysters (although they have plenty of other options). There's always a crowd here, and they don't take reservations, but you can add your name to the list and get a text when your table's ready.

FINS

www.finsrawbar.com • $$ • seafood

Fins serves up seafood from near and far, from crab dip to Australian barramundi to the fresh catch of the day.

CLAWS

www.227claw.com • $$ • seafood

Despite its prime Rehoboth Avenue location, Claws feels like your classic harbor-side, hole-in-the-wall seafood spot. Throw a sheet of brown paper down on the table, dump a pile of blue crabs, and start picking.

GROTTO PIZZA

www.grottopizza.com • $ • pizza

If there's one name that's synonymous with pizza in Delaware, it's this chain. There are locations all over Delaware and Maryland, but Rehoboth is its home. There are three locations within steps of each other on the boardwalk at Rehoboth Avenue.

NICOLA PIZZA

www.nicolapizza.com • $ • pizza

This pizza spot is another Rehoboth standby. It's known for its Nic-o-boli, a baked stuffed pizza sandwich, and its North 1st Street location is steps from the Baltimore Avenue bars.

IGUANA GRILL

Baltimore Avenue • $$ • Southwestern

This colorful, tropical Tex-Mex restaurant has indoor and outdoor seating in a Victorian house. It's an easy place for a bite, especially after happy hour at Aqua. The margs are always a good choice.

DOS LOCOS

Rehoboth Avenue • www.doslocos.com • $$ • Mexican

A popular spot for Mexican-inspired dishes, although many of them have a beachy spin (like the shrimp and lump crab burritos). There's a lot of space here, so it's good for groups.

LORI'S OY VEY CAFÉ

Baltimore Avenue • www.lorisoyveycafe.com • $ • sandwiches

Fast and fresh—and health conscious—Lori's is known for its sandwiches and chicken salad. The best part is they deliver all over Rehoboth—even if you're at the beach.

STINGRAY SUSHI

North of Rehoboth Avenue • stingrayrestaurant.com • $$ • Asian

Every day it's happy hour till 6 p.m. During this time you can get sushi rolls for $8. One of the best things about Stingray, however, isn't their early menu; it's their late-night one—it's open (for takeout, too) until 1 a.m. on Friday and Saturday nights.

FRANK AND LOUIE'S ITALIAN SPECIALTIES

Baltimore Avenue • $ • sandwiches

Across from Aqua on Baltimore Avenue, this turquoise barn-inspired deli serves some of the best sandwiches in town. While you're at it, treat yourself to some ridiculously delicious Italian desserts.

ICE CREAM STORE

Boardwalk at Rehoboth Avenue • www.rehobothbeachicecream.com • $ • ice cream

With over 100 out-there flavors, this place is worth the beach diet slip. They've got everything from mint chocolate chip with cookies and cream-cookie dough to bacon and "better than sex" (which made an appearance on *The Today Show*).

AGAVE

Lewes • agavelewes.com • $$ • Mexican

Farther north about 20 minutes in Lewes, this Mexican restaurant draws lines that are over an hour long. Wait it out; it's worth it for the six types of guac, tacos, enchiladas, and more. At this writing, another location was expected to open on Rehoboth Avenue in late 2019.

Grocery Run

Dinah Lingo's Market on Baltimore Avenue is the easiest place to get things like fresh fruit and veggies, baked goods, house supplies, or anything you forgot to pack. Prices are a bit high, though, so don't plan on using it for a larger house stock-up run.

Time for a Drink

The bars listed above are mainstays on the gay scene. Most bars in town are gay-friendly but aren't specifically gay bars.

BACK PORCH CAFÉ

www.backporchcafe.com

A couple of signature drinks make this restaurant a cocktail go-to. Their table-side flaming coffee has been called one of the best drinks at Delaware beaches (it has Kahlúa and liqueur). Their Dark and Stormy is also popular; they make the ginger beer in-house.

DOGFISH HEAD BREWERY

www.dogfish.com

Drink the popular IPAs and beachy-themed brews right from the source: Dogfish Head's, from Rehoboth. The main brewery is open to visitors; it's a massive operation in Milton, Delaware (about half-hour from Rehoboth). But there's a brewpub right on Rehoboth Avenue that serves a large selection of beers plus good food.

ZOGG'S RAW BAR & GRILL

www.zoggsbar.com

A little covered alley transports you to the Caribbean with its tiki beach bar vibe. There are good happy hour specials and live music on weekend nights.

Where to Buy Booze

The Cultured Pearl (www.culturedpearlliquor.com) is the go-to for take-home wine, beer, and liquor. It's across the street from a sushi restaurant of the same name. If you eat at the restaurant, you get a discount at the liquor store.

☰ Stay Over

House rentals are the thing to do in Rehoboth—the overwhelming majority of people opt for houses over hotels. But these book up way far in advance (think February), so plan ahead if you're going to go this route.

Not surprisingly, rents spike in peak season (summer). If you want to save, book a place away from the beach, closer to the canal on the west side of town.

HOTEL REHOBOTH

www.hotelrehoboth.com • $$$$

A few blocks from the beach, this charming boutique hotel is a good base. It's right on Rehoboth Avenue, but removed from some of the fray. There's an elegant fireplace in the lobby and a small rooftop pool.

CLOTHING-OPTIONAL STAY: THE SHORE INN

www.shoreinn.com • $$

The men-only hotel is a few blocks from the downtown action and is a fixture of Rehoboth's gay scene. The decor includes naked men all over the walls, there's a clothing-optional sundeck (there are privacy shields from neighboring buildings) and a large, frequently used, also clothing-optional hot tub. It's over in West Rehoboth, about a mile from the boardwalk.

RENTAL SCENE

Jack Lingo (www.jacklingo.com) and **Berkshire Hathaway** (www.berkshirehathawayhs.com) are the two main rental companies in town—start here, if you're looking for a house. Airbnb and VRBO also have plenty of listings.

☰ *Plan Around*

Rehoboth has become a 10-month town, although summer (Memorial Day through Labor Day) is still the biggest part of the season.

Weekends to Plan For (or Avoid):

- **Polar Bear Plunge (February):** The first Sunday in February, more than three thousand people come out and jump in 35-degree ocean water to raise money for charity.
- **Memorial Day (May):** Typically, Memorial Day weekend is the biggest weekend in Rehoboth; book a place to stay in advance if you want to join the crowds.
- **Pride (June):** At this writing, June was Pride month in Delaware. (But check the calendar; it has changed in past years.)
- **Bear Weekend (September):** Join the bear community for happy hours, bar crawls, and vendors selling everything from fetish gear to custom underwear.
- **Sundance (September):** This annual party around Labor Day includes a giant dance party that raises money for CAMP Rehoboth.
- **CAMP Rehoboth Block Party (October):** The annual block party draws a big crowd on Baltimore Avenue.
- **Sea Witch Festival (October):** One of Rehoboth's biggest weekends, this Halloween-themed fest has costume parties, parades, broom-tossing competitions, and more.

GOOD TO KNOW

- Star Power: These folks are more than just household names in Reho—they actually have houses in town. Joe and Jill Biden have a house with ocean views overlooking Cape Henlopen State Park. Tony Kornheiser, who covers sports for WashPo/ESPN; Kevin Plank, who founded Under Armour; and a slew of Congresspeople have places here, too.
- Thomas Edison was a judge at one of the country's first Miss United States swimsuit pageants, held in Rehoboth in 1880.
- So many Washingtonians escape to the beach here in the summer that Rehoboth's longtime nickname is the "Nation's Summer Capital."

BEEN HERE, DONE THAT?

- About 3.5 hours from DC, the Jersey Shore town of Asbury Park is a popular gay beach getaway. It's not quite as sceney as Rehoboth, but it is a good option on a budget.
- There's no beach here, but New Hope, Pennsylvania (about 3 hours northeast of Washington) is an artsy, gay-friendly escape.

4

Be a Beach Bum

Bethany Beach, DE

This low-key beach town is the place to be for families and folks looking for a relaxed ocean vacay.

FROM DC: 128 MILES • 2 HOURS 45 MINUTES | TRIP LENGTH: FULL
WEEKEND (OR LONGER)

DO	EAT	DRINK	BUY
read on the beach	frozen custard	Shark Attack fishbowl at Mango's	Bethany Surf Shop T-shirt

Bethany is best known as a family beach town. Instead of the bars of Dewey and the Funland rides of Rehoboth, Bethany Beach's small boardwalk and downtown consist of ice cream shops, putt-putt golf, and a small bandstand that little kids like to run around on.

It's a classic, all-American beach town—it's a bit old-fashioned, and you get the sense that not much has changed in the past 30 years (and, aside from some new restaurants and bars, it hasn't really).

If you're looking for a more low-key beach escape, especially if you have any little kids in your posse, Bethany is the place to go.

≡ Getting to Bethany Beach

Like the other Delaware beaches, it's easiest to drive to Bethany.

Check your map app after you cross the Bay Bridge. It's generally faster to go the southern route to Bethany, taking 404 to 113, then popping east to the ocean on Route 26, which comes straight into town.

As you near the shore, get ready for beach traffic, especially in summer. Saturdays can actually be worse than Fridays and Sunday in season, as a lot of beach rentals are Saturday to Saturday.

There is Uber in town, and you shouldn't have to wait too long to get a car. A ride to Dewey costs about $30.

There's paid parking here and on nearby side streets (Parkmobile works here), or you may get a parking pass if you're renting a house. Even with the pass, get there early on summer weekends.

A trolley connects some of the off-beach neighborhoods with the beach between Memorial Day weekend and Labor Day weekend (and only costs a quarter).

≡ Get Your Bearings

Bethany Beach is divided into a few districts. The heart of town is Garfield Parkway, a U-shaped drive where the main beach access, boardwalk, and shops are located.

North of the small downtown area is a strip of (often) gated private communities. To the west (a short trolley or bike ride to the beach) are more neighborhoods, which often have better house rental prices.

Just south of the boardwalk, Sea Colony's concrete high-rise condos dominate the skyline. Farther south are more neighborhoods with house rentals and beach access—some places in South Bethany also have bay and boat access.

From any of these districts, if you head east, you'll hit the ocean.

CRABS ON THE WAY HOME

Hold on to beach time for as long as you can with a detour to **Kentmorr Restaurant & Crab House**, which serves delicious crab dishes with waterfront views on Kent Island. Next door, **Dirty Dave's Tiki Bar** has palm trees, a bar, and a manmade beach.

☰ *Beach Time*

Together with Fenwick Island to the south, this part of the coast is known to be pretty quiet. Maybe it's because undeveloped state parkland buffers the towns on either side from the raucous parties in Dewey and Ocean City.

As a result, Bethany Beach is a sheltered little beach hamlet. You can ride your bike to the library, play a game of mini golf, and finish the evening with a beer overlooking the beach.

The Beach

The beach at Bethany, like its Delaware neighbors, feels endless. It stretches north and south into infinity, and if you walked for hours, you'd still be on beach. That's because the shoreline doesn't have a lot of bays or piers.

The size and shape of the beach varies based on high vs. low tide, recent storms, dredging activity, and the like. Sometimes it's short and kind of steep; other times it's been hammered flat. The ocean bottom's usually pretty sandy, although there are some crushed shells.

During the summer season, between Memorial Day and Labor Day (plus September weekends), there are manned lifeguard stands along the beach. They post up here daily between the hours of 9:30 a.m. and 5:30 p.m. (10 a.m. to 5 p.m. in September) and will blow their whistle at you if you do anything stupid or drift too far out. Guards post flags to indicate the day's water conditions. If you see a red flag, it means the surf's dangerous and the water may be closed to swimmers.

// A lifeguard stand on Bethany Beach

// Bethany Beach boardwalk

As for beach activities, you'll mostly have to bring your own. There's one cash-only company (**Steen's,** 302-539-9160) that rents chairs and umbrellas. There are no food vendors. What there ARE are good waves for body surfing and boogie boarding, ample space to toss a football, and a good chance of spotting dolphins offshore.

The Boardwalk

Like the rest of Bethany, the boardwalk here is a cleaner, smaller, and more family-friendly version of what you'll find in places like Rehoboth and Ocean City. If you walk the whole thing end to end, it's only a third of a mile long.

Everything centers around a small wood plaza with a bandstand and Bethany's iconic clock. For about one block on either side, the boardwalk's lined with ice cream and shaved ice windows, beachy souvenir stores, and french fry stands. Then the walkway continues along the beach, fronting some small hotels and rental homes. Note that dogs aren't allowed on the beach between mid-May and September. There are public bathrooms at the bandstand on the boardwalk.

>> **More info:** www.townofbethanybeach.com ; www.visitsoutherndelaware.com

>> **If It Rains:** There are a handful of shops and bars here, but many people use a rainy day as an excuse to go outlet shopping in Rehoboth (see Chapter 3).

≡ *While You're Here*

SHOP TAX FREE

Mixed in among the standard beachy souvenir shops are some local shopping institutions.

It should be illegal to visit Bethany without a stop at **Bethany Surf Shop** (www.bethanysurf shop.net), which stocks boards and wax and all the wave gear, but might be best known for its selection of surf shop T-shirts and sweatshirts. There are a billion designs in a billion colors. Tip: If you want one of those BB stickers that you see on cars around DC, come here.

Down the stairs from the surf shop is the town's small but well-stocked bookshop, **Bethany Beach Books** (www.bethanybeachbooks.com). It's the perfect place to pick up the latest beach read if you don't want to bring your tablet out onto the sand.

CHECK OUT "CHIEF LITTLE OWL"

The totem pole-like statue in the center of town honors the Nanticoke Indian Chief Little Owl and has been a Bethany landmark since the 1970s. The statue was originally placed here as part of the "Trail of the Whispering Giants" project, which donated sculptures of Native American figures like this one to every state.

PLAY GOLF . . . MINI OR DISC

It's hard to miss Captain Jack's Pirate Golf (www.captainjackspirategolf.com). The putt-putt course has a giant, 50-foot pirate ship in the middle of the lot. A round costs only $8.50.

If your preference is disc golf, there's an 18-hole course up in **Cape Henlopen State Park**, about a half-hour north of town. (The park has a $10 entrance fee, but then the disc golf is free.)

WATER SPORTS

Away from the main beach, there are plenty of ways to get on the water. You can rent kayaks and stand-up paddleboards on the protected Indian River Bay at Ecobay Kayak & SUP (www .ecobaykayak.com). Bethany Surf Shop rents paddleboards and surfboards. Indian River Inlet is a popular place to catch a wave.

Or you can get high on a parasailing trip out of **Shark's Cove Marina**, south of town, closer to Ocean City. (You can also get on a boat—and a banana boat—here.)

WORK OUT ON THE BEACH

Get in a sweat on the sand with morning workout classes on the beach. In summer, there's daily morning yoga (weather depending), plus bootcamp, pilates, and more. Most classes are around $10. Check the town website for schedules (townofbethanybeach.com).

☰ *Good Eats*

From boardwalk snacks such as frozen custard and fries to fresh seafood and some damn good pizza, there's plenty to tempt you away from that bikini diet here. (Hooray for beach workouts!)

BETHANY BLUES BBQ

Just off the boardwalk • bethanyblues.com • $$ • BBQ

This multi-level BBQ restaurant multitasks as a sports bar, a live music venue, and a popular brunch spot. (Ask for the free cornbread and honey butter)

BEACH BREAK BAKRIE & CAFE

Just off the boardwalk • $ • sandwiches

This convenient little cafe whips up made-to-order breakfast and lunch sandwiches. There isn't really space to eat in the shop, so this is best for take-away (i.e., beach picnic!).

TOM & TERRY'S SEAFOOD MARKET

North of town • www.tomandterrysmarket.com • $ • seafood

This local favorite has crab cakes that are well worth the 10-minute drive.

BLUECOAST

1 mile north of town • www.bluecoastseafoodgrill.com • $$ • seafood

One of the best seafood restaurants in the area is a short drive north of town. If there's a wait, stick it out; there's fresh fish, oysters, crab fries, and all things ocean on the other side. There's a small al fresco dining area, too.

OFF THE HOOK

1 mile west of town • offthehookbethany.com • $$ • seafood

Fresh seafood dishes like fish tacos and poke are the focus at this west-of-Bethany eatery. It's part of a popular local chain of restaurants along the Delaware and Maryland beaches.

MCCABE'S GOURMET MARKET

South Bethany • $ • deli/bakery

Sandwiches, salads, and a good selection of gourmet groceries make this a good place to stock up your house. Do not miss the freshly baked toffee cookies.

MISAKI SUSHI

South Bethany • $$ • sushi

Set in a South Bethany strip mall, this unassuming spot serves absolutely superb sushi. You can dine here or take it to go.

GROTTO PIZZA

www.grottopizza.com • $ • pizza

There are three in town; one right near the boardwalk, one in Bethany West, and one in South Bethany. There's something uniquely "Delaware beach" about Grotto. That said, a lot of people think the pizza's actually better tasting at **Surfs Up** ($), which is just off the boardwalk. If you want to go gourmet, **Pie** ($) has build-your-own specialty pizzas, including gluten-free options.

☰ *Time for a Drink*

Back in the day, Bethany was a dry town. That ended 35 years ago, but the town never really lost its wholesome vibe. If you want a wild night out, go to Dewey Beach, about 15 minutes up the road. If you want to keep it chill with a glass or two of wine or beer, there are a few places around town.

MANGOS

mangosbethany.com

Overlooking the boardwalk, this tropical bar and grille serves big sugary drinks in fishbowls. Try to snag a table on the deck overlooking the boardwalk—this is where the Bethany Beach webcam is mounted. In other words, it's the best view in town.

ROPEWALK

bethany.ropewalk.com

Right on the main drag, this lively two-story bar and restaurant has a decent selection of local beers. There are solid happy hour and football game-day specials here, plus sometimes there's live music.

BIG CHILL BEACH CLUB

www.bigchillbeachclub.com

Post up and watch the waves at this 360-degree rooftop beachside bar at the Indian River Inlet, just before the bridge to the Delaware Seashore State Park. There's a great beach here, so you can make a day and an evening of it.

Drinking on the Beach

Booze rules vary depending on where you are. In South Bethany, they're pretty relaxed about drinking on the beach. In other places, like central Bethany near the boardwalk and to the north, beach booze is a no-no (and there are cops patrolling). Also, no smoking on the beach.

Whatever and wherever you're drinking, don't bring glass to the beach—that's the last thing a bare foot wants to step on in the sand.

☰ Stay Over

To truly do the beach thing, rent a house. But if it's just you and a friend or two and you don't need the space, there are also a couple of beach motels and hotels near the boardwalk (some of them have been around for ages, others have been recently upgraded). Then, to the south, Sea Colony has plenty of options.

RENTING A BEACH HOUSE

The best way to do Bethany is to rent a beach house. They come in every size and style, from high-rise condos in Sea Colony to beachfront behemoths to cozy homes tucked in the woods a short drive from the ocean.

TIPS FOR RENTING A BEACH HOUSE

- Contact the owner directly: many owners put their houses on the gamut of sites to get them in front of different audiences. Different sites, however, come with different fees, so sometimes if you just reach out to the owner, you can bypass the fees.
- Check what's included: towels, linens, etc. are often provided. Bikes, beach chairs and boogie boards might be available, as well.
- Look for outdoor showers: it's the little details that count. Not only are outdoor showers 100% beach vibes, they help keep the sand *outside* your clean home.

Since many people come here every year, most of the houses book up a year in advance. It can also be hard to snag a weekend-only house in summer—many rentals go for a full week. It's still possible to find a last-minute place to stay—but it won't be cheap. In order to lock down a place between June and August, the further out you can plan, the better off you are.

An added bonus of some of the beachfront communities: if you rent a house here, you'll get access to a private beach. This makes a huge difference with crowds.

On the flip side, if you're looking to save money, check rentals in the Bethany West or South Bethany neighborhoods. You'll have to drive to the beach and park, but the rates are much lower.

Many of the houses here are listed on VRBO, Homeaway, and Airbnb. You can also check local rental agency, **Crowley Realty** (www.crowleyrealestate.com).

☰ Plan Around

As a family destination, Bethany Beach's numbers surge with summer vacation schedules. July and August are typically the busiest months because of this.

The water is generally warmest in August and September, although that's also when jellyfish season strikes. Hurricane season is also a wild card; if you're here in late summer and fall, keep an eye on any Atlantic storms because they can cause dangerous rip tides.

// Bethany dunes and clock

Weekends to Plan For (or Avoid):

- **Poseidon Festival (May):** Beach season kicks off with this family-friendly fest full of music, games, and a hermit crab race.
- **Fourth of July:** The town goes all Americana, with a parade and bicycle-decorating contest.
- **Delaware Seashore State Park Sandcastle Contest (July):** The free July contest transforms the state park just north of Bethany into a sand art gallery.
- **Movies on the Bandstand (September Fridays):** Every Friday night in September, the town shows movies on a big screen on the boardwalk.

GOOD TO KNOW

- If you see a firefly whose light flashes twice and is more green than yellow, think twice about trying to catch that bad boy—it's likely the incredibly rare Bethany Beach firefly. This is the only place on earth where they're found.

- To protect itself from German submarine attacks in World War II, the town instituted nightly blackout periods. You can still see the submarine watch towers along the coast as you drive north.

BEEN HERE, DONE THAT?

- Come again, or for longer! Bethany is a summer repeat jam; many people come year after year and rent a house for a week.

- A little farther south, Chincoteague has a similar family-centric beach vibe, although Bethany's a bit more polished. Still, a trip to Chincoteague comes with one thing BB can't offer: ponies (Chapter 6).

- Many people look to Lewes, which is north of Rehoboth, as another low-key beach escape. To the south, Fenwick Island is close to built-up Ocean City but still retains a quiet vibe.

5

Chill by the Chesapeake

St. Michaels, MD

Slow down and settle into this charming Eastern Shore town's easy breezy way of life.

FROM DC: 79 MILES · 1 HOUR 45 MINUTES | IDEAL TRIP LENGTH: OVERNIGHT

DO	EAT	DRINK	BUY
walk Talbot Street	crabs & oysters	10-ounce Bud or Bud Light can	Lyon Distilling Co. Rum

St. Michaels offers many of the same things as its neighbor across the bay, Annapolis. Seafood. Sailing. A cute downtown main street. But here in this small town, things move a little slower. There aren't any traffic lights. People wave as they drive by the resident crossing guard. Local mom-and-pop shops thrive while chains are few and far between.

A weekend here is like travel Xanax; grab a seat by the water, watch the boats bobbing on the gentle tides, and watch how quickly that stress washes away.

≡ Getting to St. Michaels

Your best bet for getting here is by car. Public transit involves taking the Greyhound to Easton via Baltimore (about 3.5 hours), then Ubering or cabbing to St. Michaels. Another option is to get to Annapolis (Chapter 1) and then hop a ferry over to St. Michaels.

Having a car makes it easier to explore beyond downtown, although driving's not without its annoyances, mainly because of Bay Bridge traffic.

The basic route leads you out of DC on Route 50, which takes you across the Bay Bridge all the way to Easton. Near the Easton Airport, you'll peel off and take a few turns to wind up on Route 33, heading right into St. Michaels. Waze is your friend on this drive; it can help you avoid some of the bridge traffic.

Once in St. Michaels' downtown core, you don't need a car—it's a super walkable strip and there's free parking on side streets, plus lots by the Maritime Museum and off the main drag on Fremont Street.

≡ Get Your Bearings

St. Michaels sits on a water-laced finger of land on Maryland's Eastern Shore. The town harbor fronts water, but it's not actually the bay—it's the Miles River, which flows into the Chesapeake Bay. (The bay's always nearby too, it's just out of sight if you're standing downtown.)

Most of the town's shops and restaurants line Talbot Street, the main street leading into and through St. Michaels. It takes about 10 minutes to walk the 10-block stretch of the historic district's main drag.

DINNER EN ROUTE

If you're leaving on a summer Friday, wait out traffic and leave DC around 7 p.m. Stop for a waterfront dinner just in time for sunset on Kent Island, where **Bridges** has outdoor waterfront tables and **Fisherman's Crab Deck** serves crabs dockside at the marina.

// Talbot Street shops

☰ *Unwind St. Michaels–Style*

The Miles River, which the small downtown fronts, and the Chesapeake Bay, which lies behind the town, have run the show here for centuries. St. Michaels' history is waterlogged: it evolved from a shipbuilding port to an oystering hub to a seafood packing center. Now it's a tourist hub where people come to enjoy the bay breezes and charming downtown.

There are plenty of things to do here. There are also plenty of ways to relax and not actually do a whole lot.

FLOAT ON A BOAT

There are four main ways to get your boat on in St. Michaels. It just depends on how much you want to spend, and what sort of outing floats your . . . boat (sorry).

The cheapest option is the **Winnie Estelle** (cbmm.org/visit/tours/), which used to chug around and pick up oysters from people harvesting. Now run by the Chesapeake Maritime Museum, the 45-minute ride along the Miles River costs $10 and provides information about the boat and the town's oystering heritage.

A bit more time and money ($24.50 if you buy online) gets you a seat on the **Patriot** (www .patriotcruises.com), a large power catamaran that runs a narrated 60- to 75-minute tour and has A/C and a bar. (Try their Island Music Cocktail Cruise.)

Special occasion cruisin'? The *Selina II* (sailselina.com) does sunset sails, wedding ceremonies, and more, and only takes about six people (rates start at $65).

And for a truly authentic ride, climb aboard the skipjack *H. M. Krentz* (oystercatcher.com), where captain Ed Farley leads 2-hour sails by reservation only ($47.50).

EXPLORE BY BIKE

St. Michaels is nice and flat, and the roads have incredibly wide shoulders, making the town ideal for biking. Pick up a cruiser or road bike from **Shore Pedal & Paddle** (www.shorepedal andpaddle.com) right downtown or **TriCycle & Run** (tricycleandrun.com) as you enter town. You can pedal around the historic district or dip back and ride along the St. Michaels Nature Trail, which runs parallel to Talbot Street to the west.

You can also do some bigger rides, including the wildly popular ride Oxford–St. Michaels trail. This roughly 30-mile circuit passes through picturesque little Oxford and the larger town of Easton, and it includes a historic ferry crossing in season (bring money!). Make a pit stop at the **Scottish Highland Creamery**, one of the Eastern Shore's favorite ice cream spots.

SPAAAAH

Many of the hotels in town have tempting spa menus that'll melt away any built-up weekday stress.

The Spa at Harbor Inn (www.spaatharbourinn.com) isn't stuffy (you can come in right off the boat), and they have a full slate of massage, facials, and beauty treatments. There's a small relaxation room, but it's not the sort of place you'll lounge all day.

Five Gables Inn and Spa (fivegables.com/spa) is not your standard spa setting; it's set in a cluster of 1860s-era homes. The spa itself is powered by Aveda, and has hot stone massages, facials, and body treatments.

You don't have to be a guest at the Inn at Perry Cabin to bliss out at **The Linden Spa** (www .belmond.com). The space is on the smaller side, but the relaxation rooms and post-treatment infinity pool have a luxurious ambiance that won't put you in any rush to leave.

JUST WANDER AND SHOP

Take your time popping into the little stores that line the downtown strip. You'll find everything from art made out of Old Bay canisters to beachy home decor to shorts emblazoned with the Maryland flag. Some faves include **Come by Chance**, a cool lifestyle store with a lot of shore-inspired decor, and **The Preppy Redneck** (www.thepreppyredneck.com) and **Knotty Living**, which have housewares, accessories, and gifts with an Eastern Shore preppy look.

DISCOVER TILGHMAN ISLAND

About 15 minutes beyond downtown St. Michaels, a little drawbridge over Knapp's Narrows delivers you onto Tilghman Island. While tourism has totally taken hold in St. Michaels, Tilghman retains a more authentic blue-collar vibe, with working skipjacks who make a living crabbing and oystering.

From here, you can get out on the water on the historic skipjack **Rebecca T. Ruark** (skipjack.org; cash only) or on the gorgeous **Lady Patty** (ladypatty.com) yacht. There are also plenty of captains here ready to take you out on a fishing trip. While you're here, pop into the **Tilghman Island Country Store** for some snacks or sodas. For an even quieter base, spend the night out here.

>> **More Info:** www.stmichaelsmd.com

≡ *While You're Here*

DRINK LOCAL

St. Michaels packs a punch when it comes to local beverages; you'll find a craft brewery, winery, and distillery all on the same block.

Pull up a stool or shoot some darts at **Eastern Shore Brewing** (www.easternshorebrewing.com). There are always a couple of brewed-on-site pale ales on tap, plus a rotating roster of "micro seasonals," which correspond to local happenings, like duck migration or the last days of summer.

Next door, the airy **St. Michaels Winery** (www.st-michaels-winery.com) may not serve the

// Spirits at Lyon Distilling Co.

best wine you've ever tried, but their flights offer something for everyone: dry whites, sweet wines, oak-aged wines . . . or all of 'em.

In a warehouse behind these two, **Lyon Distilling Co.** (lyondistilling.com) is a burgeoning booze favorite in the area. They're known for their rums (help yourself to a tasting—it's free), but they're also cooking up solid liqueurs and more.

EXPLORE THE CHESAPEAKE MARITIME MUSEUM

cbmm.org

The region's history and culture are on display at this waterfront non-profit museum. There are indoor and outdoor exhibits, plus you can snag some great views of the harbor from the historic pentagonal lighthouse that anchors the complex. You can also try your hand at crabbing or oystering here, and rent sailboats, kayaks, and row boats.

TAKE A NATURE WALK

Behind the town's main drag is a pleasant nature trail that's a nice place for a stroll. The whole trail spans about 1.3 miles and passes a covered bridge, a waterfront park, and tidal inlets that lead out to the bay. The trail starts at Bradley Park, although you can pick it up from many of the streets that shoot west off Talbot Street.

SNAP THE VINTAGE CARS

A newer addition to the St. Michaels scene is the **Classic Motor Museum** (www.classicmotor museum.org), a large barn-like space full of classic vehicles. The rotating collection includes a Model T, an early Corvette, and an old-school fire truck you can actually climb up onto. Admission's typically $10, but on Saturday mornings, the museum hosts "Cars and Coffee," a free gathering.

☰ *Good Eats*

It'll take a few visits to St. Michaels to exhaust the town's good eats. Seafood is plentiful, but it isn't your only option. If you're here on a summer or fall weekend and have your heart set on dining at a particular spot, make a reservation.

AVA'S PIZZERIA AND WINE BAR

Talbot Street • avaspizzeria.com • $$ • pizza

This pizza spot is one of the town's most popular restaurants, and for good reason. The crust is cooked to perfection, and the combos are endless. Crowd favorites include the Chef's

Favorite—white pizza with crispy prosciutto—and the fluffy Detroit Deep Dish. They don't do reservations, but give them a call about an hour before you arrive and they'll add your name to the queue.

LIMONCELLO

Talbot Street • limoncellostmichaels.com • $$ • Italian

Pastas, risotto, seafood . . . it's all delicious at this cheery trattoria. The menu's full of Southern Italian favorites. Pops of yellow and a painted pressed-tin ceiling add to the welcoming and casual vibe, and when it's nice out, there's sidewalk seating as well.

CHESAPEAKE LANDING

2.5 miles west of St. Michaels • www.chesapeakelandingrestaurant.com • $$ • seafood

A bit outside of town, this is where the locals go for great seafood. You won't find fresher crabs—there's a seafood packing house on-site that brings the catch right over to the kitchen. The dining room is open year-round, and from October to March there's a wildly popular Friday Night Oyster buffet.

THE CRAB CLAW

Navy Point • thecrabclaw.com • $$ • seafood

Folks will tell you this is the best place for crabs. Right next to the Maritime Museum, this family-run seafood institution has been in operation for over 50 years. Order the crab cakes and dig in at picnic tables overlooking the water (there's also A/C upstairs if it's a scorcher).

JUSTINE'S ICE CREAM

Talbot Street • justinesicecream.com • $ • ice cream

St. Michaels' go-to ice cream parlor serves homemade flavors using seasonal and local ingredients. It's best known for its Wall of Shakes, a legendary list of mixtures like the "hot" chocolate and cayenne or the mint-chocolate covered Oreo. Feel free to get creative and make your own combo.

GINA'S CAFÉ

Talbot Street • $$ • Mexican

This eccentric little cottage is known for its Eastern Shore spins on Mexican dishes. Think big plates of crab nachos, tacos, and quesadillas. Oh, and delicious fruity margaritas.

AGAVE ARTS & JUICING CO.

Talbot Street • $ • juice

Expect to have major home envy when you see the bohemian-chic interior of this juicery—it's all succulents and rustic wood accents with an exotic flair. Pick up a smoothie, sink into the comfy couch, and stay a while.

BLUE CRAB COFFEE

One block off Talbot Street • bluecrabcoffee.com • $ • coffee

This spacious coffee shop is the type of place where you want to sit and hang out. There's a good amount of seating and tables aren't on top of each other. In addition to a nice selection of coffee, they have bagels and other light breakfast options.

≡ *Time for a Drink*

St. Michaels isn't exactly a party destination. There are a few classic shore bars, and some pubs, but don't expect to be out 'til the sun comes up.

When it comes to signature drinks, aside from Lyon Rum and ESB, you may find locals throwing back the Chesapeake-area favorite: a smaller-than-normal 10-ounce can of Bud Light or Budweiser. No one can say for sure what makes this beer so popular, as there doesn't seem to be any taste difference between this beer and the beer from normal cans. But hey, when in St. Michaels . . .

// Inn at Perry Cabin

FOXY'S HARBOR GRILLE

www.foxysharborgrille.com

This casual beach-bar on the docks is a great place to sit and watch the boats. There's a rotating list of 15 beers on draft, many of which come from the Eastern Shore, Virginia, or Delaware. Frozen tiki drinks are also always a good option.

INN AT PERRY CABIN

www.belmond.com

Even if you aren't staying here, it's worth a visit. Grab a drink at the bar and claim an Adirondack chair on the lawn. Instant relaxation.

Stay Over

If your goal's truly some R&R, don't do St. Michaels as a day trip. It's just too much driving. Instead, linger overnight to soak up more of the town's laid-back vibes.

In keeping with St. Michaels' mostly local makeup, you won't find a slew of Marriotts or Holiday Inns here. There are a handful of historic inns and B&Bs scattered throughout town. And then there's the Inn at Perry Cabin, just north of town—St. Michaels' signature place to stay.

INN AT PERRY CABIN

www.belmond.com • $$$$

If budget's less of a concern, the Inn at Perry Cabin is a no-brainer. Anyone who's seen *Wedding Crashers* will recognize its romantic white colonial-style house and expansive waterfront lawns—they served as the backdrop for Craig and Christina's wedding. Hollywood fame aside, this is the premier hotel in St. Michaels, if not the Eastern Shore, and its restaurant, spa, and waterfront views are all worth the trip alone.

WYLDER HOTEL

wylderhoteltilghmanisland.com • $$$

A hip newcomer on the scene, this Tilghman Island hotel is a relaxed alternative to the refined Inn at Perry Cabin vibe. The big bayfront lawn has a fire pit and a saltwater pool, plus a crab shack run by Chef Sean Wheaton, who comes from José Andrés' restaurants in DC. Rooms are on the smaller side, but the whole hotel is so quiet that it could be sold out for the weekend and you'll still enjoy peace and space to yourself. There's a two-night minimum on summer weekends.

HARBOUR INN

www.harbourinn.com • $$$

Set on the harbor, an easy walk from Talbot Street's restaurants and shops, this three-story inn is a popular home base for St. Michaels weekenders. The inside's a bit dated but rooms are spacious, and some have water views. The pool, which is also right on the water, has a food and drink service for maximum loungeability.

RENTAL SCENE

At this writing, Airbnb rentals weren't sanctioned within the town of St. Michaels, but you can find rental homes and apartments on Homeaway and VRBO.

☰ *Plan Around*

While some places are open all year, St. Michaels really peaks in summer. Last-minute bookings during those months are a bit tougher.

There aren't any blowout events throughout the year. Instead, you'll find some cool little local festivals celebrating seafood, boats, and the waterman way of life.

Weekends to Plan For (or Avoid):

- **Return of the Fleet (April):** Every year the Inn at Perry Cabin ushers its fleet of ships back to St. Michaels for the season with fanfare.
- **Eastern Shore Sea Glass & Coastal Arts Festival (April):** Sea glass artists come in from around the country to share their wares.
- **Antique & Classic Boat Festival & the Arts (June):** Boat-owners bring their vintage vessels to the Maritime Museum for a competition about whose is the best-preserved.
- **Fourth of July:** There are fireworks over the harbor and a 1930s–style big band blowout at the Chesapeake Bay Maritime Museum.
- **Waterman's Appreciation Day (August)**: Celebrate St. Michaels' seafaring tradition with crabs and events such as a boat docking content.
- **OysterFest (October):** Ring in oyster season at the Chesapeake Maritime Museum with live music and boat rides.
- **Christmas in St. Michaels (December):** The Eastern Shore's largest holiday parade takes place the second weekend in December, and the cute little town decks its halls with festive flair.

1 Replica cannons in Muskrat Park
2 Crabs
3 Downtown houses

GOOD TO KNOW

- You might hear this is the "town that fooled the British," as St. Michaels claims to have outsmarted attackers in the War of 1812 by hanging lanterns from trees and drawing cannon fire away from town. It's a great story, but the jury's still out on whether this *actually* happened. True or not, the battle happened, and you can still see the cannons in Church Cove Park.

- There are plenty of public restrooms all over town.

- Oyster season runs between October and March. Crab season is April through September.

BEEN HERE, DONE THAT?

- For a similarly romantic weekend with much different scenery, head out to Middleburg, in the heart of Virginia's horse country (Chapter 15).

- Spend more time in Easton on an Eastern Shore sequel trip. The towns are only about 15 minutes apart, and while Easton doesn't have the waterfront preciousness of St. Michaels, it does have a growing lineup of cool restaurants and bars.

6

Find Wild Ponies at the Beach

Assateague, MD, and Chincoteague, VA

Wild ponies on unspoiled beaches. Doesn't sound like something you'd find a short drive from the sprawl of Ocean City, but hey, that's Assateague and Chincoteague for you!

FROM DC: 141 OR 172 MILES · ABOUT 3 HOURS | TRIP LENGTH: OVERNIGHT OR WEEKEND

DO	EAT	DRINK	BUY
see the ponies	oysters	Orange Crush	bug spray

Wild ponies! On the beach! Welcome to *Misty of Chincoteague* IRL, where brown and white pinto-coated ponies roam around wild barrier islands, making for a beach day unlike anywhere else in the mid-Atlantic. You can hop on a boat, grab a bike, or just lay out on the sand and have a good chance of seeing the famous local equines.

≡ Get Your Bearings

The lay of the land between Assateague and Chincoteague is confusing.

Assateague Island is a big 37-mile long barrier island that runs along the Maryland and Virginia coasts. It's wild; all of it is parkland and, aside from a few facilities, there's no major development here.

This island of Assateague is divided into three sections, each managed by a different organization:

- **Assateague State Park:** At the northern part of the island, a chunk of the land is managed by the Maryland Department of State Parks (dnr.maryland.gov/publiclands).
- **Assateague Island National Seashore:** Most of the Maryland side of the island falls under this park's management (overseen by the National Park Service; www.nps.gov/asis).
- **Chincoteague National Wildlife Refuge:** As soon as you hit the state line on Assateague Island and enter Virginia, the National Seashore stops and the National Wildlife Refuge begins (managed by the US Fish and Wildlife Service). It's named "Chincoteague," but it's actually *on* Assateague (www.fws.gov/refuge/Chincoteague).

Then adjacent to the National Wildlife Refuge is another separate island: **Chincoteague Island** proper. This is where all the stuff is, such as hotels, restaurants, and the like.

So, you've got a Chincoteague park on Assateague Island and you can't easily move between all three parks . . . suffice it to say, if you associate "Assateague" with Maryland and the north, and "Chincoteague" with all things Virginia and the south, you'll be on track.

>> More Info: Chincoteague Chamber of Commerce (www.chincoteaguechamber.com)

≡ Getting to Assateague and Chincoteague

Maps of the islands are a bit deceiving—Assateague the island goes all the way from Maryland to Virginia and is connected by bridges on each end.

But there's no road spanning the whole thing, so you can't actually drive end-to-end (although you can hike). For that, you'll have to return to the mainland and go around, which means people often pick one side rather than doing both.

To get to the northern end of Assateague, where the state park and the National Seashore are, you'll arrive via Maryland, coming in on Highway 611. To get to Chincoteague, you'll approach from the south, via Virginia's Eastern Shore (usually take Highway 12 or 13 south, then you'll cut east when you hit the NASA facility).

All of the parks themselves have parking, although you'll have to pay an entry fee at each.

>> **Leave the Pets at Home:** While dogs are allowed with strict leash rules on some parts of the beach , they aren't permitted at all in other parts—even in the car. It's best not to bring them along. Too many horses and other animals to worry about.

≡ *Meet the Ponies*

They're wild animals, so there's no guaranteed place to see the ponies of Chincoteague and Assateague. But if you know where to look, you'll usually find 'em.

There are about 300 ponies on Assateague Island, split into two main herds: one on the Maryland side and one on the Virginia side. The Maryland horses are feral; they just do their thing in the parks and are treated like wild animals, the same way a bear would be in the Shenandoah. The Virginia ponies, which live in Chincoteague National Wildlife Refuge, are actually owned by the Chincoteague Volunteer Fire Company. They get a little more special treatment, like veterinary checkups.

It's generally a little easier to see the horses on the Assateague side of things, EXCEPT in July, when the Chincoteague herd is rounded up and swum across the channel from the park to the island of Chincoteague. (More on this annual pony roundup below.)

// Wild ponies on an Assateague beach in Maryland

// The islands are flat and bikeable

There are many myths around the ponies. The most exciting of these is that they survived a shipwreck of a Spanish galleon, swam to safety here, and never left. Realistically, they probably were released here by early colonists who didn't want to pay taxes on them.

Ways to See the Ponies

BY CAR | The most common way to see the horses is to drive along the nature trails in each of the parks. There are easy-to-follow roads with pull-offs and trails where you can stretch your legs in search of the ponies.

>> **Tip:** If you see a bunch of cars pulled over on the side of the road, it probably means the ponies are nearby.

BY BIKE | Those same driving routes above are super bike-friendly, thanks to the ultra-flat island terrain. There are also additional car-free loops that open up to you when you're cycling.

You can rent bikes at **Assateague Outfitters** (www.assateagueoutfitters.com) on the Maryland side (the shop is actually located on Assateague itself). They also rent kayaks

// Chincoteague wetlands

// Assateague ponies

and sell water and snacks. In Virginia, **The Bike Depot** (www.refugebikes.com) is a short pedal from the park entrance on Chincoteague.

BY BOAT | Many people think this is the best way to see the ponies, since you're not confined to the park road. Expert captains can cruise around the island in search of the herd, and you can sometimes get a lot closer this way. **Saltwater Pony Tours** (www.saltwaterponytours .com) is a popular option.

Whichever way you're visiting, remember this is not a petting zoo. These ponies may be used to people, but that does NOT mean they want to be petted, ridden, or posed for your Instagram. Pony bites hurt, just give them some space (the rule of thumb is at least a bus length) and everyone will be happier.

Attending the Annual Pony Swim

Every July the Chincoteague herd is rounded up by local "saltwater cowboys" and swum across the channel from Assateague Island (where they live) to Chincoteague Island (where people live).

They're then paraded down Main Street, penned, and some are sold at auction. (This is necessary to keep the herd size from overrunning the natural resources on Assateague.) The proceeds of these sales support the Volunteer Fire Company and pony veterinary care. Then the rest of the ponies swim back across the channel to go back to their normal lives until next year's roundup.

The nearly 100-year-old event draws about 40,000 visitors and comes with a week's worth of carnival events and celebration.

ATTACK OF THE FLIES

The biting bugs here (mostly flies and mosquitos) are NO JOKE in July and August. Take one step into the woods and you will get swarmed and bitten—even through your clothing. Bring bug spray. Or else.

≡ *While You're Here*

CHILL ON CHINCOTEAGUE ISLAND

Whether you're passing through or spending the weekend, the low-key town of Chincoteague is worth a visit. There are strips of all the expected beach businesses: souvenir shops with floaties and T-shirts, mini-golf, ice cream shacks. You can pose in the 10-foot-tall "love" chairs and watch sunset at Robert N. Reed Waterfront Park. You can putz around in the little salt-air-worn island eateries. Whatever you do, make sure you're not in a rush—everything moves on island time in Chincoteague.

EAT OYSTERS

Crabs have gotten a lot of love in this chapter, but let's not forget Delmarva's other seafood star. Thanks to its protective barrier islands, its salty location next to the Atlantic Ocean, and its lower water pollution (hat-tip to the wildlife refuge for that), Chincoteague oysters are known to be briny and delicious. Between October and March, you'll find fresh oysters at excellent price points on nearly every seafood menu in town.

WATCH A NASA ROCKET LAUNCH

Driving into Chincoteague Island, you'll probably notice the giant field of radar dishes. This area is run by NASA, and is part of the **Wallops Flight Facility** (www.nasa.gov/centers/wallops /home). While most of the facility is off-limits, there's a Visitor Center here where you can watch real-live rockets launch into space. (You can also see the rockets launch from spots on Chincoteague Island.) Check the center's launch schedule for specific dates and times.

PAY HOMAGE TO MISTY

If you grew up a fan of the book *Misty of Chincoteague*, make a quick visit to the small **Museum of Chincoteague** (chincoteaguemuseum.com). For the $4 admission, you can see Misty and her foal, Stormy, plus exhibitions of the local area, seafood culture, and, of course, the ponies.

CLIMB THE ASSATEAGUE LIGHT

Stop by this iconic red and white candy-striped lighthouse in the Wildlife Refuge. It's a huff and puff up the 175 steps to the top, but you'll be rewarded with 360-degree views of the park and surrounding islands.

≡ *Good Eats*

If you didn't notice the slow pace of life on Chincoteague, you'll certainly notice it at some of these eateries. In peak season, it's not unusual to stand in line up to an hour at some of the island's popular eateries. In off-season (late October through April), many of the eateries here shut down.

Fine dining isn't really a thing here—there are a few white tablecloth spots, but you can still wear your jeans. Many of the island's best places to eat are seasonal trucks or shacks that pop up and serve great fresh food.

If you're spending all your time on the Maryland side, Ocean City is closer and has a gazillion dining options (see Summer Weekend Getaways).

// Casual Chincoteague dining

SEA STAR CAFE

Chincoteague • www.seastarcafeci.com • $ • sandwiches

The super fresh sandwiches are generously sized. This place is more of a food stand than an actual cafe; you order at a window and either take your food to go or sit at one of a few picnic tables next to a little lake. They're open between March and Thanksgiving.

PICO TAQUERIA

Chincoteague • picotaqueria.com • $ • tacos

There's pretty much always a line at this popular taco spot, but it's worth the wait. The motto here is "You can put anything on a taco," and many of the ingredients come from local farms. They're seasonal; open April to October.

SANDY PONY DONUTS

Chincoteague • sandyponydonut.com • $ • donuts

This small turquoise truck sells hot, made-to-order donuts in a variety of creative flavors. With options such as Porky Pony (bacon, cinnamon sugar, and honey glaze) and the Fruity Pebbles–covered Yabba Dabba Doo-Nut, the treats are just as much eye candy as they are tasty. They're seasonal; open April to October.

ISLAND CREAMERY

Chincoteague • islandcreamery.net • $ • ice cream

It's been called the best ice cream in Virginia and one of the top ice cream spots in the country. Accolades aside, this colorful ice cream parlor is legit, serving small-batch homemade scoops. Also legit: the lines—especially after dinner time, when hordes of dessert seekers keep this place open well past its 10 p.m. closing time. Here's your excuse to have ice cream for breakfast: if you go first thing, you can generally beat the rush.

WOODY'S SERIOUS FOOD

Chincoteague • $ • BBQ

A beachy, seasonal shack on the side of the road serves generously sized BBQ favorites, plus seafood. The meat here is cooked to perfection on the smoker, plus there's a slew of sides. There are hammocks and picnic tables (the whole place feels like a hippie beachy campsite), or you can take it to go.

CAPTAIN ZACK'S SEAFOOD

Chincoteague • www.captzackseafood.com • $$ • seafood

This seafood window is basically an extension of the beach, with a sandy floor and tiki-umbrella'ed picnic tables. The menu revolves around the ocean, with seafood sandwiches, tacos, platters . . . and enough to satisfy the non-fish eaters in your crew, too.

MAIN STREET SHOP & COFFEE SHOP

Chincoteague • www.mainstreet-shop.com • $ • coffee

It's part coffee shop, part boutique, selling a curated collection of home goods, note cards, and women's clothing. There isn't a ton of seating, but it's a great place to get your coffee to go.

// Marsh at Assateague Island National Seashore

≡ Time for a Drink

If you really want nightlife action, head to Ocean City. There's a bar for every type there, with **Seacrets** (seacrets.com), **Macky's** (mackys.com), and **Fager's Island** (www.fagers.com) leading the party scene (see Summer Weekend Getaways).

Chincoteague is not a late-night town—most places close up by 10 or 11 p.m. That said, there are a few places to pony up for a pint.

BLACK NARROWS BREWING CO.

blacknarrowsbrewing.com

Tucked off the main drag, this local brewery serves about nine rotating beers. It's a great nighttime hangout spot: fewer tourists, plus they're open until 11ish on weekends.

ROPEWALK

chincoteague.ropewalk.com

Get your toes in the sand at this palm-tree-strewn tiki bar. There's cornhole, Adirondack chairs with sunset views, and a floating bar. The same live bands that play at Seacrets in Ocean City come through here, too.

≡ Stay Over

There's no formal lodging on Assateague Island, aside from camping. Most pony fans base themselves either on Chincoteague Island or in Ocean City.

Chincoteague overall is fairly no-frills, and the lodging scene's no different. The main drag is lined with budget chain motels, B&Bs and family-owned inns, with beachy house rentals nearby. Hotel prices on the island can skyrocket during peak summer months.

If you really want to spend quality time with the pony population, consider camping, which is available at both parks on the Maryland side. These coveted campsites book up months in advance. (The Chincoteague park does not allow camping; there are RV-style campgrounds on Chincoteague Island, but you'll still have to head into the park to see the ponies.)

1   Assateague Light for big views
2   Chincoteague's Waterfront Park is great for sunset
3   Assateague is a good spot for a beach day

REFUGE INN

www.refugeinn.com • $$

Tucked on a wooded lot a short drive from the Chincoteague Wildlife Refuge, this inn is a convenient and affordable option. It's not the most modern (although few places on the island are), but everything is clean and comfortable, and many of the rooms have balconies overlooking the woods and wetlands.

MISS MOLLY'S INN

missmollys-inn.com • $$

This B&B's claim to fame is that it's where Marguerite Henry stayed when she wrote *Misty of Chincoteague* in 1946. It's a beautiful Victorian-style inn, and they'll set you up with bikes or whatever beach gear you need.

CAMPING

Imagine waking up to a pony grazing outside your tent. There are two camping options on Assateague, both on the Maryland side: one in Assateague State Park and the other at the Assateague National Seashore. You can reserve campsites and a few small cabins at both. One difference is in the showers: the State Park has warm showers and the National Seashore's are cold. But alcohol and bonfires aren't allowed in the State Park.

GOOD TO KNOW

- Assateague Island itself is in a state of flux. The island is actually slowly moving westward due to sea level rise and storms. In fact, the island only became an island in 1933; it was attached to Ocean City until a storm carved an inlet between the two.
- The average cost for a pony at the annual Pony Auction has gone up from $1,413.85 in 2008 to $4,309 in 2018.

BEEN HERE, DONE THAT?

- If the beach is more a focus than the wildlife refuge, consider renting a house in Bethany (Chapter 4), Rehoboth (Chapter 3), or Fenwick Island (just up the beach from Ocean City).
- If you've seen the wild beach ponies on Assateague, check out the wild mountain ponies in Grayson Highlands State Park, down near the Virginia–North Carolina border.
- For another nature preserve escape, visit Blackwater National Wildlife Refuge, which, like Chincoteague, is known for its birds.

As for campsite location, try to snag a seaside campsite—the breezes make it far less buggy. Most of the sites are on sand, so you'll need extra-long tent poles.

Between May and October, sites can fill up six months in advance, so if you see a spot, snag it.

RENTAL SCENE

At this writing, VRBO and HomeAway had more options than Airbnb, if you're looking to stay in Chincoteague. Most rentals here are cottage-y bay homes; nothing beachfront. Ocean City has hundreds of options across all the sites, ranging from high-rise condos to homes that are steps from the beach.

☰ *Plan Around*

The ponies live here, so you can see them all year round. Summer is definitely peak season though, coinciding with school vacations. Prices spike and lines lengthen, but it's also when all the businesses around Chincoteague Island open—many shut down between October and April.

The annual Pony Swim event is the area's biggest production and is going to be the hardest time to find lodging and the like.

Weekends to Plan For (or Avoid):

- **Seafood Festival (May):** Fish, clams, oysters, chowder, and more are served to your stomach's content at this annual bash. Wash it all down with some beer and live music.
- **Pony Roundups (July):** More than 40,000 visitors flood into town. The main event is on a weekday, but there'll be residual crowds on the surrounding weekends. There are usually two other smaller roundups—in April and October, although these don't draw crowds.
- **Oyster Festival (October):** The Chincoteague Oyster Festival has been celebrating the beginning of the oyster season for over 40 years. There are food tents, beer, and prizes.
- **Christmas Parade (December):** Fire companies come out from all over the Eastern Shore to ring in the holiday season with a family-friendly parade through Chincoteague.

Part Two
Outdoorsy Fun

7

Take an Epic Scenic Road Trip, Part I

Skyline Drive and Shenandoah National Park, VA

Tackle the twisty-turny mountain roads, take in the killer views, and pop off for a hike along the region's most scenic driving route.

FROM DC: 70 MILES · 1 HOUR 20 MINS | TRIP LENGTH: DAY TRIP OR OVERNIGHT

DO	EAT	DRINK	BUY
drive	Blackberry Ice Cream Pie at Skyland Resort	local wine	vintage National Park postcards

Together with the Blue Ridge Parkway, Skyline Drive is the G.O.A.T. road trip in the DC area—maybe even the East Coast. Set in Shenandoah National Park, the scenic drive snakes along the Blue Ridge Mountains for 105 photo-primed miles. There are 75 designated scenic overlooks to wow you along the way, plus waterfall trails, tree tunnels, and wildlife from bears to birds. Come fall, there isn't a better place to see the leaves change, but the drive is open—and worth an adventure—any time of year.

Getting to Skyline Drive

There's no public transit here, plus it's a road trip—you need your own wheels (car, motorcycle, or bike all do the trick).

Since this is national park land, you've gotta pay to play here. (It's $30 per car, $25 per motorcycle, and $15 if you're biking into the park.) There are four entry points with pay stations along the drive:

- Front Royal: MP (a.k.a "milepost") 0
- Thornton Gap: MP 31.5 (near Luray and Sperryville)
- Swift Run Gap: MP 65.5 (near Harrisonburg, Massanutten, and Elkton)
- Rockfish Gap: MP 105.5 (near Waynesboro, Staunton, and Charlottesville)

The closest entrance to DC is Front Royal—it's about 1 hour and 20 minutes' drive from the city. This entrance can also get insane during leaf peeping season; on a peak weekend, the line to get into the park can stretch for miles. Likewise at Thornton Gap. Insider tip: Swift Run and Rockfish Gaps usually have shorter lines, even during peak foliage. If you enter at either of those entrances, drive north on Skyline.

The speed limit here's only 35 miles per hour, and there's too much to see to rush. You can drive the whole route in 3 or 4 hours. If you plan on hiking, plan for at least a full day.

Get Your Bearings

Skyline Drive forms the backbone of Shenandoah National Park, traveling 105 miles from Front Royal down to Rockfish Gap near Waynesboro (where this route ends and the Blue Ridge Parkway picks up).

The road runs north–south, although it winds around so much it's easy to lose track of what direction you're facing. In general, as you head south, the Shenandoah Valley is to your right (west) and the farmland of the Piedmont is to your left (east).

Stone mileposts tick off your mileage as you go, and all directions around the park (and in this guide) are listed by the closest "MP" (milepost).

PARK GRAMS

Check out @shenandoahnps on Instagram—not only do they share great park views, you'll get tips on park status, foliage status, weather closures, animal sightings, etc.

Most of the time the road curves its way along the ridges of the Blue Ridge Mountains, dipping in and out of forests. Elevation ranges from 561 to 3,680 feet (and higher if you're climbing a peak)—your ears will probably pop a few times along the way.

Over 75 overlooks are stationed along the park and are pretty evenly distributed, although some say the best views are in the northern section. Honestly, most of them are pretty impressive. About 500 miles of hiking trails also lace the park, including the Appalachian Trail, which has many crossings with other trails. There are trailhead parking lots along the drive, too.

// MP marker

In short, Skyline Drive will lead you through some of the best the park has to offer.

≡ *Road Trip: Shenandoah*

Many of the views are so amazing that you may even find yourself with scenic overlook fatigue. ("Yawn, this beautiful 180-degree mountain view looks like the one we saw 2 miles ago.")

There's no right or wrong place to stop along the route. The best view or the best hike depends on the time of year, time of day, type of clouds in the sky, etc. That said, there are

// Thornton Hollow Overlook sunrise

some particularly popular sites along the drive. The best way to do Skyline Drive, however, is to not stress about "must sees" and instead, stop where you want and skip what doesn't speak to you.

MP 4.5: DICKEY RIDGE VISITOR CENTER:

There's some pretty immediate view-gratification at this end of the drive. If you need a bathroom, this visitor center, which overlooks the Shenandoah Valley, is a good place to stop.

MP 5.7: SIGNAL KNOB OVERLOOK:

Signal Knob is a few miles in and is a good place to get your first real "OMG these views" kicks. The long roadside vista looks west over the Shenandoah Valley and the town of Strasburg. If you're up for a big hike, there's a 10-miler that climbs up all over Signal Knob; access is outside of the park.

MP 14.9: BROWNTON VALLEY OVERLOOK:

With a westward valley view, this is a good place to stop for sunset.

MP 20.9: HOGBACK OVERLOOK:

Unlike Little Hogback, which is just to the north, this expansive westward-looking vista is a contender for the best in the park. You can see some actual blue ridges here, plus the snaking Shenandoah River.

MP 24: ELKWALLOW WAYSIDE:

It's nothing fancy, but it has a little bit of every-thing. This pit stop has bathrooms, a store with groceries and grilled food that you order from a counter, souvenirs, and camping gear. There are also picnic grounds.

MP 31.3: THORNTON GAP:

You can enter the park here, via either Luray to the west or Sperryville to the east. (FYI: the park headquarters are here too, just east of Luray.) On Skyline Drive, you'll find bathrooms at Thornton Gap, plus this is where you can start **Mary's Rock Trail**, a 2.9-mile out-and-back that has a great 360-degree view of the park.

MP 32.2: TUNNEL PARKING OVERLOOK:

Just on the south side of the boul-dery tunnel near Thornton Gap is a pull-off where you can get a picture of said tunnel, plus a look at the mountains to the east.

MP 35: PINNACLES OVERLOOK:

There's a solid view of a handful of mountains at this curve-in-the-road viewpoint—including a good glimpse of Old Rag. Foliage fans like this spot in the fall (although obviously the leaves change year to year). Just down the road, the **Pinnacles** picnic spot has covered table areas, grills, and a giant fireplace.

MP 38.5: STONY MAN OVERLOOK:

A big Shenandoah Valley vista, plus views of the Stony Man rocky outcrop greet you at this pull-off. Some of the pull-offs can feel a little claustrophobic but this one has a ton of parking. If you climb to the top (it's not too far), you can claim your "I hiked the Appalachian Trail (at least a little bit of it)" bragging rights.

MP 41.7: SKYLAND RESORT:

Welcome to the highest point on Skyline Drive. It's also one of the most built-up places—you'll find a restaurant, tap room, and lodge, all with spectacular mountain views (especially at sunset). The resort here dates back to 1888; if the surrounding nature doesn't remind you you're in a national park, the classic timber and stone construction of the building will.

MP 45.5: HAWKSBILL GAP PARKING: Pick up the trailhead to climb the park's highest mountain here, or in the Upper Hawksbill lot a mile or so down the road. This is a super popular hike so the lots get crowded.

MP 46.4: OLD RAG OVERLOOK: Look to the left from this roadside pull-off and you'll see the park's most famous peak.

MP 50.4: DARK HOLLOW FALLS PARKING: The park's most popular waterfall trail starts here.

MP 51: BIG MEADOWS AND BYRD VISITOR CENTER: It's hard to miss this place: it really is a big meadow, so it looks different from all the other woodsy or viewpoint stops. You can rest up, eat up, and fuel up here at the lodge/campground, restaurant, and gas station. This is also the best spot in the park to view the night sky.

MP 77.8: ROCKYTOP OVERLOOK: A number of mountains converge into view here.

MP 79.5: LOFT MOUNTAIN: The southernmost wayside in the park, this stop has a large gift shop and offers a grill with both indoor seating and outdoor picnic tables. The campground here has views you definitely won't mind waking up to. A little ways north on the drive, around MP 74, Loft Mountain Overlook is also a stunner.

MP 92: MOORMANS RIVER OVERLOOK: This is one of the best views in the park, thanks to the pop of water you'll see nestled between the rolling peaks.

MP 104.4: ROCKFISH GAP: Welcome, or goodbye—you've reached the southern entry point of Skyline Drive. Keep going south and you'll quickly enter the Blue Ridge Parkway (keep reading, Chapter 8 covers it). To the east lie Crozet and Charlottesville; to the west is Staunton. To get back to DC, you can go east or west; check the traffic, and if it's comparable, we recommend taking the eastern route.

SKYLINE GAS

There is only one gas station in the park—at Big Meadows. It's not cheap up here, though, so try to fuel up before you get into the park.

Best Hikes

- **Mary's Rock Trail (MP 31.5):** Near the ranger station at Thornton Gap, this popular 3.7-mile hike to a rocky outcrop gives you a good look at the Shenandoah Valley, as well as the entrance to Skyline Drive. It's a well-trafficked hike.
- **White Oak Canyon Trail (MP 42.4):** There are two ways to access this 9.5-mile, waterfall-loving trail. You can start at the top, just beyond Skyland on Skyline Drive, and hike down (but then you'll have the harder leg on the way back up). Or you can pick up the trail outside the park in Syria and hike up to Skyland, have a bite, then head back down. If 9 miles sounds scary, you can always do a shorter out-and-back.
- **Dark Hollow Falls Trail (MP 51.4):** It's totally fine to chase waterfalls on this popular hike down to a 70-foot cascade. At 1.4 miles round trip, it's a relatively short excursion; just get ready for the trek back uphill after you tromp down to the falls. Photographers love this shady spot, though it can get pretty busy.
- **Old Rag:** The most popular summit hike in the park. You can see Old Rag from Skyline Drive, but the Skyline Drive isn't the easiest way to reach the trail. See Chapter 10 for more details.

>> **Fall Foliage:** Peak leaf color out here is similar—but not always the exact same—as DC. Weather and elevation have a big effect on the trees. Usually higher elevations change first, and the trees up here may be bare when the lowlands are turning. Really windy, rainy, or cloudy weather can make the leaves fall or not turn quite as vibrant.

// Shenandoah National Park hiking

Driving Tips

// Black bear

- **Make way for bears! (And other animals.)** The park's wildlife—including deer, wild turkeys, and black bears—don't understand the laws of traffic and won't wait to cross the road. Keep an eye out.
- **Go slow and let the speedsters pass.** The speed limit is 35 mph, and there's really no reason to rush. Not only are those overlooks scenic, they make good places to pull over and let the impatient tailgater behind you pass.
- **Watch out for cyclists.** This route's popular among cyclists. Respect their space—not only because it's badass that they're biking these hills in the first place, but also because you don't want to whip around a curve and have to swerve when there are thousand-foot drops below.

☰ *While You're Here*

CAVES

Maybe you've seen the **Luray Caverns** (luraycaverns.com) ads on TV? It's the biggest and best-known cave on the East Coast, with 10-story ceilings and a "stalacpipe" organ. Luray's a quick drive from the park's Thornton Gap entrance, but there are other caves throughout the Shenandoah Valley. If you're closer to Front Royal, **Skyline Caverns** (www.skylinecaverns .com) has extremely rare crystal formations. On the southern side of the park, **Grand Caverns**

SKYLINE DRIVE INFO

Cost: $30 per car, $25 per motorcycle

// Deer along Skyline Drive

- The **National Park Service** has driving and hiking maps, weather updates, ranger programs, and more on their park website: www.nps.gov/shen
- www.goshenandoah.com has information about all the park's dining options, lodges, and more.

(www.grandcaverns.com) has been drawing visitors since 1806—it's the oldest tourist cave in the country.

VIRGINIA'S HORSESHOE BEND

As the Shenandoah River squiggles its way down the valley, it offers up a beautiful horseshoe vista at **Shenandoah River State Park** (www.dcr.virginia.gov/state-parks/shenandoah-river). There's a scenic overlook where you'll get a good photo op, plus the park has hiking trails, camping and picnic areas, and a kayak put-in spot.

SMALL TOWN EXPLORING

Pop out of the park to putz around the smattering of small towns on either side of the mountain ridge. To the west, **Front Royal** and **Luray** have small but bustling historic downtowns. To the east, **Sperryville** has emerged as a tiny foodie haven, as has **Washington** (home of the Inn at Little Washington, Chapter 27).

☰ *Good Eats*

Skyline Drive has a handful of food options along the way, mostly at the casual waysides or a couple of sit-down restaurants. These are all seasonal though; most open in the spring (March through May) and close in November (dates are online).

There are also a number of great picnic setups, including some with grills and shelters. If you're going to picnic, you can grab-and-go from Skyland or Big Meadows, but for more options, just BYO food from outside the park.

Pop outside the park and your options increase exponentially in the towns on either side of the route. That said, if you're doing this as a day trip, don't waste your time leaving the park mid-way and re-entering to do the rest of the drive; just eat when you enter or exit.

In the Park

POLLOCK DINING ROOM

MP 4 • www.goshenandoah.com • $$ • American

The menu at Skyland's main dining room is what you'd expect at a national park lodge; a decent mix of American classics plus local go-tos. The view is beyond expectations, especially at sunset. The must-eat here is the signature blackberry ice cream pie.

SPOTTSWOOD DINING ROOM

MP 51 • www.goshenandoah.com • $$ • American

The other main dining room is down the road at Big Meadows Lodge. It's run by the same group who does Skyland, so some menu options overlap, although each venue is a little different. A new outdoor terrace offers dining al fresco.

Outside the Park

SPERRYVILLE

Blink and you could miss this tiny creekside town. So keep your eyes open—there's some serious food business happening here. **Three Blacksmiths** (www.threeblacksmiths.com • $$$$) does a knockout $99 five-course dinner in an intimate hearth-warmed dining room on weekends. Nearby, **Rappahannock Pizza Kitchen** (RPK) (www.rappahannockpizzakitchen.com • $) uses locally sourced ingredients in their artisanal pizzas.

LURAY

To the west of the Thornton Gap entrance, downtown Luray has some cute spots. **Gathering Grounds** (ggrounds.com • $) has enormous made-in-house sandwiches and a fun eclectic vibe. If you're here in the morning, try **Uncle Bucks** ($), home of the Redneck Benedict and Southern comfort food faves.

CROZET

Just east of the southern entrance, little Crozet has some good food picks—plus it's on the route back to DC. **Crozet Pizza** (www.crozetpizza.com • $) has been called some of the best 'za in the country. Nearby, **Smoked Kitchen and Tap** (smokedkt.com • $$) graduated from a Charlottesville food truck to this brick-and-mortar BBQ spot. The Rooftop, on the roof of Smoked, has views of those mountains you just drove through. For more options, Charlottesville isn't much farther along.

☰ *Time for a Drink*

Nightlife in Shenandoah National Park consists of stargazing and listening for wildlife. Two taprooms at the park's resorts anchor the beverage scene here, and they aren't open all year.

If you want to cap off your adventure with a glass of something, come down out of the mountains—either side of Skyline is rich wine and beer country.

MOUNTAIN TAPROOM

www.goshenandoah.com • Closed late November through March or April

Doesn't get much better than a drink with a view at this ridge-top bar at the Skyland Resort. They serve a handful of park-inspired specialty cocktails, such as the Blue Ridge Mule, plus local beers and live music most nights.

NEW MARKET TAPROOM

www.goshenandoah.com • Closed November through mid-May

Over at Big Meadows, this bar has a more robust drink menu than its Skyland counterpart. There are craft beer flights, local and private label wines, and another batch of mountain-themed cocktails. Nightly live music is also a draw here.

SKYLINE WINE TRAIL

As Route 211 approaches Skyline Drive from the east, it strings together more than 10 vineyards and breweries. Highlights include **Hopkins Ale Works**, **Copper Fox Distillery**, and **Gadino Cellars**. You can use this route as an entryway to the middle part of the park, or start your trip on Skyline Drive in Front Royal and then hit up some Route 211 wineries on the way home.

☰ *Stay Over*

Sure, you can do the drive in a day, but a trip to Skyline Drive is best when it's done as an overnight or a Shenandoah Valley weekend escape.

Most of the in-park accommodations are found in the central section of the park. There are two main lodges, plus a handful of campsites and rustic cabins. They're all seasonal, so they close for the winter and early spring.

Outside the park, take your pick from any of the towns between Winchester and Charlottesville. There are cute creekside cabins, chain hotels, tree houses, inns, farm stays, vineyard stays . . . basically you'll have no problem putting a roof over your head.

If you're craving some camping action, the national park-caliber campgrounds here are a great place to pitch a tent.

SKYLAND RESORT AND BIG MEADOWS LODGE

www.goshenandoah.com • $$

These two resorts are the anchors of the national park's dining, lodging, and activities scene. Skyland sits at the highest elevation point on Skyline Drive, and has rooms and suites in the lodge, plus cabins. Some of them have pretty spectacular valley views. Big Meadows is a popular place to view the night sky and has similar rooms and cabins. Few rooms here have air conditioning.

CAMPING

None of the campgrounds are open all year—most open in late March or April and close in October or November. Around the park's halfway point, **Lewis Mountain Campground** has tent sites as well as cabins you can rent. In the southern part of the park, **Loft Mountain** is one of the biggest and best-equipped campgrounds along Skyline Drive. Usually campsites cost around $15; some take reservations (via www.recreation.gov), while others are first-come, first-served.

RENTAL SCENE

There are tons of options across all the big home-sharing sites here—Airbnb, HomeAway, VRBO. What's more, you can find some cool sweet digs, like cute riverside cabins near Luray, tree houses with views for days, rustic yurts, and mountain homes with hot tubs overlooking the Blue Ridge.

☰ Plan Around

Over a million people visit the park every year, and if you come here on a beautiful fall weekend when the leaves are turning, you'll swear there are a million people there in a day. Peak fall foliage is when Skyline Drive is at its most scenic—and most crowded.

Aside from that, holiday weekends, nice-weather summer weekends, and free-entry weekends get busy. There are also a handful of fun events and festivals in the park, although none of them draw anywhere near as many people as the leaves.

Weekends to Plan For (or Avoid):

- **National Park Week (April):** This week kicks off with free entry for a day. There are events and special hikes around the park.
- **Wildflower Weekend (May):** Flower walks and art exhibitions celebrate the park's 850 types of flowering plants, which are usually starting to bloom around this time.
- **Night Sky Festival (August):** Join the park rangers for some stargazing as well as daytime solar viewing and talks on all things space.
- **Apple Butter Festival (September):** Try apple butter straight from the pot (or make some yourself). There's also apple fixin's galore within the BBQ and bar offerings.
- **Fall Foliage (varies, usually around October):** If you don't like crowds, this time might not be for you. If you can stand some traffic, then this is when the park really shows its stuff. Check the park's Instagram before you arrive; they often give tips on which entrances are less crowded.

1 Dark Hollow Falls
2 Fall foliage on Skyline Drive
3 Mountain ridges

GOOD TO KNOW

- Cell phone service is very spotty throughout the park. Pick up a park map from the entry stations in case your phone GPS doesn't work.

- The National Park Service does free entry days a few times throughout the year. (Usually it's MLK, Jr. Day, Veterans Day, and then a few others.) Check their website to save the fee. On the flip side, if you want a bigger outdoors kick, consider getting an annual Shenandoah pass. At $55, it turns into a discount on your second visit.

- There's a free Shenandoah National Park app by the National Park Service, which has road and park closure updates, maps, and more. Download it before you get out here.

- Leave no trace is a common outdoors mantra (enjoy the nature, don't litter/mess with things). Shenandoah National Park Service is one-upping the concept by asking visitors to follow a social media leave no trace—this means not tagging specific locations in the park, in order to keep certain spots from getting overrun.

- The park is technically open every day, but weather can affect that. Check before you head out here—if there's a major storm they may shut down parts or all of Skyline Drive. Likewise for government shutdowns—when these happen, the park closes.

BEEN HERE, DONE THAT?

- Keep going! The Blue Ridge Parkway lies just to the south and is a natural continuation of Skyline Drive (Chapter 8).

- Many people cruise through Skyline Drive, then turn around and head back to DC. Instead, think about staying in a cabin around Luray or Sperryville, then popping into the park for a hike (a Getaway cabin is a fun option, Chapter 28).

- Tackle Old Rag. You've seen it from Skyline—now see it up close (Chapter 10).

8

Take an Epic Scenic Road Trip, Part II

Blue Ridge Parkway, VA

Find out why this scenic mountain route, which runs all the way from Virginia to North Carolina, is nicknamed "America's Favorite Drive."

FROM DC: 137 MILES · 2.5 HOURS | TRIP LENGTH: OVERNIGHT OR WEEKEND

DO	EAT	DRINK	BUY
drive and hike	orchard fruit	local beer	Appalachian goods at a general store

Like its sister Skyline Drive to the north, the Blue Ridge Parkway runs along the ridge of the Appalachian chain's Blue Ridge Mountains, delivering big views and big thrills. But this drive is Skyline on steroids—and, it's free. Spanning 469 miles and two states, the Parkway laces together some of the highest mountains and deepest gorges east of the Rockies. You'll see hazy blue mountain ridges. Hike to perches for sky-on-fire sunsets. Swim in creeks and discover hidden waterfalls. Soak in the music, food, and heart of Appalachian culture.

So fuel up the car, take a big breath of that mountain air, and get your camera ready—these views will feed your soul. No filter needed.

≡ *Getting to the Blue Ridge Parkway*

The Blue Ridge Parkway runs from the bottom of Shenandoah National Park (at Rockfish Gap, near Waynesboro, VA) all the way to southwestern North Carolina.

To do the full Parkway in one trip, you'll need more than a weekend. For a standard weekend trip from DC, focus on the section between the northern terminus and Roanoke, VA (about four non-Parkway hours from Washington)—that's what this section will focus on. This drive is about 120 miles and will take you 3 to 4 hours; more if you stop a lot.

There's no "right" direction to travel this route. You can either drive south on a standard route such as I-81, then cut in and make your way back north along the Parkway, or pick up the Parkway at the northern end and go south. There are entrances every 20 miles or less, so it's pretty easy to hop on and off the route.

If you're relying on a GPS to get here it can be tough to actually find an entrance (you can't always just type "Blue Ridge Parkway"). Google Maps recognizes the northern entrance (type "Blue Ridge Parkway north entrance"); otherwise it can be easier to use coordinates or drop a pin manually. Once you get to the Parkway, don't bother using Google Maps. It'll try direct you off the Parkway to faster routes.

Try mapping to the coordinates below for some commonly used entry points:

NORTH ENTRANCE (AFTON) | MP 0 (Afton, Skyline Drive, and gas are nearby): 38.030000, -78.857362

REID'S GAP (ROUTE 664) | MP 13 (Wintergreen Resort is nearby): 37.9021852, -78.9852227

MONTEBELLO (ROUTE 56) | MP 27.2 (Crabtree Falls and gas are nearby): 37.8868303, -79.1511592

BUENA VISTA (HIGHWAY 60) | MP 45.6 (Lexington, VA, and gas are nearby): 37.7425404, -79.3012466

GLASGOW (HIGHWAY 510) | MP 63.7 (Lynchburg, VA, Natural Bridge, and gas are nearby): 37.5542078, -79.3730326

BUCHANAN (ROUTE 43) | MP 90.9 (gas nearby): 37.4833350, -79.6686730

VINTON (ROUTE 24) | MP 112.2 (gas nearby): 37.2825540, -79.8524910

NARROWS (HIGHWAY 220) | MP 121.4 (Roanoke and gas are nearby): 37.2179220, -79.9450740

Oh, and this is a road trip, so suffice it to say you need your own wheels. Cars are most common, although you'll see a lot of bikers—both motorcycles and road bikes—tackling the twists in the road.

Get Your Bearings

The Blue Ridge Parkway squiggles its way up and down the mountains, running diagonally from Rockfish Gap near Waynesboro down the slanted western region of Virginia and North Carolina to the Tennessee border, near Great Smoky Mountain National Park.

Since the road curves so much, it's incredibly easy to lose your sense of direction up here—you may be driving a southern route on the Parkway but physically going north at times. For this guide's purposes, directions assume you're going south, so anything that's "to the right" is relatively west-ish and "to the left" is the eastern side of the Parkway.

// Skyline Drive

// Blue Ridge Parkway

SKYLINE DRIVE VS. BLUE RIDGE PARKWAY

They're sister routes, but not the same.

- Blue Ridge Parkway is free; Skyline Drive, as part of Shenandoah National Park, has an entry fee.
- Skyline Drive's speed limit is 35 mph; the Parkway is 35–45 mph.
- Skyline Drive is closer to DC, so it's an easier day-trip option.
- The Parkway intersects a lot of roads; it's pretty easy to hop on and off it. Skyline Drive only has four entry/exit points, so once you're on it, you're on it.
- The Parkway is about 4.5 times longer than Skyline Drive, which means there is more to see.

Just as on Skyline Drive, everything on the Parkway is measured by mileposts (MP), the stone posts with numbers on them that line the west side of the road. You'll typically see them every mile, although there may be some stretches where a few miles go by without one visible. MP 0 is at the northern entrance, then they go up as you go south.

☰ Road Trip: Blue Ridge Parkway

Drawn up during the Great Depression, this scenic route was created to connect two of the East's great parks: Shenandoah and Great Smoky Mountains. But the Parkway's just as enjoyable as its bookends; in fact, some may even like it more—in 2017, it was the most visited unit in the National Park System.

There isn't really one "if you miss this you blew it" stop along the Parkway. Sure, some hikes and overlooks and towns are more frequented than others, but for the most part the name of the game is to explore on your own and stop where you feel like it.

That said, of the 200 overlooks and stops along the drive leading to Roanoke, here are some of the most notable ones:

MP 0: ENTER THE PARKWAY: The northern entrance is at Rockfish Gap, a little south of Waynesboro. This is where Skyline Drive ends and the Blue Ridge Parkway picks up. There's a very small Visitor Info station before you get onto the Parkway.

MP 0.2: AFTON OVERLOOK: It only takes a few minutes on the Parkway before BAM! View! This viewpoint looks east out over the town of Afton.

MP 6: HUMPBACK ROCKS: This is a popular picnic and hiking hub, especially for folks who live in nearby Charlottesville. There's a small visitor center here (which means bathrooms!), where you can pick up maps and info. A couple hundred yards down the Parkway from the visitor center is a pull-off with a large parking lot and the Humpback Rocks trailhead (see below).

MP 11: RAVENS ROOST: This is an overlook you'll want to stop for. The rock-walled ledge looks westward over layers of mountains as well as the Shenandoah Valley.

MP 13.7: WINTERGREEN RESORT: A short drive from the Parkway brings you to this popular mountain resort. More info on this below.

To the west, Sherando Lake is a good detour; there's hiking, swimming, and camping here.

MP 19: TWENTY-MINUTE CLIFF: You're really in the mountains now; this viewpoint overlooks a stretch of the Blue Ridge that doesn't have a lot of development, making it feel nice and remote. The name comes from the big rock beneath the overlook, which is used to tell time by the residents in the little town of White Rock down below. When the sun hits this rock, it means there are 20 minutes left before it sets behind the mountain.

// Hiker at Humpback Rocks

MP 27: PARKWAY ENTRANCE AT VA-56: CRABTREE FALLS (MP 27.2):
Not to be confused with the Crabtree Falls in North Carolina (also along the Parkway), this is
one of the best places to see waterfalls along the Virginia stretch of the Blue Ridge Parkway.

MP 36: YANKEE HORSE RIDGE: A nice place to stretch your legs. There's an old
railroad line here, plus a little bridge and a trail up to a waterfall. Some people stop here for a
picnic.

MP 45.6: PARKWAY ENTRANCE AT US 60: Get on or off here at Buena Vista to
detour to Lexington.

MP 61: OTTER CREEK: There are actually multiple Otter Creek pull-offs, starting at
around MP 57, but just before MP 61, there's a campground and picnic tables here along the
shady creek.

MP 63: JAMES RIVER OVERLOOK: This is the low point of the Parkway—elevation-
wise, that is. The James River slices through the mountains, creating a pretty landscape of
water and peaks that you can view from a bridge. It's especially picturesque in the fall when
all the foliage reflects off the water. There's also a visitor center here, plus picnic tables, short
hiking trails, and a series of canal locks you can explore.

MP 63.7: PARKWAY ENTRANCE AT US 501: Just across the James River is an
entry/exit point that, if you take it west, will take you to **Natural Bridge**. This impressive 215-

foot-tall stone arch was once surveyed by George Washington, whose initials are etched in the rock wall. Allow at least an hour to hike around Natural Bridge.

MP 76(ISH): JUST A CURVE IN THE ROAD: Not every viewpoint has a name. Here, you'll get one of those quintessential Parkway curve experiences, with the road curving into what seems like oblivion, and expansive western views below.

MP 78: SUNSET FIELD OVERLOOK: True to its name, this westward facing viewpoint can be a good spot for sunsets. There's also a 1.5-mile trail here to Apple Orchard Falls, a 200-foot cascade.

MP 82.5: FALLINGWATER AND FLAT TOP TRAILS: There are two parking lots a short distance apart; this first one is best if you're hiking the Fallingwater Trail, because the trailhead starts in the parking lot. The farther one is better if you're hiking Flat Top. (It's a short walk between lots, so either works.) **Fallingwater** is about a 1.6-mile loop down along a cascading stream, then back up through the woods. It takes about an hour. **Flat Top** is one of the three Peaks of Otter—the trail here is about 5 miles out and back, and takes about 3 hours. It's tough and very rocky but rewards you with a view.

MP 86: PEAKS OF OTTER: Set in the shadow of the three Peaks of Otter (Flat Top, Sharp Top, and Harkening Hill), this is the most "built-up" spot along the Blue Ridge Parkway in Virginia. There's a visitor center with a gift shop, plus a pretty lakeside lodge, a campground, and a restaurant and bar overlooking the mountains. There are also a handful of popular hiking trails up the peaks and around the lake here.

If you're driving south, you'll see the lodge first, then the visitor center is on the other side of the road a little bit farther. Around lunch time this place (and its parking lot) gets very busy.

MP 90.9: PARKWAY ENTRANCE AT VA 43: Route 43 actually follows the Parkway for a little, so if you're heading east, toward Bedford (a good place to pop out for a bite), the exit is near the Peaks of Otter campground. To go west from the Parkway, toward Buchanan, you'll exit a little farther down the road.

MP 90: PORTER MOUNTAIN OVERLOOK: This shady viewpoint has a great valley view, plus it's at a curve in the Parkway. If you look toward your right (south down the route), you can see the roadway pop out along the mountain ridges. That's where you're heading next, into a stretch of great views along the mountain ridge.

MP 95: HARVEY'S KNOB OVERLOOK: A fantastic view to the west, overlooking a massive valley. Keep an eye on the sky too; this is a really good place to spot hawks.

MP 106: PARKWAY ENTRANCE AT US 460: This is the first of a handful of exits around Roanoke, the largest city on the Virginia's piece of the Parkway. There's gas nearby if you really need it, but otherwise hold out for the next two entrances, since they're closer to downtown Roanoke.

MP 112.2: PARKWAY ENTRANCE AT VA 24: To pop into Roanoke from the east or the north, use this Parkway exit.

MP 115: EXPLORE PARK: A big Parkway Visitor Center is here, with historical and nature exhibitions in addition to maps and drive info. Stretch your legs on the hiking and biking trails around the park, or spend the night in a pod cabin or a yurt.

MP 120: ROANOKE MOUNTAIN OVERLOOK: Most people who go to Roanoke take a look at the city from the **Mill Mountain Star**. While this view (and the giant star) is impressive, a less-crowded option is about 4 miles off the Parkway and has stunning sunrise AND sunset views.

Best Hikes

There are over 350 miles of trail along the Parkway, including the granddaddy of all trails, the Appalachian (you could follow this route all the way down to Georgia, or up to Maine).

// Appalachian Trail

Here are some of the best hikes on and near the Parkway, though you really can't go wrong:

- **Humpback Rocks (MP 5.9):** This 2-mile out-and-back is steep—it's a workout for sure—but the reward is an expansive view of the Shenandoah Valley at the top from its namesake, Humpback Rocks.
- **Sharp Top (MP 86):** A wildly popular (and challenging) 3.5-mile out-and-back hike brings you to the stunning summit of one of the highest peaks around. There are 360-degree views from the top. Start across from the Peaks of Otter visitor center. You can combine this hike with a Flat Top climb, too, for a longer adventure.
- **McAfee Knob, Roanoke:** Alright, it's not ON the Parkway—it's about a 30-minute drive from the Parkway entrances in Roanoke. But this awesome 7.5-mile hike takes you to the most photographed spot on the Appalachian Trail, so it's worth a detour. Just make it an early outing; the small parking lot fills up as soon as the sun comes up on weekends.

TIP: GAS UP

There aren't any gas stations on the Parkway itself, but there are some in Waynesboro, a short drive from the entrance. If you run low along the drive, you'll have to hop off at one of the Parkway exits. Many, but not all, have gas stations nearby.

// Blue Ridge Parkway

Driving Tips

- **Drive carefully, and keep your lights on.** These different elevations often create cloud banks, fog, or even storms in the higher elevations, so you could have dark, low-visibility driving even if it's sunny at the base of the mountains.
- **Grab a paper map.** Cell service isn't great up here, and it disappears completely for long stretches. Mapping apps are still usable, but you can't beat paper when you're out in the wilderness. Paper maps are available at all the Parkway visitor centers.
- **Speed limit: 45 mph.** The views alone should deter you from speeding; this is not a route to rush. But more important, there are a lot of animals who live along the parkway, plus hikers and police patrols. Drive the speed limit.
- **Park smart.** Sometimes that view is just so good you need a photo ASAP, but that doesn't mean you can just pull over wherever and leave your car. All four car wheels need to be parked off the pavement if you're going to stop on the shoulder.

≡ *While You're Here*

LOOK FOR WILDLIFE

The Blue Ridge Parkway is home to black bears, deer, wild turkeys, bobcats, and a whole host of birds and other animals. Keep your eyes peeled on hikes or as you drive—often there'll be animals to the side of the road (or crossing it, so watch out!).

SEE THE NIGHT SKY

It's a road, so it's open at all hours (except in really bad weather). This means you can come up to the Parkway after hours and see great glimpses of the night sky.

If you're into astrophotography, come up here during the daytime to scout your shot, then return, and you'll likely have the place to yourself at night.

FLOYD FRIDAY NIGHT JAMBOREE

www.floydcountrystore.com

Flatfoot into the weekend at the Floyd Country Store's legendary weekly jam sesh. There are string bands playing bluegrass as folks clog, square-dance, and two-step into the night. Getting here is a stretch—it's another hour past Roanoke, but if you're seeking authentic Appalachia, this is worth the early DC departure.

≡ *Good Eats*

As any road tripper knows, snacks can be the make-or-break to keep hanger at bay. Options are pretty limited along the Parkway itself, so you're best off bringing some snacks or a picnic—restaurants may not be plentiful, but picnic tables are. That said, there are a LOT of places to eat if you venture just beyond the Parkway.

MORE INFO

- The **Blue Ridge Parkway Association** (www.blueridgeparkway.org) has a ton of information on their site, including an interactive map and trip planner.
- The **National Park Service** manages the parkway and has a lot of useful info on their site (www.nps.gov/blri).

On the Parkway

PEAKS OF OTTER LODGE

There are a few options here. You can sit down in the big buffet-style dining room, which has lake views, but it can have a wait if you're here at lunch rush hour. If you'd rather not sit, the to-go coffee counter sells snacks such as hummus and pretzels.

Off the Parkway

BEDFORD

An easy exit from the Parkway at MP 87 drops you in Bedford, a small and friendly mountain town with a surprisingly large number of places to eat. It may look modest and homey, but the sandwiches at **Town Kitchen & Provisions** (townkitchenprovisions.com) can compete with your favorite big-city deli. For crowd-pleaser tacos and Mexican food (including vegan and gluten-free options), try **Azul**.

LEXINGTON

About 15 minutes from the Buena Vista Parkway entrance is Lexington, VA, a charming university town that has something for everybody. **The Red Hen** (redhenlex.com) serves upscale farm-to-table fare and made headlines in 2018 for its encounter with White House staff. Meanwhile, there are college-budget friendly places such as **Macado's** (www.macados.net), where you can get sandwiches, and **Salerno's** (www.salernolex.com), where you can get pizza and beer from the pour-your-own-beer bar.

☰ *Time for a Drink*

On this stretch of the Blue Ridge Parkway, nightlife isn't really a thing. The Peaks of Otter and Wintergreen have lodge bars, but otherwise it'll be just you and nature out here once the sun goes down.

Off the Parkway, it's another story. The road runs by many of the spots covered in other chapters, like Staunton and Charlottesville, all of which have booming beer and wine scenes. Roanoke, too, is emerging as a beer town.

BOOZE TRAILS

There may be as many miles of wine and beer trails surrounding the Blue Ridge as there are miles of Parkway pavement. The area has craft-beverage fever. (Some say that the water quality of the Blue Ridge Mountains makes for better brewing.)

One of the best drink trails is near the northern portion of the Parkway: the **Nelson 151** (nelson151.com) connects about 13 breweries, wineries, and more on a road that runs along the base of the Blue Ridge. Near the Peaks of Otter and MP 86, exit the Parkway for the **Bedford Wine Trail** (thebedfordwinetrail.com), which pairs seven wineries with mountain views.

DEVILS BACKBONE BREWING COMPANY

dbbrewingcompany.com

Near Wintergreen and the MP 13 exit, the base camp of this beer company is much more than a brewery. There's a campground, bonfires, and a compound with multiple bars.

ROANOKE

In addition to local brewers such as Twin Creeks (www.twincreeksbrewing.com) and Big Lick (biglickbrewingco.com), the Roanoke area has emerged as an HQ2 of sorts for some West Coast names. **Deschutes** (www.deschutesbrewery.com) opened their East Coast operation in downtown Roanoke, while **Ballast Point** (www.ballastpoint.com) debuted a large tasting room, restaurant, and rooftop bar in nearby Daleville.

☰ Stay Over

The lodging options ON the Parkway are reminiscent of a national park: There's a rustic lodge, a full-on resort, and a handful of cabins and campsites.

During summer and peak fall foliage, these can book up a few weeks out, but with so many towns a short hop from the route, you'll have no problem finding a place to spend the night. Charlottesville, Lexington, Bedford, and Roanoke are all good bases with hotels at all price points.

PEAKS OF OTTER LODGE

www.peaksofotter.com • $$

Rooms are on the basic side, but the location's unbeatable at this Parkway hotel. Many rooms have views of the lake and Sharp Top mountain. There's a bar and restaurant on-site.

WINTERGREEN RESORT

www.wintergreenresort.com • $$

Sprawled across 11,000 acres of mountainside, this four-season escape ticks all the "resort" boxes, with mountain views at every turn. You won't run out of things to do here. There are two golf courses, skiing, snowboarding, a giant snow tube track, one of the best tennis programs around, a spa, zipline, and more. When it comes to sleeping, you can do a room at the main Mountain Inn, or rent a condo or a house.

CAMPING

There are two main campgrounds on this part of the Parkway: one at **Otter Creek** near the James River Visitor Center and one at **Peaks of Otter**. Choose Otter Creek for something a little more natural (you can pitch your tent right next to the water). Peaks of Otter is good if you want to be close to a restaurant/bar. There are first-come, first-served sites, or you can reserve online at www.recreation.gov. Campgrounds cost about $20 per night and are only open between May and October.

RENTAL SCENE

You won't find an Airbnb *on* the Parkway, but options are plentiful just outside the park land. Here's your chance to get creative and stay in a teepee, a treehouse, or even a Hobbit home.

☰ *Plan Around*

Some visitor centers close for winter, but the Blue Ridge Parkway itself is open year-round.

Every season has its draws. Spring sees an eruption of wildflowers around the mountain slopes. Summer's long days and warm nights are perfect for hiking and camping. Fall means foliage, just like Skyline Drive. Winter is a wild card—sections of the Parkway can close due to

// Overlook along the Parkway

bad weather. (The National Park Service posts a closure status map at go.nps.gov/brp-map.) But brave the cold and you'll get clear views and trails to yourself.

Weekends to Plan For (or Avoid):

- **Summer Concerts (May to August):** There's free mountain music on summer Sunday afternoons at Humpback Rocks (MP 6) and Roanoke Mountain Picnic Area (MP 120).
- **Wintergreen Summer Music Festival (July):** This month-long fest brings classical and mountain performances to the resort and nearby venues.
- **Fall Foliage (October):** Peak leaf dates vary, so keep an eye on the park reports. This is the most crowded time of year on the Parkway, but since there aren't pay stations like Skyline Drive, there typically aren't as many lines to get in.

GOOD TO KNOW

- The mountains *do* look blue. This is because the trees release a chemical into the atmosphere that creates the blue hazy look.
- At this writing, the Blue Ridge Parkway is the most visited site in the National Park system. More people came here than the Grand Canyon or the Lincoln Memorial (which was #5, by the way).
- The Blue Ridge Parkway Association also has a free **mobile app** that you can download (www.blueridgeparkway.org). It has information about the different sections of the route, as well as dining and lodging nearby.
- Elevation changes a lot as you drive. Not only can this make your ears pop, it can create wild weather shifts and temperature drops. Wear layers and drive carefully.
- Don't count on your phone working for much of the drive—cell service is spotty.

BEEN HERE, DONE THAT?

- Keep going! The views and twisty road thrills continue all the way down through North Carolina (including funky Asheville!) to the Tennessee border and Great Smoky Mountain National Park.
- If you've done the Blue Ridge Parkway but haven't tried Skyline Drive, do the northern leg. The two routes are Virginia's one-two road trip punch (Chapter 7).

9

Four-Season Lake and Mountain Fun

Deep Creek Lake, MD

Whatever time of year it is, there's always a reason to grab a crew and head to the lake.

FROM DC: 179 MILES · 3 HOURS | TRIP LENGTH: WEEKEND

DO	EAT	DRINK	BUY
boat or ski	FireFly cheese	cocktails at the Honi Honi	giant inflatable floatie

Okay, it's not quite Lake Tahoe, but Deep Creek Lake follows the same MO: in summer, Maryland's largest lake sparkles against its mountain backdrop. In winter, those mountains take center stage, with skiing, snowboarding, and mountain tubing. In between, you'll find nature opportunities galore, and one of the region's most popular fall festivals.

At any time of year, Deep Creek Lake has a woodsy, up-north vibe (bears! cabins!), with farmland pumping in fresh food and orchard goodies. There's spotty cell service. People have time to pause and chat. It's the type of place where traffic stops to let a raccoon cross the road. And it's a wildly popular spot to rent a house with a whole lot of friends and live up that lake and mountain life.

Getting to Deep Creek Lake

You really need a car to get here and around. Public transit is actually more expensive and takes longer.

The route from DC takes you up 270 to I-70 and I-68 west. You run the risk of traffic until around Hagerstown; then it's generally smooth sailing. The drive takes you through scenic rolling mountains of the Alleghenies. If you're coming from Northern VA, take 66 to the newly constructed Corridor H (a.k.a. US 48) up across West Virginia. There's usually no traffic—the road drops you into Deep Creek at Oakland.

If you get in at night, be careful—there are no lights on the country roads and this place gets dark.

Once you're here, don't bother Ubering; you won't get a ride. On weekends there's a shuttle service run by **A Touch of Class Limousines** (www.atouchofclasslimousines.com).

>> **Cumberland, MD Pit Stop:** About an hour from Deep Creek, Cumberland is a charming little town nestled in the mountains.

Get Your Bearings

Deep Creek Lake is long and narrow, running north–south with a fork at its bottom end and fingers that fan out into little inlets all around.

Highway 219 forms the spine of Deep Creek, connecting the north and south ends of the lake. A series of bridges make it super easy to get around. You don't have to drive all the way around the lake to get from one end to the other, so nothing's really more than 20 minutes away no matter where you are.

That said, there's no central downtown on the lake. It's more smatterings of little plazas. There isn't really a town center (the closest of those is downtown Oakland, but that's not on the water). Do some research on what you want to do. Even though there's plenty within a short drive, you have to know where to find it. (According to locals, "McHenry is more of a zip code than a town.")

Pick a Season

Maryland's largest freshwater lake, Deep Creek, is manmade but doesn't feel like it. With 3,900 acres of lake and 65 miles of shoreline, there are ample places to swim, boat, and rent a lakefront home. (Translation: there's space here; the more the merrier.)

Look up from the lake and you'll see the area's other big draw: mountains. (Or, if you're

// Bill's Marine boat rentals

from the western United States, you may just call them hills.) Whatever they're called, they get snow, so winter brings all sorts of frozen fun.

Unlike a lot of summer vacay hubs or ski towns, Deep Creek Lake is open for business all year long. As the seasons change, you'll find a fresh new list of things to do. Here are the must-dos:

SUMMER: Summer here's all about living your best lake life. Boating, floating, water skiing, fishing . . . you can even whitewater raft on an Olympic course.

- **Boating:** There are a lot of boat rental businesses around the lake, but **Bill's Marine** (www .billsmarineservice.com) is the area's go-to. You can rent everything from pontoons to powerboats to jetskis. Rentals can be as short as 2 hours (or half-day or a full day), but anything under two days is first-come, first-served. If you're here on a nice weather midsummer weekend, get there early.
- **Beach:** There's a good stretch of sand on the east side of the lake at **Deep Creek Lake State Park** (dnr.maryland.gov), with a roped-off area for swimming (with a sandy bottom), shady spots, picnic tables and grills and a volleyball net. It costs $5 to get in.
- **Fishing:** Catch your dinner, or at least your next Bumble profile pic. The lake's full of bass, crappie, walleye, catfish, and trout. Fishing season runs all year (a.k.a. ice fishing in winter). You can get equipment and a fishing license (need one of these) at bait shops such as **Bill's Outdoor Center** (www.billsoutdoorcenter.com), which rents water trampolines, too. Just sayin'.

- **Adventure sports:** At the top of Wisp mountain, **ASCI** (www.adventuresportscenter.com) has a whitewater course that was built for Olympic caliber whitewater athletes. Grab some friends and do a raft run, try your hand at kayaking rapids in a duckie or in your own boat, or tackle the surrounding woods with rock climbing, rappelling, and mountain biking.

FALL: Fall means foliage at Deep Creek Lake. If you're lucky, the weather will stay warm enough for boating, with a stunningly technicolor mountain backdrop.

- **Autumn Glory:** Every October, about 80,000 visitors flock here for one of the country's top fall festivals: Autumn Glory. This five-day fest takes over the little town of Oakland on the south side of Deep Creek Lake with parades, concerts, art fairs, and a "turkey trail," a series of turkey dinners run by local orgs.
- **Fall foliage:** Aside from the events, the area is just gorgeous come foliage time. The hills rising up from the dark cool lake water turn into a kaleidoscope around October. The tourism office has put together some foliage driving routes, available online (www.visitdeepcreek.com) or in their office in McHenry.

WINTER: With an average snowfall of 100 inches per year, Deep Creek Lake sees more of the white stuff than Anchorage, Alaska. In recent years, the snow has lasted into March.

- **Wisp Resort:** The ski resort here, Wisp (www.wispresort.com) is winter central. Aside from the 34 slopes and trails for skiers and snowboarders, there's a mountain coaster (an alpine rollercoaster of sorts), ice skating, and a snow-tubing course. The slopes are about 90-percent lit at night, so night skiing is big here.

SPRING: While there's still plenty to do this time of year, spring is the area's low season. This means you'll find lower prices. If you just want a chill weekend to hang out and go to a cabin, spring's your season.

- **Hiking:** Shed that winter weight by hitting the area's extensive hiking trails. You can hike in Deep Creek Lake State Park, nearby Swallow Falls State Park, and along the 14-mile Meadow Mountain Trail, which runs through the scenic Savage River State Forest. (Don't worry, there are multiple access points, so you don't have to do the full 14 miles.) Garrett Trails (www.garretttrails.org) has info and maps of the region's trails.
- **Mountain Biking:** There's no shortage of tough-terrain trails for mountain bikers up here. A popular loop runs 8 miles around Deep Creek Lake State Park, with switchbacks, some rocky sections, and views for days.
- **Golf:** Deep Creek Lake's courses open for the season around April, and some are considered among the best in Maryland. Tee off to sweeping mountain views at Wisp's **Fantasy Valley Golf Course,** a slope-side par 70 championship course, or lake views at the resort's mountaintop **Lodestone Golf Course** (www.wispresort.com/Lodestone). Down in Oakland,

the 18-hole **Golf Club at Oakland** (www.golfatoakland.com) is a local fave that costs a fraction of what a round at Wisp does. On the southeast corner of the lake in Swanton, **Thousand Acres Golf Club** (www.thousandacresgolf.com) has nine holes in a natural setting.

>>   More Info: www.visitdeepcreek.com

While You're Here

CHASE WATERFALLS AT SWALLOW FALLS STATE PARK

Pay the $5 per person and stretch your legs in this well-kept state park about 15 minutes from the lake. Here you can get up close to not one, but four waterfalls, including the 54-foot Muddy Falls, Maryland's highest free-falling cascade.

If you're traveling with your dog, you won't actually be able to go *in* the park during summer. There's a trail along the opposite river bank that's dog-friendly and still offers views of the falls. Park just east of the one-lane bridge before the park entrance and pick up the trail across the street, or ask at the park pay station.

// Swallow Falls Park

TRY ACCIDENT CHEESE

One of the best cheesemongers around is **FireFly Farms** (www.fireflyfarms.com) in tiny Accident, a small town about 10 minutes north of Deep Creek Lake. (The town's called that because in the pre-Google Maps era, two surveyors independently, and accidentally, plotted the same tract of land.) You can taste their cheese, from Merry Goat Round soft brie to Manchego, plus buy cheese, breads, wine and beer, and other gourmet goods.

LOAD UP ON LAKE KITSCH

Bear Creek Traders (www.shopdeepcreek.com/bearcreek.html) is a giant gift shop that has everything from water shoes and giant inflatable flamingo floaties to wine glasses and signs with cheesy lake slogans like "Life is better at the lake."

≡ *Good Eats*

Farm to table is big here, mostly because the food doesn't have to travel far from the neighboring farms. Because there's no one center of town, most restaurants are spread around the lakeshore in little town centers and shopping clusters. You'll find a lot of options on the western shore of the lake in Oakland.

MOONSHADOW

McHenry (northeast end of Deep Creek Lake) • www.moonshadow145.com • $$ • Local farms/gastropub

Don't be discouraged by the out-of-the-way location among college houses. This farm-to-table spot is a top choice for brunch, and they have live nightly music every weekend, all year.

CANOE ON THE RUN

McHenry (north end of Deep Creek Lake) • $ • sandwiches & salad

Just off the lake in McHenry, this place is known for its fresh salads and sandwiches. It's also one of the few places you can grab an espresso or cappuccino.

NEED SOMETHING TO READ?

Black Bear Wine and Words (www.blackbearwineandwords.com) sells $1 paperbacks and $2 hardcover books. Also, there's wine, with most bottles under $30.

TRADERS COFFEE HOUSE

Oakland (west side of Deep Creek Lake) • www.traderscoffeehouse.com • $ • cafe

This place is packed every morning. It's one of the best places for coffee. They also have breakfast and lunch sandwiches and pastries (including a breakfast cookie, which has to be healthy because "breakfast," right?).

BRENDA'S PIZZERIA

Oakland (west side of Deep Creek Lake) • www.brendaspizzeria.com • $ • pizza

Right next to Traders, Brenda's does New York pizza two ways: red or white. (They have specialty pies, too.) You can order ahead online or by phone and come pick up, or you can walk in and grab a slice or pie from the subway-tiled storefront. There's also an upstairs dining room with sit-down service.

UNO PIZZERIA & GRILL

Oakland (west side of Deep Creek Lake) • deepcreekuno.com • $$ • pizza

Yes, it's a chain, but it's one of the most popular, best-situated restaurants in town, so ignore the fact that you've been to an Uno before and dig into the Chicago-style deep dish pies. It's lakefront, so expect a crowd.

ACE'S RUN

Oakland (west side of Deep Creek Lake) • www.acesrun.com • $$ • American

Ace's is a bit fancier than its neighbors, but lake-fancy, like you can step off your boat and dine, not jacket-and-tie fancy. It's in the Will O' the Wisp Hotel, and has a great view of the water. The menu is large and covers the American bases: burgers, sandwiches and some mid-Atlantic musts like crab cakes.

LAKESIDE GRILL

Oakland (west side of Deep Creek Lake) • $ • sandwiches

Stop in this quick-bite food cart for fresh health-conscious sandwiches and Mediterranean options like souvlaki. There are picnic tables with lake views. This place is seasonal.

MARKETS

If you're staying in a house, there are a few groceries up here where you can load up on food. (Some people also load up in DC before the trip.) Keep in mind that you can't buy booze in grocery stores. You need a liquor store for that.

Up in McHenry, there's a **Shop 'n Save**, a typical supermarket where you can find food and some decently priced freshly made entrées. **Arrowhead Market** in Oakland has a smaller, more specialized selection. You can get all the staples plus some deli and premade foods, but the price is a bit higher than a standard grocery.

≡ *Time for a Drink*

You don't really come to Deep Creek for the nightlife—unless you bring it yourself at a house party. But there are a few local standbys for raging:

BLACK BEAR TAVERN & RESTAURANT

McHenry (north east side of Deep Creek Lake) • www.blackbeartavern.com

A sports pub/restaurant by day, Black Bear has a "Nite Club" that gets the dance party started around 10 p.m. on weekends. They bring in DJs and stay open until 1 a.m.

HONI HONI BAR

Oakland (west side of Deep Creek Lake) • www.honi-honi.com

The Honi is a local classic. Adjacent to the equally popular Uno Pizzeria, the tiki bar has live music and a lawn overlooking the lake and boat docks. The parking lot fills up but you can park at the movie theater across the street, too.

MOUNTAIN STATE BREWING CO.

McHenry (north west of Deep Creek Lake) • mountainstatebrewing.com

Honestly, the house beers from this West Virginia brewer won't be the best you've ever had. But this spacious brewpub has a great selection of guest taps, plus the wood-fired flatbreads are worth a trip, even if you're not a beer person. The farmhouse-style building set in a field at the base of a mountain is pretty damn scenic, too.

// Mountain State Brewing Co.

☰ *Stay Over*

If you don't know Deep Creek Lake, it can be a bit confusing to decide at which part of the lake to base yourself. The good news is it doesn't matter all that much—it's so easy to get from one side of the lake to the other, you won't ever be too far from whatever you want to do.

That said, there are some hubs to keep in mind, if you're here for the following reasons:

- **Mountain:** Especially during ski season, stay at or near Wisp or off Marshall Road on the northwest side of the lake. You'll be right by the lake but also near the lifts.
- **Restaurants and bars:** Stick around west Deep Creek Lake, near the intersection of Highway 219 and Quarry Road.
- **Easy lake and dock access:** You'll find this all over, but a good bet is along the east side of the lake, south of McHenry and in the Swanton area south of Deep Creek Lake State Park.
- **Autumn Glory Festival:** Stay near downtown Oakland, though keep in mind you'll be about 20 minutes from the water.

LAKE HOUSE AND CABIN RENTALS

The Deep Creek rental market has homes of all shapes and sizes, from a two-person bungalow to a 10-person house.

It's really easy to get a lakefront home, especially if you book over one month in advance. The more last-minute you book, particularly in summer, your options get more limited but you should still be able to find *something*. And while most people go for the lake access, don't hesitate to get a house on the mountain. What you'll give up in water access you'll gain in awesome views, plus it only takes a few minutes to get down to the lakeshore.

The local rental market is dominated by **Railey Mountain Lake Vacations** (deepcreek.com/rentals/), although you can also use sites such as Airbnb, HomeAway, and VRBO. The best bet is to check all these sites. Some houses are listed on all of them; others are only available through one.

WHAT IF IT RAINS?

Outdoor activities are the main thing to do in Deep Creek Lake. So what if the weather doesn't cooperate? Truthfully, it limits your options. There are the bars, or you can cozy up with a board game or book or Netflix with a lake view. If you're really bored, there's a movie theater in Oakland.

THE LODGE AT WISP

www.wispresort.com • $$

While the lake houses are great for lazing and boozing, Wisp is where you go to not be bored. The area's premier resort, Wisp is Deep Creek's one-stop shop for staying, eating, and playing. The lodge here sits at the foot of the mountain, steps from a few of the chair lifts. Some of the rooms have views of the slopes.

WILL O' THE WISP

willothewisp.com • $$$

Sort of an in-between from the all-out resortiness of Wisp and the DIY-style house rentals, Will O' the Wisp is an upscale condo complex overlooking the lake in Oakland. Every unit has lake views and a patio or balcony, and you can combine multiple units for larger groups.

ELLA'S ENCHANTED TREEHOUSES

eetreehouses.com • $$$

These treehouse rentals are perched in the forest about 15 minutes from the lake. Fully furnished, the treehouses even have bathrooms, and they sleep five to six people.

☰ *Plan Around*

Summer, fall, and winter are pretty consistently popular here. Things get crowded on big holiday weekends, especially during the summer but also during ski season. Overall, it doesn't get so insane that you should stay away; it's more that these busy weekends require more planning ahead.

Weekends to Plan For (or Avoid):

- **Fourth of July:** All summer holiday weekends are busy, but the Fourth is usually the busiest weekend of the year. Book your stay long in advance if you come during this time.
- **Autumn Glory (October):** As mentioned above, this is the area's top festival, and it draws tens of thousands of people. The activity's centered around Oakland, so if you're elsewhere on the lake, you won't be quite as affected.

DOGS AT DEEP CREEK

Not only is this a popular spot for friends' weekends, Deep Creek Lake is incredibly dog-friendly—as are many of the rental homes.

GOOD TO KNOW

- Cell service is pretty spotty in parts of Deep Creek Lake.
- Deep Creek has an eerie chapter of its history. It was the site of a big CIA scandal. Back in the 1950s and '60s, the CIA ran mind-control experiments on oblivious subjects. They then dosed a CIA biochemist with LSD at Deep Creek; he was found dead a few days later. The Netflix show *Wormwood* is based on this story.
- If you were a fan of *Jersey Shore*, you may like Snapchat's Deep Creek Lake "reality" show, which follows a highly dramatic group of friends on their vacay here.

BEEN HERE, DONE THAT?

- Come back and try another season. Base yourself on another part of the lake and get to know the scene there.
- On the Virginia side of the world, there's Lake Anna, which has similar boating, fishing, and lake activities, although it doesn't have the mountain action that Deep Creek does.
- If you're into the "rent a big house with buddies" thing, give a beach house a try. The Bethany Beach chapter (Chapter 4) has tips on rentals.

10

Climb Old Rag

Shenandoah National Park, VA

The Mount Everest of the Shenandoah—this one's a beast to climb and a boast once you've made it to the top.

FROM DC: 94 MILES · 2 HOURS | TRIP LENGTH: DAY TRIP

DO	EAT	DRINK
hike	summit snack	lots of water

What a hike. It's the most popular. The most difficult. The most dangerous in the area. A 9-mile slog up and down the rocky mountain will turn your legs into gummies . . . but those views. The 360-degree look at Shenandoah National Park from the open bouldery is what draws so many day-trippers to the park's most famous trek. Well, that, and bragging rights.

Getting to Old Rag

You'll need a car to get to Old Rag. One, because there is no easy public transit, and two, because cell phone service isn't reliable to call an Uber.

Take I-66 west out of the city and make your way down to Sperryville (the best route varies based on traffic patterns—use Waze to get there fastest). From there, you'll continue down Route 231 to Peola Mills and then Nethers Road, where you'll find the Old Rag lower parking lot (the only lot; the upper one is closed).

The parking lot is free, but you'll have to pay the park entrance fee ($15 if you're just walking in). If the lot's full, some of the nearby houses charge fees to park on their land.

Get Your Bearings

Old Rag sits on the eastern edge of Shenandoah National Park. You can see the mountain from Skyline Drive in the park, but you can't get here from there.

Doing the Hike

It takes most people anywhere from 5 to 8 hours to do the full Old Rag circuit. Along the way, you'll gain about 2,400 feet of elevation and tackle about nine switchbacks.

This isn't a spur of the moment stroll—you need to be prepared physically (i.e., be in good shape), well-supplied (more on that below), and have enough time (seriously, start the climb early).

Follow the Blue Blazes

From the parking lot, hike about a mile up to the trailhead. Pick up the Ridge Trail, which will take you around the full loop clockwise (most people do it clockwise; you can go against the flow, but it can be annoying to dodge all those people coming the other way).

Once you're on the Ridge Trail, it's up you go, winding back and forth on a steady wooded climb up the switchbacks. This lasts for about 2 miles; the higher you get, the prettier the views.

Next up, it's the boulder field. Get ready to scramble, hop, and pull yourself up and down over granite boulders the size of SUVs. Good upper body strength—or a friend who can pull you over some of the tall ones—is a must-have here.

After a mile or so of rock scramble you'll reach the summit (don't be fooled by the false summits along the way—they're pretty but the real thing is better). The views are huge in all directions. It's a good place to lay down a blanket, give your legs a breather, and have a little snack.

The way back down follows a smooth, gradually sloping fire road in the woods. To be honest, the last hour of the trek is kind of boring—no more views or rocks, but your alternative is re-navigating the boulder field, and by this point, your legs will likely be having none of that.

Hiking Tips

- Get here early—like before 8 a.m. The lot fills up, and you could get towed if you park on the side of the road. Plus, the mountain gets super crowded on nice weekends. Sometimes the line to climb through the rock field is almost an hour long, so the earlier start you get, the less waiting you'll do.
- The rocks can tear cotton leggings (and bare legs), so wear thicker pants or leggings for the scrambling.

Mountain Safety

The National Park Service airlifts multiple people off Old Rag every year—try not to be one of them. Safety here is serious business, so in addition to all the park rules and regulations (which you should read before hiking), here are some tips:

- Don't hike if it's wet or icy out. The rocks are slippery enough in good weather.
- Summer storms bring lots of lightning. Getting struck would suck, so get off the mountain ASAP if you see any.
- Watch out for bears! Black bears live here, and sometimes they come say hi to hikers. Keep your distance; if you make some noise as you hike, it'll likely keep them away.

>> **More Info**
The Shenandoah National Park website (www.nps.gov/shen) has hiking info and trail maps.
All Trails is a great hiking app. Download the trail map on your phone before you go.

OLD RAG PACKING LIST

Leave that big pack at home; packing light's the way to go (you'll need your hands and nimble-ness for the rocks). But on a big hike like this, there are a few essentials:

- Good, grippy shoes: at least running shoes, at best hiking boots
- 2 liters of water per person
- Snacks such as trail mix, cheese sticks, or granola bars
- Sunscreen
- Layers (it can be chilly at the top)

// View from Old Rag

≡ *While You're Here*

CHECK OUT SKYLINE DRIVE

Enter at Thornton Gap and take the scenic route home after your big hike. See Chapter 7 for more. (If you do this, pay for the vehicle park pass instead of the walk-in pass, to cover the full experience.)

≡ *Good Eats*

There aren't all that many places to eat right near Old Rag; you're either in the mountains or in farmland.

Sperryville (mentioned in Chapter 7) has a couple restaurants. Go for pizza (**Rappahannock Pizza Kitchen**), burgers and bar fare (**Headmaster Pub**), or coffee (**Before and After**).

You could also swing over to **Culpeper** (Chapter 21), which has two breweries in addition to its main street full of restaurants.

Make sure you eat and hydrate the night before your hike, too.

≡ *Time for a Drink*

The closest option for an immediate post-hike drink is **Sharp Rock Vineyards** (sharprockvineyards.com), five minutes down the road from the hike's parking lot. Can't say no to an Old Rag

Red! Nearby, **DuCard Vineyards** (www.ducardvineyards.com) hosts live music on their outdoor patio every Saturday night.

If beer is more your jam after a long hike, head up to Sperryville, where **Pen Druid** (www .pendruid.com) goes wild with beer fermentation.

Stay Over

The only reason you'd need to spend the night is if you wanted to do a sunrise hike to beat the crowds, or if you just feel like making a Shenandoah weekend out of it. Otherwise just day trip it.

If you're really outdoorsy, you can get a backcountry permit and camp out here, but that's only recommended if you really know what you're doing. There are easier camping options along Skyline Drive (Chapter 7).

Plan Around

If you think it'd be a good idea to climb Old Rag during fall foliage, just remember that about 2,000 other people a day will have the same idea. The mountain gets so jammed on peak weekends that there's sometimes a line to get to the summit.

Weekends to Plan For (or Avoid):

- **Peak Foliage Weekends (October):** The prettier the fall leaves, the more crowded the mountain.

GOOD TO KNOW

- Dogs aren't allowed on this hike. You'll see why once you get to the boulder field.
- Tina Fey reminisced about a hike up Old Rag in *Bossypants* (she did it to impress a guy).

BEEN HERE, DONE THAT?

- It's not as challenging, but the views are great from Sugarloaf Mountain, too (Chapter 11).
- Old Rag may be the most famous hike, but it's far from the only trail out here. There are more than 500 miles of hiking trails in Shenandoah National Park. See Chapter 10.

// Boulders on the trail

11

Hike Sugarloaf Mountain

Dickerson, MD

An easy escape from DC where you can stretch your legs and find decent views. Even better: entry is free!

FROM DC: 45 MILES · 1 HOUR | TRIP LENGTH: DAY TRIP

DO	EAT	DRINK	BUY
climb to the summit	Rocky Point ice cream	wine from the vineyard	home decor

One of the most accessible hiking hubs near DC, Sugarloaf is pretty easy in every sense.

You can easily make it here, up and around the mountain, and head back to DC with the afternoon to spare. But don't overlook the surrounding countryside. It's full of local charm and places that'll tempt you to linger after your climb.

☰ Getting to Sugarloaf Mountain

Sugarloaf Mountain is an easy 45-minute to an hour drive northwest from DC. A car's the best way to get here, although Uber/Lyft is an option (you just may wait 20-plus minutes for a ride home).

You'll take Highway 270 most of the way, then follow Comus Road through scenic countryside to the base of the mountain. Keep an eye to the right and you'll soon see the smooth mound of Sugarloaf popping up over some farm fields.

Be careful if you're using Google maps—there are a few entries for "Sugarloaf Mountain," and some may lead you to a random spot on a wooded road rather than the parking lot. Your best bet is to map directly to the parking lot (East View or West View) you plan on using. You'll bear right through the park gates at the four-way stop to head up the mountain to the view lots.

This place isn't a secret, so arrive early (i.e., before 10 a.m.), especially on nice summer days or during fall foliage weekends.

>>   Shop Along the Way: Load up on new hiking gear (or, you know, whatever) at the Clarksburg Premium Outlets. The mall is about 20 minutes south of Sugarloaf on 270.

☰ Get Your Bearings

Sugarloaf sits in farmland, right on the border of Montgomery and Frederick counties. Even though it's a short drive to the main highway, it feels remote. There are very few commercial outlets around here, and you may need to drive 20 minutes or so for more food options.

☰ Sugarloaf Trails

When Gordon Strong set up a nonprofit to protect Sugarloaf Mountain back in 1946, he did it so that the public could enjoy and learn from nature's beauty, because people who did that "will be better people, people who will treat each other better." Can't argue with that, right?

Now, thanks to this nonprofit, Sugarloaf is still free, open to the public, and naturally beautiful. And it's easy to take it all in, thanks to a well-maintained network of trails that laces up, down, and around the mountain.

There are four main color-coded trails, marked by blazes. They all intersect, so you can mix and match nearly unlimited options of routes. (In fact, despite the fact that signage is pretty prominent, some hikers inadvertently end up on a different color trail than they started out on. No biggie, they all loop together, although it can add miles to your trek.)

BLUE (NORTHERN PEAKS TRAIL): This 5-mile loop picks up at the West View parking lot and climbs up and down around the whole mountain. There are a number of good views from this trail, including White Rocks, a beautiful overlook of Frederick Valley. It'll take between 3 and 5 hours to hike this one.

PURPLE: Looking for a higher step count? Take this alternate route to White Rocks. If you add Purple to Blue, you'll get an extra 0.5 mile, or if you do the Purple as a standalone, it's 1.5 miles.

WHITE (MOUNTAIN LOOP TRAIL): Pick up this shaded 2.5-mile trail from the East View parking lot, then follow it as it loops around the summit (and connects to the Orange and Green summit routes). The trail overlaps with the Blue and Yellow trails at times, so it can get a bit confusing. Most people combine the White trail with another loop in the park (sometimes accidentally).

YELLOW (SADDLEBACK HORSE TRAIL): At 7 miles, this is the longest trail in the park. There are some steep rocky parts, but typically this trail is less crowded than the ones at the top. Keep an eye out for wildlife, including black bears, and wildflowers, especially in the spring when the azaleas pop. Parking at the base of the mountain can be limited.

Summit Trails

None of the above trails actually take you to the summit (and what's the fun in climbing a mountain if you don't get to the top?). To get here, follow one of three trails that fan out like a spoke from the top: **Green** (from the West View parking lot), **Orange** (from the East View lot), or **Red** (which just connects to the Blue trail). The climb is steep, especially on the Orange trail.

Once you reach the top, there are views of the surrounding countryside. There are rocky outcrops you can sit on, though on busy days, they crowd up.

Park Hours

Whatever you're doing on the mountain, just make sure you're done at least an hour before sunset. That's when the park gates close. You don't want to get shut in.

>> **More Info:** You can find maps and park info at www.sugarloafmd.com.

1 Orange summit trail
2 Picnic tables on Sugarloaf Mountain
3 Sugarloaf Mountain

≡ *While You're Here*

OTHER MOUNTAIN ACTIVITIES

Hiking is what brings the most people here, but there are a bunch of other things to do on the mountain itself. You can ride a horse along the Yellow trail, a.k.a. the Saddleback Horse Trail, which loops for 7 miles around the mountain's base. Once there's some decent snowfall in the winter, cross-country skiing is an option (you'll have to bring your own skis). Finally, while you can't go inside unless you're here for a wedding, there are some historic mansions here that you can gaze at from afar.

POST-HIKE WINE TASTING

At the base of the mountain is **Sugarloaf Mountain Vineyard** (smwinery.com), a popular spot for hikers and local residents. There are small bites such as cheese, hummus, and charcuterie available too. You can post up with your pup outside (as long as you have a leash), and there's often live music on weekends.

BROWSE AQUATIC GARDENS

Primarily a shop for water gardening enthusiasts, **Lilypons Aquatic Shop** (www.lilypons.com) is a pleasant place for a stroll around the lily pads and koi ponds. Sometimes there are events such as live music or car shows. Open hours vary; some weekends, it's only open on Saturdays.

HOME DECOR EMPORIUMS

About 15 minutes away, in Buckeystown, you'll find two shopping gems. The **Buckeystown Design Co-Op** (www.buckeystowndesigncoop.com) features 6,000 square feet of furniture, rugs, and home goods from local designers. Once a month, it's vintage home goods Christmas at **Chartreuse & Co.**'s (chartreuseandco.com) tag sales. Three barns are converted into an antiques/decor bazaar, with homemade food and sometimes live bands.

≡ *Good Eats*

One of the best ways to eat at Sugarloaf is to pack a picnic and dine with a view at one of the tables in the East View parking lot. There aren't a lot of real restaurants (or even grocery stores) nearby, but if you feel like a sit-down meal, you'll have a few options.

ROCKY POINT CREAMERY

Tuscarora • rockypointcreamery.com • $ • ice cream

Cool off at this cute cow-themed ice cream shop about 20 minutes from the mountain. The homemade ice cream, soft serve, and sundaes are fresh from the family-run farm (as are the eggs, cheese, and milk). Check before you arrive; hours vary by season.

BUCKEYSTOWN PUB

Buckeystown • buckeystownpub.com • $ • seafood & pub grub

The big crab on the roof of this no-frills neighborhood bar will tell you why most people come. Slide into a wooden booth or outdoor picnic table, and settle in with a pitcher of beers and a platter of all-you-can-eat crabs. It's a 15-minute drive from Sugarloaf.

COMUS INN

Dickerson • thecomusinn.com • $$$ • contemporary American

Gaze out on the mountain you've conquered from this historic country inn (although you may feel a tad out of place in your hiking clothes). Local farms source the menu, which features fine-country dining such as crab hush puppies, shrimp and grits, and filet mignon. Sunday brunch is a popular time to dine.

≡ *Stay Over*

Sugarloaf is usually done as a day trip from DC, so there aren't a ton of lodging options nearby. There are plenty of chain hotels along I-270, around Frederick (see Chapter 17 for lodging ideas) or Hagerstown. You can also camp at the nearby **Little Bennett Campground** (www .montgomeryparks.org).

≡ *Plan Around*

Almost a quarter-million people come to Sugarloaf every year. On a good-weather weekend day, it can feel like they're *all* there at the same time. Other times, you'll have the mountain in relative solitude, especially in winter or if there's a little bit of rain.

Weekends to Plan For (or Avoid):

- **Labor Day:** Every year, Sugarloaf Mountain Vineyard hosts a Grape Stomp Festival, featuring wine, food, and live music.
- **Peak Fall Foliage:** Beautiful? Absolutely. Crowded? Incredibly. On good-weather fall days, it can be pretty insane here; trails can be packed and the parking lots are a nightmare.

GOOD TO KNOW

- Dogs are allowed on the trails here; they just have to be on a leash.
- This spot came close to being a presidential retreat, but the mountain's owners convinced FDR to use nearby Catoctin Mountain instead. (That one is now known as Camp David.)
- The mountain was used as a lookout point for both Union and Confederate troops during the Civil War. The log cabin at the base of the mountain was used as a field hospital.

BEEN HERE, DONE THAT?

- So you've aced the summit trail. Try a bigger challenge with a hike up Old Rag (Chapter 10).
- Many people compare Sugarloaf to the Maryland Heights hike at Harpers Ferry, which has better views.
- Not too far from Sugarloaf, in Catoctin Mountain Park, a 4-mile hike takes you to Chimney Rock, an outcrop that has stunning views of the surrounding mountains.

12

Go River Tubing

Harpers Ferry, WV

The best way to spend a hot summer day is on a scenic, lazy-river-style float through nature.

FROM DC: 67 MILES · 1 HOUR 10 MINUTES | TRIP LENGTH: DAY TRIP OR OVERNIGHT

DO	EAT	DRINK	BUY
get on the water	pepperoni roll	cold beer	historic candy

If your face feels like it's melting off in the DC summer heat, grab some friends and book it out to Harpers Ferry. Here, the Shenandoah and Potomac rivers meet in a watery adventure hub, where you can raft, paddle, and lazily float down the cool waters in a landscape that's all nature. The water here is cool and clean, and there are enough rapids to make it a fun (but not too scary) ride.

≡ Getting to Harpers Ferry

Since none of the river outfitters are right in town, the easiest way to get here is to drive. The route takes about 1 hour and 20 minutes; you'll either go up via Maryland (take the Beltway up to 270, then cut west on Highway 340), or via Virginia (a few options get you to Leesburg, where you'll take routes 7 and 9 north to Harpers Ferry Road).

There *is* a train from DC to Harpers Ferry (and it's only about $14 each way), but there's only one route a day and it arrives in Harpers Ferry too late to do a same-day float trip.

If you're with a large group, River Riders (more info below) has shuttle buses that run the round-trip from DC. It's pricey though—from DC, the cost starts at around $900 for 14 people or fewer.

≡ Get Your Bearings

Harpers Ferry is the meeting point of three states (West Virginia, Maryland, and Virginia) and two rivers (Potomac and Shenandoah).

The town itself sits on a wedge of land created by the river confluence. It's split into three general districts: Lower Town, right along the water's edge; Upper Town, the higher ground that's set back from the water; and Bolivar, another historic village to the west that's now largely residential.

Overall, this place is hilly; get ready to climb. The good news is that many of the hills come with good views.

Parking in Harpers Ferry itself is tough; you may need to park in an overflow lot and take a free shuttle to town. The good news is that if you're coming to Harpers Ferry for water fun, you probably won't be parking right downtown; at least to start. Depending on which company you use, you can either park on-site at the operators' lot and they'll drive you to and from the river, or you'll head to a waterside meeting point.

≡ Riding the River

Sure, rafting and kayaking are fun. But they involve work.

River tubing, on the other hand, requires no skill, and little effort. You just sit in an inner tube and float. It's best done on a hot day with a crew and a cooler and is by far the most popular way to ride the river out here.

What to Expect

Where and how you float depends on which outfitter you use, but essentially, you'll have a choice between a flat water or a whitewater trip. Flat water's good for little kids; the whitewater's usually a more fun bet for everyone else. The rapids here range between Class I and III. While it sounds scary, it makes for some fun little bumps and drops, but is not unmanageable.

Standard trips are unguided (you can pay extra for the guide but there's no need, it's easy to DIY). Before your float you'll get a safety overview that outlines which side of the river to stay on, which rocks to watch out for, and, most importantly, where you'll need to get out of the river in order to get picked up.

Then, you're off! Life jacket-up, drag your tube to the water, plop butt-first into it, and kick or paddle your way out into the current.

The river will carry you past scenic wooded hillsides that plunge down to the water. You'll see Harpers Ferry and Maryland Heights. There are big rocks along the way where you can pull up, hop off your tube, and hang out.

And that's it—just float, and enjoy the company, nature, and whatever you brought to drink.

>> **Cheaper Rates Online:** Most operators offer a discount if you book in advance online (you can usually save $5 or so).

// Tubing with River Riders

Tour Operators

A couple of different companies run trips out here, and each is a little different.

RIVER RIDERS

Check-in in Harpers Ferry • just west of town • www.riverriders.com • $29 and up • late May–
September

River Riders claims to have the "longest" trip on the river, since they drop you farther
upstream. The 5-mile float can take anywhere from 1.5 hours to 4 hours, depending on how
much you dawdle along the way.

The check-in is located just west of Harpers Ferry, a little way from the water; it's an outdoors center with supplies, snacks and beer, and a zip-lining course. They rent a handful of
tube options, plus cooler tubes and paddles.

HARPERS FERRY ADVENTURE CENTER

Check-in in Purcellville • 3 miles east of Harpers Ferry • harpersferryadventurecenter.com • $30 and
up • May–October

Rather than a one-and-done float, shuttles run between the put-in and take-out points all day,
so you can do as many river runs as you can fit in before last call.

The operator is based right on the river in Purcellville (on the Virginia side of the Tri-State).
Trips end right where your car is parked—no long shuttle rides. In addition to renting tubes
(and cooler tubes), HFAC has a lot of other activities on-site, including zip-lining, a high ropes
course, camping, and fishing.

RIVER AND TRAIL

Check in at Manidokan Camp • 4 miles north of Harpers Ferry • www.rivertrail.com • $29 and up •
late May–late September

These unguided trips typically last 1 to 2 hours. Note that coolers and any sort of non-water
drinks are not permitted on these tours.

If you look up River and Trail on Google Maps, it'll take you to the company's main site.
There's limited parking here; on weekends, tubers are instructed to check in at Manidokan
Camp, about 20 minutes north of Harpers Ferry. River tubing is one of the many tours this
operator runs—they do everything from bike to food tours, too.

// Harpers Ferry water gap

What to Bring

It's pretty straightforward: you'll sit in a tube and float. But there are a few goodies you can bring to make the trip even more fun.

- A cooler, and drinks: if you've got your own cooler, you can rent a tube that's specially fitted for it.
- Some small garbage bags, for any cans. Leave no trace!
- Water shoes: you'll have to wade a bit to get back to shore, plus there are lots of rocks to push off of along the way. Flip-flops are a recipe for losing a shoe, plus some outfitters won't let you on a tube with them on. Wear water shoes or Tevas.
- Waterproof speakers and a dry bag for your phone: load up the river playlist.
- Swimsuit and quick-dry clothes: You. Will. Get. Wet.
- GoPro or another waterproof camera.
- Sunscreen: there's no shade on the river, and water reflects those rays. Carry some 'screen so you can reapply.
- Leave the valuables at home: anything that can't get wet can't come on the river with you and has to stay in a locker or in the car.

// Lower Town Harpers Ferry

≡ *While You're Here*

EXPLORE HISTORIC HARPERS FERRY

www.harpersferryhistory.org

The town of Harpers Ferry has a cool vibe that's part National Historic Park site and part out-doorsy mountain town. Not only does the **Appalachian Trail** (www.appalachiantrail.org) cross through here, the trail's conservancy group is headquartered here; it's a major crossroads for serious hikers reentering civilization for a little bit.

At the same time, it's the site of an armory established by George Washington and a later ill-fated raid on said armory by abolitionist John Brown, who was trying to spark a rebellion against slavery. Much of the town is now managed by the National Park Service (www.nps.gov /hafe/index.htm).

HIKE THE HEIGHTS

If you're not worn out from the river, there are some excellent hiking options in Harpers Ferry.

One of the most accessible routes is the walk to **Jefferson Rock**. It's a short and steep walk through town along the Appalachian Trail to a view overlooking the rivers and town. There's a large rock slab here where Thomas Jefferson stood in 1783 and remarked at how awesome the view here is.

Across the bridge on the Maryland side of the river is an ass-kicker of a hike, the **Maryland Heights Trail**. The climb takes you up to an iconic viewpoint overlooking Harpers Ferry, the Potomac, and the Shenandoah. It's about 6.5 miles round trip, and takes most people about 3 to 4 hours. It's awesome at sunset, but be careful hiking down in the dark.

BIKE THE C&O CANAL

Yep, *that* C&O Canal. In theory, you could bike this trail all the way to Georgetown. (That ride would be 59 miles.) Of course, you can also do something a little shorter. **River Riders** and **River and Trail** rent bikes.

VISIT THE JOHN BROWN WAX MUSEUM

www.johnbrownwaxmuseum.com

While the wax figures here are bit creepy, this small museum skillfully sums up the story of John Brown's raid on Harpers Ferry.

≡ *Good Eats*

Bringing food out on the river's a bit of a hassle, but there are a handful of restaurants in Harpers Ferry or on your drive back to DC that you can hit up once you dry off. Many of the restaurants in town are a bit tourist-centric; there are buds of the "locavore" craze but it's not as widespread as elsewhere.

If you really want to go local, try a West Virginia classic: the pepperoni roll. Try this log of dough baked around slices of pepperoni at some of the restaurants and bars below.

GUIDE HOUSE GRILL

Knoxville, MD • www.guidehousegrill.com • $$ • American

Just outside of town on the Maryland side, this small rustic restaurant is a good post-tubing place to refuel. Ignore the no-frills appearance; the food here's the real deal, from crab soup to burgers to zoodles.

ROAD FOOD

A few tents and food stands sell food along Harpers Ferry Road in Virginia. At the intersection of this road and Route 340, you'll find a tent selling kettle corn that's worth a stop. At Route 9 and Harpers Ferry Road, there's a good BBQ stand.

PURCELLVILLE

Only a 10-minute drive away, the eateries in Purcellville, such as **Monk's BBQ** and **Petite LouLou Creperie**, are an easy stop if you're getting to or from Harpers Ferry via Virginia. (See Chapter 16.)

BRUNSWICK

On the Maryland side, a little east of River & Trail, Brunswick is another potential post-rafting stop en route to DC. There are a few places to eat here, like **Potomac Street Grill** and **The Mini-Dip**, plus **Smoketown Brewery** and a coffee shop in an old church called **Beans in the Belfry**.

≡ *Time for a Drink*

Some of the tubing outfitters sell cases of beer (officially intended for post-float consumption). If you want a supply of cans and didn't bring any from home, **Hillside Liquors** opens early and is located near River & Trail in Knoxville, Maryland.

   If you want to check out the town after the trip, there are a few places in the area to grab a drink, although the local beer scene is a bit lacking compared with other nearby towns.

THE BARN

Bolivar • Harpers Ferry • www.harpersferryeventbarn.com

A full bar plus acts like live music, karaoke, and line dancing make this a good hangout spot. You can also bring in outside food. Its rustic style makes this a popular event space, so check the online events calendar to make sure no one has it booked for a wedding.

HARPERS FERRY BREWERY

Purcellville • harpersferrybrewing.com

You can go from inner tube to bar stool in a matter of minutes; this spacious brewery is right next to Harpers Ferry Adventure Center. The beers are great, but that view! The river-view tables are reason alone to come here, even if you're not into the hoppy stuff.

LOUDOUN COUNTY VINEYARDS

The vineyards around Purcellville and Leesburg aren't too far. You could drive down there after your float, but bring a change of clothes—many of the vineyards aren't soggy river wear–appropriate (Chapter 16).

// Harpers Ferry Brewery

≡ *Stay Over*

If tubing's your main focus, there's no real need to spend the night. You can easily drive out in the morning and head back to the city after your ride or after some time in the town of Harpers Ferry.

But if you have a little more time, the town makes for a charming overnighter, especially once the day-trippers leave. In keeping with the town's historic character, the in-town lodging options are mostly homey B&Bs, historic inns, and well-priced Airbnbs.

THE LIGHT HORSE INN

www.lighthorseinn.com • $$

Set in a building that was here around the time when George Washington passed through, this seven-suite inn has comfy beds and an updated historic charm. It's up in Bolivar, right near the Barn.

THE LEDGE HOUSE

www.theledgehouse.com • $$

For a view that's tough to beat, try the Ledge House's tree house–like deck, which overlooks the river and town. The B&B has three suites, some of which have private balconies.

RENTAL SCENE

You can rent cottages, carriage houses, cabins, and houses here—and, for the most part, they're very affordable.

≡ Plan Around

Tubing season runs from around May to October. Usually water levels are higher in the spring, but it just depends how much rain the area's gotten. If the water's too high, the river can be too fast and dangerous to tube. Likewise, too little rain can mean the water's too low to float down.

If you're worried, call a day or two before you drive out there.

Weekends to Plan For (or Avoid):

- **Fourth of July:** Not only is this one of the most popular days on the river, the Fourth is a big deal all over Harpers Ferry, given the town's patriotic history.

GOOD TO KNOW

- Legally, we should note, you aren't allowed to operate a tube while under the influence of alcohol. Journalistically, we will note that some people do not obey that rule.

BEEN HERE, DONE THAT?

- You can also float on the Shenandoah farther south, from places such as Front Royal.
- A short drive from Charlottesville, the James River is a very popular float zone. For more white water rapid action, pick up the James in Richmond, which has arguably the best urban whitewater in the country.

13

Explore the Ghost Ships of Mallows Bay

Nanjemoy, MD

Most Washingtonians don't realize that the Western Hemisphere's largest shipwreck fleet is right in our backyard. And it's open for visitors.

FROM DC: 43 MILES · 1 HOUR | DAYS HERE: EASY DAY TRIP

DO	EAT	DRINK	BUY
kayak	BBQ	water	cupcakes from Michelle's

After World War I, a fleet of unused warships was scrapped, towed to this corner of the Potomac, and left to rot.

Now, after 100 years, nature has commandeered the ships. The hulls have become rich ecosystems, home to beavers, bald eagles, osprey, and plenty of fish. Under the water, barely submerged and still visible when the tide is right, lies a ship graveyard bigger than any other on this side of the world.

The area is on its way to becoming a protected National Marine Sanctuary, but the ships are easy to access. All you need is a kayak and a paddle.

☰ Getting to Mallows Bay

The only way to get to this part of Maryland is by car. It's about an hour's drive south of DC along the Potomac. You'll head out of the city on I-695, then cut south on 295. At National Harbor and the MGM casino, you'll keep going south on Highway 210 (also called Indian Head Road) and Highway 224, until you reach the turnoff for Mallows Bay (look for the sign).

>> **Water Levels:** When the water's high, it can be harder to see some of the ships. If it's been especially rainy, you may want to wait for the water levels to drop.

☰ Get Your Bearings

Mallows Bay is on the eastern bank of the Potomac River, just a little south of the Quantico Marine Corps base (on the other side). It's part of the Nanjemoy Peninsula in Charles County, a rural, river-laced area in southern Maryland.

There's ample parking at the bay; if you park in the main lot, there's an overlook with a telescope viewer that points out at the ships. There's also a small boat launch at the water; this is where kayak tours generally leave from, too.

☰ Kayak in a Ship Graveyard

If you were to fly over Mallows Bay today, you'd see the distinctive outlines of about 200 ships just beneath the water's surface, laid out like cars in a parking lot. From the water, the scene is much more intimate. Rather than vessels, many ships look more like small islands. You can touch the rusty hulls and see where plants and animals have taken over.

But why are they here?

Some of the ships here date back to the Revolutionary War, but the most famous residents at Mallows Bay are the World War I-era steamships.

In 1917, with World War I raging, the United States revved up its shipbuilding business to counteract deadly destruction by German U-boats. Hundreds of ships were built to help in the war effort, but the war ended before many of them could be sent over to Europe. The government had to figure out what to do with them.

Ultimately, the ships were sold for scrap to Western Marine & Salvage Company. The Alexandria-based company towed them to the Potomac River.

The ships were salvaged a few times and raided during the Depression (people stripped away the metal and wood). They were burned a few times. Finally, Mother Nature took over, covering the hunks of scrap with trees and bushes and birds' nests.

// Kayaks at Mallows Bay

In the 1960s, efforts started to remove the ships. But by now, the natural environment had set in, and lawmakers saw how valuable the vessels were to the surrounding ecosystem. Removal plans were scrapped. And here the ships lie today.

Where to Find a Kayak

There's nowhere to rent self-guided kayaks nearby, but if you have your own, you can bring it and explore solo. (Just make sure it's a hardshell—inflatable kayaks don't stand much of a chance against the rusty submerged metal ship scraps.)

Two main tour operators run guided tours here; these include the boats and gear. **Charles County** (www.charlescountyparks.com/parks/guided-tours) runs trips on Sundays, and **Atlantic Kayak Company** (www.atlantickayak.com) runs trips on weekends (they partner with the county on some trips).

Both companies have the same pricing ($75 for a 3-hour tour, $49 for a 1.5-hour tour). If you have the time, opt for the 3-hour tour; you'll get closer to the S.S. *Accomac*, a rusty old car ferry that's the most "ship"-looking ship of the fleet (it's the least submerged).

A handful of organizations such as Smithsonian and Sierra Club also run occasional trips out here. These tend to be a lot more expensive, but they do sometimes include transportation.

☰ While You're Here

FISH MATTAWOMAN CREEK

This northern neighboring estuary to Mallows may not have ghost ships, but it's got a different claim to fame. The creek is also said to be one of the best largemouth bass fishing spots on the East Coast. On weekends from spring to fall, there are frequent bass tournaments. You need a freshwater fishing license to participate here.

HIKE THE INDIAN HEAD TRAIL

Flat, paved, and scenic, the 13-mile rail trail runs from Indian Head to the town of White Plains. Along the way, there are bridges, wetlands, and benches to take in the scenery.

EXPLORE PORT TOBACCO

About half hour to the east of Mallows is one of the East Coast's oldest communities. (And smallest, at population: 13.) You can visit a few historic buildings like the reconstructed 1819 courthouse (now a small Civil War museum).

GAMBLING

It's the opposite of a nature day, but the massive MGM Casino is on the route about halfway between Mallows Bay and DC. It's the closest place to gamble around Washington.

☰ Good Eats

Once you get out of the capital region, dining options along the route are light. So if you're day-tripping, you might skip the eating out and just bring a snack. That said, you're entering BBQ country, and there are a few local faves that'll fuel you up before or after your paddle.

MORE INFO

- **Find Your Chesapeake** has some great videos and 360 photos of the ships online (www.findyourchesapeake.com/places/mallows-bay-park).
- **Charles County**, which manages the Mallows Bay park, has a great self-guided kayaking map and facts about the ships (www.charlescountymd.gov/GhostFleetofMallowsBay)

// Sunset at Mallows Bay

B&J CARRYOUT

Accokeek • www.bjcarryout.com • $ • ice cream

Pop into this little corner spot right off the main road for ice cream and BBQ. Ice cream season conveniently overlaps with kayaking season; from April through November, you can get cones, shakes, sundaes, and malts. There's no seating, so you'll want to take your food to go.

GEORGE'S BBQ

Indian Head • www.georgesribs.com • $ • BBQ

A popular BBQ joint in the area is George's, which serves juicy ribs, smoked chicken, seafood, and too many sides to choose from. It's the type of place where the food's served in styrofoam take-out boxes and the seating's all checkered tablecloth-covered picnic tables.

DALE'S SMOKEHOUSE

Indian Head • $ • BBQ

A minute or so down the road from George's, Dale's is a homey spot with American flags on every table and pig knickknacks all over the walls. They're known for their slabs of ribs—people drive for miles to devour them.

// Kayaking around a submerged ship

MICHELLE'S CAKES

Indian Head • www.michellescakes.net • $ • cupcakes

If you're passing through on a Saturday, stop at this family-run cakery. Most of their treats are made to order, so you have to call ahead; you can, however, get cookies or cupcakes (their menu has 50 flavors . . .) if you stop in. If it's a Sunday, don't bother—they're closed.

≡ *Stay Over*

Mallows Bay is really a day trip; there aren't a ton of hotel options right here, nor do you need one. The main reason to spend the night is if you want to do some camping in one of the nearby state parks.

CAMPING

You can't camp at Mallows Bay itself, but about 15 minutes up the road is **Smallwood State Park** (dnr.maryland.gov), which has campsites for tents, plus six cabins, some of which have water views.

☰ *Plan Around*

Mallows Bay Park is open all year, so if you have your own boat, you can bring it whenever. If you need to rent a boat, you'll have to go in season, which is typically May through October. Other things to plan around: rain and tides. It's tougher to see the submerged ships at high tide, while rain can also cause higher water levels (and also who wants to pay to kayak in the rain?).

GOOD TO KNOW

- During World War I, it cost the government $700,000 to $1 million to build *each ship*. A few years later, the 233 ships sold for salvage recouped only $750,000 total.

- Each sunken ship supports its own ecosystem, called island "flower pots."

BEEN HERE, DONE THAT?

- The Mattawoman Creek to the north also has kayaking trips.

- Across the state, on Maryland's Eastern Shore, is the beautiful Blackwater National Wildlife Refuge, which has a lot more chances to kayak among eagles.

- If you want less kayaking and more history, check out Staunton (Chapter 19). The Woodrow Wilson Presidential Library & Museum has a lot more background on World War I, and the historical setting against which the ships were built (Wilson was the one who commissioned the ships in the first place).

Part Three
Wine & Beer Trails

Brewery Hop in Virginia's Beer Capital

Richmond, VA

Richmond has emerged as one of the East Coast's best beer towns, with 30 breweries—and counting.

FROM DC: 109 MILES · 2 HOURS | TRIP LENGTH: WEEKEND

DO	EAT	DRINK	BUY
walk along the James River	Vietnamese pub food at The Answer	all the beer	crowlers or six-packs

Prepare your liver. The beer scene here isn't just the best in the region—breweries in Richmond are gaining national attention. Each company puts its own spin on their beers, so rather than a common regional style, you'll see different brewers trying different things all over town.

Beyond the beer, the city is legit cool. While outsiders may think of it first as the Virginia state capitol, or even throw it back to when this was the capital of the Confederacy, those in the know recognize that there's a new identity charging through. Little hipster enclaves are popping up all over Richmond (a.k.a. RVA), bringing with them coffee shops, street art, bike shops, galleries, and specialty food purveyors, like pie shops and popsicle stands.

But this weekend, we're here for the beer.

≡ Getting to Richmond

Leave the car at home, you don't need it for this trip! Amtrak runs an easy 2-hour(ish) route between DC and Richmond and tickets start at $24. Greyhound and MegaBus buses also go back and forth for about $20; the trip's typically a little longer than the train.

You can also get here by car, but I-95 between DC and Richmond is a notoriously terrible traffic zone. What should be a 2-hour drive can often take much longer. If you do insist on driving, don't forget your EZ-Pass!

Once you're here, it's easy to get around with no car. Uber and Lyft are plentiful, and there are bike share docks spread around town, although it is a bit hilly. (Buy passes at the kiosks—it's $1.75 per ride or $6 for a full day.)

≡ Get Your Bearings

Like any city, Richmond's made up of a jigsaw of neighborhoods. The state capitol and government buildings sit in the middle of all of it.

From here, Church Hill is an up-and-coming 'hood to the east. Heading northwest, a chain of districts shoot out along the Broad Street thoroughfare: the Fan District (home to VCU); Carytown, an Adams Morgan-esque strip of restaurants and bars; the Museum District, which is not surprisingly home to some (but not all) of the city's big cultural institutions; and Scott's Addition, the trendy warehouse-turned-brewery district.

The James River runs to the south of downtown, and in it, the popular Belle Isle, which is Richmond's equivalent of Teddy Roosevelt Island.

≡ BEER!

Even if you hit up a different brewery every hour, you still couldn't get to all of Richmond's beer hotspots in a day. At this writing, there were over 30 breweries in the Richmond area, with more on the way.

They're scattered throughout the city, although the biggest concentration is in Scott's Addition, a walkable industrial–style neighborhood that might as well be called the brewery district (plus there are cideries and a meadery).

You can pick one or hop around, but whatever you do, leave room in your bag for some, er, "souvenirs." Most places sell cans or crowlers, so you can taste your way through what's on tap and bring home your faves. Bottoms up!

>> **Brewery Jams:** Many of the breweries bring in live music on weekends. Check them out on Facebook or Instagram to see what music (and food trucks) might be there.

IF YOU JUST GO TO ONE BREWERY: THE VEIL BREWING CO.

Scotts Addition • www.theveilbrewing.com

// The Veil brewery

The Veil is one of the best-known breweries in Richmond—beer nerds trade their cans across the country like baseball cards. Known for their creative and flavorful hop-forward beers, the menu changes constantly.

You can order from the draft list, although a lot of people go straight for the cans—buy a pallet of some of the day's drafts and take them outside to the covered picnic tables to avoid constant trips back to the draft line.

IF YOU LIKE IPAS: TRIPLE CROSSING BREWING COMPANY

Downtown • Fulton • triplecrossing.com

Abundantly hopped IPAs are the focus at this acclaimed local brewery. Started by some buddies who were into home brewing, Triple Crossing churns out serious beers in a low-key atmosphere. There are two locations, the original Downtown and a larger, newer one in Fulton.

IF YOU'RE HUNGRY: THE ANSWER BREWPUB

Off Broad Street, near Westwood • theanswerbrewpub.com

The beers at The Answer sound more like cupcake flavors than lagers and ales. They brew stouts with things such as coffee, maple syrup, and toasted coconut, and make their sours so fruity that it's hard to tell there's alcohol in them. Aside from the beer, the food menu's fantastic—probably the best of RVA's breweries. The founder hails from the nearby Mekong restaurant, so expect delicious Vietnamese favorites such as ramen, dumplings, and bahn mi.

IF YOU LIKE SOURS: VASEN BREWING

Scotts Addition • www.vasenbrewing.com

This Scandinavian-hip brewery trades the traditional wood pub style for towering high ceilings, white walls, and mod-Nordic decor. Opened in 2017, it was named one of the best new breweries in the country by Beer Advocate. They focus on funky sours and farmhouse saisons.

IF YOU WANT SOMETHING FAMOUS: STONE BREWING

Fulton • www.stonebrewing.com

Need proof of Richmond's beer cred? West Coast brewing behemoth Stone, one of the country's largest craft brewers, opened their East Coast command center here. The massive industrial-chic riverfront space includes a beer production plant, a taproom, a store, and an upcoming farm-to-table restaurant.

IF YOU'RE WITH A GROUP: ARDENT CRAFT ALES

Scotts Addition • ardentcraftales.com

This is the type of place you'd want to hang out at all day—which is why it's not surprising to see groups of people with small babies, dogs, and the like post up at large picnic tables in the beer garden. Known for their IPAs and saisons, Ardent also has a rotating cast of food trucks to help hold you over.

IF YOU WANT GOOD VIEWS: LEGEND BREWING CO.

South Richmond • www.legendbrewing.com

This brewery is across the river, in Manchester (you can walk from the T Pott pedestrian bridge, but once you cross the river it's not a pretty walk . . . we recommend driving). The main draw here is the view; an open-air patio overlooks the James and the city skyline across the water.

☰ *While You're Here*

HANG OUT ON THE RIVER

On a warm summer day, the James is the place to be. You can rent kayaks or stand-up paddle-boards from **Riverside Outfitters** (www.riversideoutfitters.net) or **RVA Paddlesports** (rvapaddlesports.com), or you can join a whitewater rafting boat down the Class III and IV rapids. Best of all, you can reward yourself with a cold beer after a rapid run; **Stone** is easy to access from the water.

A network of parks and pedestrian bridges also take advantage of the river. **Belle Isle**, which you can get to via a suspended pedestrian bridge that runs under the highway, is a favorite place to picnic, mountain bike, or lay out on the river rocks.

Brown's Island, on the Downtown-side of the river, also has trails, plus public art displays and events like Friday night concerts in the summer. From here, you can walk across the new Potterfield (a.k.a. T Pott) pedestrian bridge to find more trails and viewpoints on the other side of the James.

MUSEUMS & HISTORY FOR DAYS

Founded in 1737, Richmond has been the site of pivotal moments in American history. (Patrick Henry's "Give Me Liberty or Give Me Death" speech happened here; it was also the capital of the Confederacy during the Civil War.) Now all that history's commemorated in

// River rafting on the James

an impressive museum scene, which covers everything from internationally recognized art to Civil War history to local culture.

Possibly the best-known institution is the **Virginia Museum of Fine Arts** (VMFA). Anchoring the city's aptly named Museum District, it's one of the country's largest art museums, known for its contemporary art, although you can find everything from Impressionist paintings to an Ancient Egyptian sarcophagus here. Best of all, it's free.

Other interesting stops on the museum circuit include the newly opened **Institute for Contemporary Art** at VCU, the **Black History Museum**, and the **Valentine**, which covers 400 years of Richmond's history.

Not officially a museum, but **St. John's Church** in the Church Hill district is the site of Patrick Henry's famous speech, and there are great views from nearby Libby Park.

CHECK OUT THE STREET ART

Murals and street art are all over the place in Richmond. Back in 2012, the **Richmond Mural Project** set out to create over 100 murals within five years. Now every year new artists come in from around the world; their works range from the evocative woman sitting in a jar of moonshine to the poppy crosswalk intersection in Scotts Addition. Many—but not all—of the works are documented on the Mural Project's website (richmondmuralproject.squarespace.com).

☰ *Good Eats*

If you're going to be beering all day, you need something hearty in your stomach. Some breweries have gone the "brewpub" route and serve full menus. Others cart in food trucks or specialize in one dish like pizza or grilled cheese.

Overall, it's easy to eat well in Richmond, and it's easy to do so without spending a lot of money.

ZZQ TEXAS CRAFT BBQ

Scotts Addition • www.zzqrva.com • $$, BBQ

What started out as a casual pop-up backyard BBQ is now the hottest name in Richmond restaurants, having been named the best BBQ in Virginia by *Food and Wine*. Cooked true Texas–style, the brisket's a must. One Texas food critic named it the best Texas BBQ outside of the Lone Star State. It's on the same block as Ardent Craft Ales, so it's the perfect brew-crawl stop.

KUBA KUBA

The Fan • www.kubakuba.info • $$ • Cuban

This corner Cuban favorite is a great choice for brunch or dinner. The bodega-inspired inside will transport you to the island, with lively music and colorful knickknacks like photos, murals, and canned goods. Portions are big and include island classics such as Cuban sandwiches, ropa vieja, and eggs all kinds of ways.

STELLA'S

Malvern Gardens • stellasrichmond.com • $$ • Greek

Greek staples in huge portion sizes dominate the menu (plus they have the largest plate of spaghetti you've ever seen). Tables book up; either reserve ahead or get here when the bar opens for happy hour. You can get the whole menu at the bar.

SAISON

Downtown • www.saisonrva.com • $$ • modern American

Southern cooking meets Latin American flavor at this hip American gastropub. Open for dinner only, expect dishes like jalapeño and pineapple chicken wings or crispy rice bowls. But what draws many RVA locals to the cozy brick eatery is the burger, which is said to be the best in the city. The beer and cocktail menus are both thoughtfully curated.

BRENNER PASS

Scotts Addition • www.brennerpassrva.com • $$ • modern European

What pairs well with a day of beer drinking? Warm, gooey CHEESE. This trendy Alpine-inspired restaurant serves a range of meats, cheeses, pastas, and small plates. Plus fondue. Fondue in pots. Fondue in a burger. Fondue frites. There's also a coffee shop if you need a jolt while you bar-hop around Scotts Addition.

PERLY'S

Downtown • www.perlysrichmond.com • $$ • Jewish deli

It's one of Richmond's most beloved brunches: a New York–style deli with a menu full of Jewish deli classics (think latkes and reubens), plus some inventive options like a crab-cake-take on whitefish. One meal here will hold you over for awhile, the portions are so big.

KING OF POPS

Scotts Addition • kingofpops.com • $ • popsicles

Farm-to-stick popsicles have taken hold in RVA, with "pop"-up carts around the city and a permanent window in Scotts Addition. Flavors are either cream-based (cookies 'n cream) or fruit-based (blueberry lemonade) and rotate with the seasons.

THE ROOSEVELT

Church Hill • rooseveltrva.com • $$ • Southern

Known equally for their Southern food and cocktail list, this Church Hill standout brings Virginia flavors to life. James Beard–nominee Chef Lee Gregory serves dishes such as roasted chicken and seared scallops in a charmingly converted turn-of-the-century house.

LAMPLIGHTER COFFEE ROASTERS

Scotts Addition • The Fan • lamplightercoffee.com • $ • coffee shop

Man-buns, flannel shirts, and all other hipsterisms are welcome at this local coffee chain, which caters to a diverse crowd. The three locations around the city not only serve great coffee, they have amazing breakfast sandwiches and plenty of veggie/vegan-friendly menu options.

☰ *Time for a Drink*

In addition to all the beers, Richmond's a college town, a political town, and a trend-aware town. So whether you want something cheap and boozy or to go somewhere to see and be seen, this city's got it.

QUIRK HOTEL

Downtown • www.destinationhotels.com/quirk-hotel

One of the trendiest local hotels has shot to the top of the city's bar list, thanks to an eighth-floor open-air rooftop bar with a panoramic view of the city. It's a sceney place, so you'll want to dress the part. The lobby bar, with its white groin-vaulted ceilings and rosé-color finishes, is also a great place to people watch.

THE JEFFERSON

Downtown • www.jeffersonhotel.com

Class it up at this grande-dame hotel's lobby bar. This luxury hotel has been serving visitors (including 13 Presidents) since 1895. If the rooms are out of your price range, grab drinks at the hotel bar or stop in at the Sunday champagne brunch. Make sure to check out the Tiffany-stained glass ceilings in the hotel lobbies.

THE CIRCUIT ARCADE BAR

Scotts Addition • www.thecircuitarcadebar.com

With 50 craft beers on tap plus a cavernous arcade space, this place is like Chuck E. Cheese for grownups. The beer wall is self-serve; no waiting for a bartender's attention.

THE JASPER

Carytown • jasperbarrva.com

RVA's craft cocktail establishment of choice is backed by an all-star roster of local bartenders. Despite its mixology caliber, the vibe is decidedly unpretentious, with everything from $3 cans of light beer to cocktails made with absinthe or chili liqueur.

☰ *Stay Over*

As a major city, Richmond has a bed for every budget.

Most of the city's hotels are clustered in the city center area near the Capital, and in The Fan. If you want a more neighborhood-y vibe, look for an Airbnb in either Church Hill, the Fan, or Carytown. There's typically somewhere with availability, which makes RVA good for a last-minute getaway.

THE COMMONWEALTH

www.thecommonwealthsuites.com • $$

Situated across from the Capitol building, this 100-year-old landmark hotel recently reinvented itself. Rooms are large and well-appointed, and the hotel is full of local touches, like tattoo-inspired decor and furniture from local craftspeople. Since this is a government area, it's a bit quiet on weekends, but the city center bars and restaurants are within walking distance.

THE GRADUATE

www.graduatehotels.com • $$

Relive your college glory days at this alumni-themed hotel. It's far better than any dorm room you ever had, with ultra-hip decor and a rooftop bar and pool. Set in the Monroe Ward district a few blocks from VCU, you'll be right in the thick of the city's action.

HI RICHMOND

www.hiusa.org • $

Hostels aren't only for study abroad in Europe, FYI. This a cool, clean, and cheap spot. It's located downtown, a few blocks from Triple Crossing. Six-bed dorms start at around $30, or there are private rooms, too.

RENTAL SCENE

Renting a place can be the best way to stay in some of Richmond's neighborhoods, like the Fan and Church Hill. It's also crazy cheap here, with a lot of options under $100 per night. Most of the rentals are apartment–style or a full town-home. Airbnb has the most options, although check HomeAway and VRBO too.

1 Brews and bites at The Answer
2 Kegs at the Veil
3 Bar at Ardent

≡ Plan Around

Richmond's big enough to handle most of the events that happen here. There are a few major events around the universities that may cause congestion or hotel prices to spike, but for the most part, this is a major city with a full calendar.

Weekends to Plan For (or Avoid):

- **VCU Commencement (May):** Lines lines lines, plus booked hotels—that's graduation weekend in Richmond. There's also a commencement weekend in December.
- **Richmond Marathon (November):** Unless you're running, steer clear. Street closures and large crowds make getting around a pain. (If you *are* a runner, this run's a fun one—bands and DJs line the course, and you'll get beer on Brown Island when you're done.)

>> **Beer Releases:** Beer releases are an excuse to party. Check out your prospective breweries' websites or Facebook pages to see if there are any new brews to line up for.

GOOD TO KNOW

- Baltimore may get the Edgar Allen Poe link, but the poet was born and grew up in Richmond. While it's no NFL team, there is a museum celebrating the writer.

BEEN HERE, DONE THAT?

- About an hour north on I-95, Fredericksburg continues the beer theme, with seven breweries including an outpost of RVA's Strangeways. It's a great pit-stop on the drive to or from DC (Chapter 25).
- As Richmond is Virginia's beer capital, Frederick claims the title for Maryland. There are around 15 breweries in the town, with more on the radar (Chapter 17).
- The Nelson 151, which runs along the Blue Ridge Mountains near Charlottesville, connects breweries along a beautiful driving route.

15

Drink Wine in Horse Country

Middleburg, VA

The road to Middleburg is lined with rolling hills, white-fenced horse farms, country estates, and a winery for every occasion.

FROM DC: 46 MILES · 1 HOUR | TRIP LENGTH: DAY TRIP

DO	EAT	DRINK	BUY
winery-hop	cheese at a winery	wine	riding-style designs

Middleburg's one of DC's most accessible vineyards clusters, but once you're here, "wine country" doesn't quite fit the bill. Despite the fact that some of the vineyards here are over a decade old, wine's a relative newcomer on the Middleburg scene, which is all about horseback riding, fox hunting, and an elegant country charm.

The town has an appreciation for tradition; society revolves around events like the hunt and steeplechase horse races. It feels a bit like you've traveled to the English countryside, with cozy stone inns and horses grazing in pastures. The vineyards provide a perfect portal into all this, with a trail of wineries that carries you through the historic heart of the town.

Getting to Middleburg

This is Uber-accessible wine country. A standard Uber or Lyft ride from DC costs about $60. And while you may feel worlds away from the city, Dulles airport is close enough that you shouldn't have a problem Ubering back home, especially on weekends.

If you plan on vineyard hopping and want someone else to DD your whole trip, try a wine tour (more on that later).

If you want to drive on your own, you can take US-50 W much of the way, but stoplights can slow down your arrival to wine time. Taking I-66 and then cutting up on 15 might be faster . . . but 66 traffic can be nightmarish, so check a map app before heading out.

Get Your Bearings

US-50, a.k.a. Mosby Highway, is essentially vineyard alley. Starting about 7 miles east of town, at least five vineyards line the route into Middleburg. Many of them are visible from the road.

As for location, this is the base of the Blue Ridge. If you were to keep driving west, you'd hit the Shenandoah River and could make your way to Skyline Drive. Due north are Purcellville and another wine cluster around Leesburg (Chapter 16). Keep going north and you'll eventually get to Harpers Ferry.

The Highway 50 Vineyard Crawl

Welcome to wine country, Virginia–style. You won't find chateaux or villas out here; instead, vineyards are influenced by the local farms and horse culture. Tasting rooms often resemble barns or farmhouses (or, in one case, a log cabin). Most vineyards have great outdoor seating, with views of the Blue Ridge Mountains.

DOGS + WINE

Virginia considers beer and wine "food," so they're cracking down on dogs being involved in your tasting day. Some once-dog-friendly wineries in this area have become a little less so, but you can check schedules and find special events, like **Barrel Oak Winery's** (www.barreloak .com) dog adoption weekends.

// Cana patio

Most wineries don't specialize in one type of wine. They cater to popular styles (pretty much everyone has a rosé), and also serve local varietals, including Viognier (Virginia's signature grape), Norton (Virginia's less elegant sounding but best growing grape), and Petit Verdot.

As it passes through Middleburg, US-50 West plays connect-the-vineyard-dots, stringing together about seven venues (plus a cidery). Here's what you can expect to find at each:

IF YOU'RE LOOKING TO PARTY: QUATTRO GOOMBAS

Aldie • goombawine.com

Known for their wine slushies, delicious fluffy pizza, and a full brewery to satisfy the beer drinker in your group, there are plenty of reasons to stay for another round. The vibe here is social. Started by four friends (the name's an Italian slang word for buddies), there's a big deck and cornhole, and you can carry your drinks between the winery and brewery.

IF YOU WANT TO BE OUTSIDE: CHRYSALIS

Middleburg • www.chrysaliswine.com

The long windy drive in leads to an impressive winery, with an outdoor terrace, bar, patio, and deck. Tastings here are done at scheduled time slots on weekends, which feels corporate and a bit less intimate. Instead, grab a glass (or a bottle) and load up on meats and cheeses from the farm market here, then post up at a table outside and enjoy the view.

PAIR WITH LIVE MUSIC: 50 WEST

Middleburg • www.50westvineyards.com

Set in a sand-colored farm-style cottage up a hill, this spot has nice views over its surrounding vineyards and rolling green hills. Every Saturday and Sunday, they bring in live bands, which pump up the Bordeaux–style wine. It's a decent in-between option: upscale but not stuffy. A metallic horse sculpture out front is a reminder that you're in horse country.

FOR WINE YOU'VE NEVER TRIED BEFORE: CANA

Middleburg • canavineyards.com

Helmed by an award-winning female winemaker, this winery throws it back to Biblical times by aging some of its wines in amphoras, or big clay pots. (You can see it pictured on the bottle labels here.) The tasting menu's always changing, and they also do a wildly popular rosé release in early May.

FOR SOMETHING FANCY: GREENHILL WINERY & VINEYARDS

Middleburg • www.greenhillvineyards.com

The wine here is some of the best in the area; the winery's blanc de blanc was served in an 2016 Oscar nominee gift bag, so you can drink the same bubbly that Jennifer Lawrence and

// Boxwood Estate Winery

Leonardo DiCaprio received. Despite ample signage and notice online, people seem to keep showing up here with their kids. Don't bother—they won't be let in, which makes for a quieter, more refined (also, more expensive) wine-tasting experience than some of the nearby vineyards. Tastings are seated and served affairs in the airy tasting rooms or on the verandah; you can also buy wines and bring a picnic for the lawn.

CLOSEST TO TOWN: BOXWOOD ESTATE WINERY

Middleburg • boxwoodwinery.com

Down a side road off the town's main street, this modern barn-style winery sits in the middle of a field of vines. Owned by former Redskins owner John Kent Cooke, the winery is located on the Boxwood Estate, a National Historic Landmark, considered one of the earliest horse farms in the Middleburg area. Wines here are done in the Bordeaux style.

A COZY SETTING: SLATER RUN TASTING ROOM

Upperville • www.slaterrun.com

A short drive west of town, this adorable little tasting room looks like a stone cottage. It's owned by a family whose Middleburg farm roots date back to the early 1700s. In addition to Slater Run wines, the tasting room sells small bites and bottles from other local wineries. The vineyard itself is located off Highway 50, but it's only open on weekends in the summer.

MIDDLEBURG VINEYARD TIPS

- Check the hours: most vineyards close at 6 or 7 p.m. (5 p.m. in the winter). While a geographic tour might make sense at first, you can maximize your time more by starting at the earliest opener and ending at the last last call.
- A good rule of thumb is to pick three vineyards. Any more than that, and you'll probably stop noticing what sets each wine apart.
- If your wine-tasting crew is six or more people, book a reservation before you get to the vineyards. Many of them can't accommodate groups without a heads up.

WINE TOURS

Birthday partiers, bachelorettes, and anyone in need of a DD, rejoice! Not only are there plenty of vineyards to explore around Middleburg, there are a lot of companies that want to drive you around.

RESTON LIMO

www.restonlimo.com

This transportation company runs two-vineyard wine tours (featured vineyards rotate), or you can do a private tour and pick how many and which wineries to visit. They'll pick up from the West Falls Church Metro station. Tours start at $62 and include tasting fees.

CORK & KEG

www.corkandkegtours.com

Dedicated specifically to Loudoun wine and beer exploring, this husband-and-wife–run tour company has special access at some vineyards. They'll skip the line and pick up your wine or beer. All you have to do is show up, grab a table, and get served. Tours start at $110 and do not include tasting fees.

≡ *While You're Here*

EXPLORE DOWNTOWN MIDDLEBURG

Even if you have no reason to buy anything, it's fun to peruse the shops in the historic downtown. You'll find saddles and riding gear, galleries with photos depicting scenes of the hunt, sporting-inspired clothing haberdasheries like **Highcliffe** (www .highcliffeclothiers.com), plus the original location of local boutique chain **Lou Lou** (loulouboutiques.com).

// Downtown Middleburg

// Red Fox Inn & Tavern

BROWSE THE NATIONAL SPORTING LIBRARY & MUSEUM

www.nationalsporting.org

Immerse yourself in the area's fox hunting and sporting culture at this small fine arts museum and library. The paintings, sculptures, and other works of art depict scenes of hunting, horses, and hounds, plus other outdoors pursuits like fly fishing.

TAILGATE FOR TWILIGHT POLO

www.greatmeadow.org/twilight-polo

Come out for an evening of polo, wine, and dancing at Great Meadows. Every Saturday night between May and September, the polo center hosts nighttime matches with a party. There's usually a theme, a food truck, and a winery pouring—or you can BYO picnic.

HIKE AT SKY MEADOWS STATE PARK

www.dcr.virginia.gov/state-parks/sky-meadows

This scenic state park in the Blue Ridge Mountains has 22 miles of hiking trails (including access to the Appalachian Trail) through forests and meadows. Visitors can also bike, fish, camp, and visit the historic Mount Bleak House in the middle of the park. Make sure you make it to the Piedmont Overlook, which provides a panoramic view of the Piedmont Valley eastward from the Blue Ridge.

☰ *Good Eats*

Most of the wineries serve small bites, and some let you bring outside food (not drinks though) for a vineyard picnic. Middleburg's main street isn't a foodie mecca, but it's getting better, and there are a few great options in nearby country villages.

KING STREET OYSTER BAR

Middleburg • kingstreetoysterbar.com • $$ • seafood

This relative newcomer on Middleburg's main drag is one of few spots open "late" in Middleburg, which draws a young, energetic crowd. Specialties include, you guessed it, seafood. There's a sister location in downtown Leesburg.

MIDDLEBURG DELI

Middleburg • middleburgdeli.com • $ • deli

If you don't want to stop for a sit-down meal, swing through this sandwich shop on the main drag. There are over 30 combos on the menu, plus a good lineup of sides.

THE UPPER CRUST

Middleburg • $ • bakery

This spot has been around forever; its baked goods are a local favorite. There's a decent menu of sandwiches and a small back patio you can eat on. It's closed Sundays.

MARKET SALAMANDER

Middleburg • www.salamanderresort.com/dine/market-salamander • $ • grocery/cafe

Most vineyards let you bring in food, so stop at this high-end grocery for bread, cheese, and other bites. There's a Safeway down the road, but the gourmet items here are perfect for picnics. It's also a cafe, so you can eat on-site.

MIDDLEBURG COMMON GROUNDS

Middleburg • www.middleburgcommongrounds.com • $ • coffee shop

For pretty good coffee in the heart of Middleburg, this is the place. There's often live music, and they're dog-friendly (as are many Middleburg spots).

MARSHALL

The little town of Marshall, about a 20- to 30-minute drive from Middleburg, is emerging as a foodie hotspot. Try **The Whole Ox** for one of the best meat-forward menus around. **Red Truck Bakery** serves great coffee, fresh pastries and bread, and has a small market with local jams and seasoning. A local secret is **Nick's Deli**, at Glascock Grocery, where you can get out-of-this-world fried chicken, tacos, and BBQ.

THE PLAINS

Another small-country crossroads, The Plains has one main intersection—and it's full of food options. **The Front Porch** offers exactly that: a comfortable perch to eat locally sourced salads, sandwiches, and entrées. Next door, **Happy Creek Coffee** is a cool bike/coffee shop hybrid that's 100 percent gluten-free. **The Rail Stop's** chef, Tom Kee, has been featured on Oprah and The Food Network, and the gourmet country cuisine is served with little trains running around the dining room.

☰ *Time for a Drink*

Vineyards are plentiful here. Bars aren't. Most of the restaurants listed above double as bars, but Middleburg and the surrounding area aren't known as a late-night destination. Your best bet is to do your drinking at vineyards during the day, then enjoy a low-key nightcap.

MT. DEFIANCE CIDERY & DISTILLERY

www.mtdefiance.com

It's not a winery, but this giant wood cider barn is lumberjack-hip, with its Edison lights and bluegrass soundtrack. Cider flights include some out-there blends, like a five-pepper cider or a blueberry-infused combo. They also have a tasting room in the center of town.

☰ Stay Over

The vineyards around Middleburg are really day-trip destinations; they don't go full-estate with lodging as well. If you do decide to extend your stay in wine country, your primary options are historic inns and the Salamander resort. (And they don't come cheap!) To save money, look at home rentals and B&Bs.

RED FOX INN & TAVERN

www.redfox.com • $$$$

The oldest building in Middleburg (it dates back to 1728), this inn has hosted its fair share of power-guests, including Jackie Kennedy Onassis, Elizabeth Taylor, and Confederate General

GOOD TO KNOW

- Middleburg's long been an escape for wealthy Washingtonians. Jackie Kennedy and JFK owned a farm estate out here while JFK was president. Today, famous folks like Robert Duvall and Linda Tripp have homes out here.
- Stock your bar—some wineries let you keep your glass after a tasting.

BEEN HERE, DONE THAT?

- Have you tried the Leesburg vineyards, too? The biggest difference between the towns' wine options is just location; you have clusters in both areas but not as much in between. Leesburg vineyards are a bit more spread out and aren't all as much on the horse train as the Middleburg ones (Chapter 16).
- From Middleburg, the wineries continue to the south and west. You can essentially winery-hop all the way to Tennessee if you really wanted to. **RdV Vineyards** (www.rdvvineyards.com) is a good splurge; the estate is absolutely stunning and makes fantastic wines.
- To the south, check out Sperryville, a burgeoning foodie hamlet surrounded by a cluster of wineries.

J. E. B. Stuart. Rooms are scattered throughout a few different buildings, from the main stone inn to private cottages.

SALAMANDER RESORT & SPA

www.salamanderresort.com • $$$$

This country resort and spa is one of the most popular home bases for a weekend stay in Middleburg. There's horseback riding, a spa, tennis, golf, and a handful of on-site bars and restaurants. Some feel the character's a bit forced; the hotel feel outweighs the country estate atmosphere. If you stay there, they'll chauffeur you to nearby vineyards. Pets are pampered here, too.

RENTAL SCENE

You'll find little cottages, renovated barns, manor homes, and even a treehouse to rent on sites like Airbnb, VRBO, and Homeaway, but they might not all pop up if you just search "Middleburg." The trick here is to shift the map around; there are a number of other places in the towns nearby if you poke around in places such as Upperville, Aldie, Delaplane, Marshall, and the Plains.

☰ Plan Around

You can visit the wineries all year long, although summer and fall see the biggest crowds. October is Virginia Wine month, and some of the vineyards and restaurants offer specials to celebrate.

Weekends to Plan For (or Avoid):

- **Gold Cup (May and October):** There are actually horse races throughout the year, but this is the best known and most attended. The May event can see up to 50,000 people come out; October's races aren't quite as crazy.
- **Fall Foliage (September–October):** The highways can jam up with leaf peepers making their way to Shenandoah National Park during peak foliage. Roads around the vineyards themselves shouldn't be too bad, but getting here can take longer than usual.
- **Middleburg Film Festival (October):** A growing favorite on the film fest circuit, this four-day event draws Oscar winners and big Hollywood names.
- **Christmas in Middleburg (December):** Middleburg puts on one of the most popular Christmas parades in the region, with a special appearance by hunt riders on horseback and their hounds.

16

Escape to Wine Country, DC-Style

Leesburg, VA

DC's easiest-to-access wine region makes it hard to choose just one vineyard.

FROM DC: 10 MILES · 50 MINUTES | TRIP LENGTH: DAY TRIP

DO	EAT	DRINK	BUY
vineyard tours	fried green tomatoes	wine	Luckett's home decor

If you tried a different Leesburg winery every weekend starting in January, it'd take you until September to do them all (and by that point, there might be new ones to add to the list). Up the road from the Middleburg wine trail, Leesburg has (at this writing) about 35 wineries scattered around the city and the surrounding towns. Not only will you find some of the heavy hitters of NOVA's wine scene here, but you'll also have plenty to choose from when it comes to wine-tasting style.

☰ Getting to Leesburg

To get here by car, you can go the fast way or the cheap way. Both routes start by taking I-66 west. For the "fast" way, use the Dulles Toll Road and Dulles Greenway (about $9). For the cheap option, follow Route 7 (Leesburg Pike), which takes longer and has some traffic circles along the way.

If you're going to be drinking a lot, Uber and Lyft are good alternatives to driving. It costs about $60 to Uber from DC to downtown Leesburg; the vineyards around Purcellville and what not will be an additional $20 to $25. Since Leesburg's only 15 miles from Dulles Airport, there shouldn't be too long of a wait to request a ride home. (Although the farther out you are, the longer you may have to wait.)

The same wine tour companies we mention in Chapter 15 also operate in this area. Or you can always bike—see Chapter 18 for how to get here on the W&OD Trail.

>> **Cheers to Discounts:** If you're going to be hitting up multiple wineries, the three-day LoCo Wine Pass (visitloudoun.org) can be a good deal—it includes gift cards at many Leesburg wineries.

☰ Get Your Bearings

Leesburg sits on the western edge of DC's Virginia suburbs, and, for the most part, the city looks like what you'd expect in the 'burbs. The historic downtown is full of redbrick charm; the rest of it is largely town centers and residential communities. There aren't any wineries *in* Leesburg (just one tasting room and a bunch of breweries), but it's a good hub to do your vineyard exploring from.

As you head west out of town, the land starts to get a little more rural, with wineries mixed in among farms and residential communities. Same deal as you head north; you'll start to see some more forest as you near the Potomac River.

For overall bearings, once you hit the Potomac River out here, you could shoot west and soon hit Harpers Ferry (Chapter 12) or follow Route 15 across the river into Maryland and you won't be too far from Sugarloaf Mountain (Chapter 11).

☰ Go for the Grapes

It's hard to say what's booming more: the Leesburg area's wine scene or its housing development. It's getting to the point where there seems to be a winery or a residential development (or both) on almost every road you turn down.

// Stone Tower Winery

This means the wineries are kind of a mixed bag, scenery-wise. Some, like **Stone Tower** and **Bluemont**, are set among rolling hills and fields. Others are clearly more suburban, situated between homes in neighborhoods.

OK, but what's in the glass? Reds and whites get equal play, with a lot of focus on Virginia's strongest grapes. Viognier rules the whites, and reds are a mix of Cabernet Franc, Petit Verdot, and Norton. (But really, you'll find everything from Chardonnays to Sauv Blancs to rosé because everybody seems to love a good, or even mediocre, rosé.)

MOST POPULAR: STONE TOWER

15 minutes south of Leesburg • www.stonetowerwinery.com

On weekends in the summer and fall, there's a tailgate-like atmosphere at this vineyard. It feels like everyone who lives in the greater DC area is here. The venue itself is a beautifully renovated barn—well, actually, two barns: one's a bit more upscale and hosts weddings while on the other side of the lawn there's a more rustic "bring your dogs and kids" venue.

They serve a mix of reds and whites grown and bottled on-site, plus their Wild Boar labels, which use grapes from around the world.

BEST WINE: BREAUX

20 minutes northwest of Leesburg • www.breauxvineyards.com

Take a break from the barn-style wine tasting at this large Napa Valley–esque estate. The owner's originally from Louisiana, so you'll see French influences in the wines and Cajun touches, such as the crawfish logo and Mardi-Gras-bead–strung tasting bar. The place is huge, with multiple seating areas and enough breathing room that there can be a 50-person birthday party going on, kids running around outside, a live band playing throwback jams, and you'll still have space to yourself.

They've been making wines here for about 20 years, and the experience shows. The Viognier's a staff favorite, but from the steel barrel–aged non-buttery Chardonnay to the Cab Sauv made with the property's original vines, there are a lot of good pours.

BEST TASTING DEAL: TARARA

17 minutes northwest of Leesburg • www.tarara.com

If you're budget-minded, this should be the first winery of your day. The weekend "Penny Tastings" run from 11 a.m. to noon and cost—wait for it—a penny. Normally the tasting's $15, so if you can get out here early, it's a no-brainer.

Once the penny crowds die down, the peaceful elements of the winery's location start to shine a bit more (except during the summer concert series—that's a party). It's tucked away on a woodsy property, so you can hear birds chirping and a creek gurgling. As for the wine, Tarara specializes in Bordeaux and Burgundy styles and is one of Virginia's longest continuously operating wineries.

LOW KEY HANGOUT SPOT: FABBIOLI

12 minutes northwest of Leesburg • www.fabbioliwines.com

Hanging out at Fabbioli feels a bit like you're drinking at a neighbor's house . . . maybe because the winery's located in a rural subdivision and there are residential homes nearby. They've won many awards for their Tre Sorelle Merlot, Tannat, and Chardonnay. There are a few outdoor seating areas with loungers overlooking a field. This is a good bad-weather spot; the views from inside are comparable to the ones outside.

COME FOR THE VIEWS: BLUEMONT VINEYARD

23 minutes northwest of Leesburg • www.bluemontvineyard.com

The views here are just wow. The winery's perched atop a pretty steep hill overlooking grape vines, apple orchards, and a valley. When it comes to wine, the slushies and sangria seem to be more popular than the varietals, but most people aren't too picky about their drinks because, well, views. There's also a good menu here, with gourmet flatbreads, crab cakes, and farm fare. The food's a bit pricey, but . . . views.

// Fabbioli

A FOODIE'S WINERY: 868 ESTATE VINEYARDS

21 minutes northwest of Leesburg • 868estatevineyards.com

There's a lot of character here: the pretty country estate grounds have a beautiful natural feel, with gardens and an old manor house. As for the wine, you can level up between four different tiers of tastings, from the standard six-wine flight to the elevated version that comes with food and truffle pairings. This is one of the best spots to eat well on your tasting tour—either the property's restaurant Grandale or snack on paninis, cheese boards, and warm pretzels in the tasting room.

☰ *While You're Here*

REDECORATE YOUR APARTMENT

The Old Lucketts Store (www.luckettstore.com) feels like a place that Chip and Joanna Gaines would shop for all their fixer uppers if they lived in DC. It's an emporium of "antique hip" pieces—think big rustic wall clocks. Reclaimed wood doors and farm tables. A shed full of succulents. Check the calendar before you go—there are a lot of fun classes, such as one on how to repaint furniture, and a huge Design House at Christmas and Spring Market that brings out hundreds of vendors.

// Lucketts shopping

If vintage isn't your style, maybe outlet shopping is? The **Leesburg Corner Premium Outlets** (www.premiumoutlets.com) have about 100 name-brand stores, from Le Creuset to J. Crew Factory.

PICK YOUR OWN . . .

Apples. Pumpkins. Christmas Trees. The farms around Leesburg aren't just working farms: a handful of them welcome visitors. Across the street from Bluemont Vineyards, **Great Country Farms** (greatcountryfarms.com) has U Pick fruits like apples, peaches, and cherries. Nearby, **Snickers Gap Christmas Tree Farm** (www.snickersgaptrees.com) lets you saw your own (don't worry, they provide the saw).

POP INTO A STATELY HOME

A short drive from Stone Tower, **Oatlands** (www.oatlands.org) is home to a historic Federal–style mansion and beautiful formal garden. **Morven Park** (www.morvenpark.org) bills itself as Leesburg's equivalent of Central Park. There are two museums and a Greek Revival mansion that are open to visitors.

☰ *Good Eats*

There's no need to stray from a vineyard to eat; many of them have light menus, fridges full of meat and cheese, and in some cases, full-on restaurants. Elsewhere in the area are kitchens that specialize in farm-to-fork ingredients from nearby farms.

If you don't want to spend a lot, pack a picnic: many of the wineries allow outside food to be eaten outside.

THE WINE KITCHEN

Downtown Leesburg & Purcellville • www.thewinekitchen.com • $$ • local/American

Farmers often stop by with the latest crops, which keeps the menu ultra fresh. Wine's as big of a deal as the food here; in addition to glasses and bottles, you can choose from 10 different flights to pair with your meal.

BITES

Downtown Leesburg • www.bitesgrilledcheese.com • $ • grilled cheese

Mmmm . . . a bar dedicated to grilled cheese and wine. Twelve different warm melty cheesy sandwiches anchor the menu—from a classic four-cheese on sourdough to a version with bacon and apple butter spread.

SIDEBAR

Downtown Leesburg • $$ • New American

This downtown Leesburg eatery puts a hip slant on its colonial digs, with boozy brunch, happy hour specials, and seasonally inspired fare. Dine al fresco in the cute little courtyard, cozy up in the homey dining room and bar, or grab a coffee to go from the coffee shop.

PETITE LOULOU CRÊPERIE

Purcellville • www.lapetiteloulou.com • $ • French

Strip mall on the outside, Parisian brasserie on the inside. This charming cafe is utterly French in every way, from the tinkling bistro music to the painted floor to the piles of macarons. Crêpes are the cuisine du jour, although you'll a good variety of sandwiches, soups, and salads as well. There's a sister cafe in Union Market.

GRANDALE VINTNER'S TABLE

Purcellville • www.grandalerestaurant.com • $$ • local/American

Steps from the tasting room at 868 Estate Vineyards, this upscale country restaurant has become a dining destination in its own right. You can watch the chef prepare the seasonal fare, from crab cakes to filet mignon.

≡ Time for a Drink

Given that vineyard-touring involves plenty of drinking, you should be all set. However, if you're with some non-winos or you want to try some other local liquids, this area is full of places to imbibe.

LOCAL BREWS

Loudoun County bills itself as DC's wine country, but in recent years the local breweries have given wineries a run for their money. There are around a dozen breweries around Leesburg and Purcellville. See Chapter 18 for more info on the area's beer.

14 LOUDOUN

If the lines at whatever new Shaw pop-up bar are too daunting, check out this theme-loving Leesburg option. Ordinarily the bar rocks live music and an outdoor fire pit, but they pull out all the stops for holiday takeovers, like "summer camp," a Halloween haunted house, and a "Fa La La" Christmas setup worthy of Buddy the Elf.

CATOCTIN CREEK DISTILLERY

Purcellville • catoctincreekdistilling.com

Helmed by a female distiller, this Purcellville distillery has won roughly a billion awards for its Roundstone Rye (they claim it's Virginia's most awarded whiskey). The tasting room does flights—it's a good idea to reserve a time slot in advance.

≡ Stay Over

One of the best things about the Leesburg wineries is, like the ones a little farther south in Middleburg, they're really easy to do as a day trip (or even just for a couple hours). But if you want to make a country weekend out of it, there are options galore, from budget-friendly chains near the Leesburg Outlets, to B&Bs, historic inns, and a major destination spa and resort.

LANSDOWNE RESORT & SPA

www.destinationhotels.com/lansdowne-resort • $$$$

Spanning nearly 500 acres of lush land along the Potomac River, the Landsdowne is one of those "everything you need is right here" resorts. If all you want to do is drink wine, that's cool. There are vineyard tours that depart from the resort on weekends ($60), and Leesburg area vineyards' wines are served on-site. But there's also a plethora of activities here, from the standard resort golf/spa/tennis amenities to more unusual offerings, like soccer-golf and fly fishing.

FARM STAYS

The farther out you get from Leesburg, the more farmland takes over from subdivision. There are a handful of farm-stay country escapes out here, such as **Alta Terra Farm B&B** (altaterra farmbandb.com • $$$), which is right next to a winery and brewery (Hillsborough).

The Cottage at Dunthorpe Farm (dunthorpecottage.com • $$$) turns a restored barn with Blue Ridge views into a beautiful weekend home. You can find it on Airbnb, too.

Just outside Purcellville, **Creek Crossing Farm B&B at Chappelle Hill** (www.creekcrossing farm.com • $$) scores points for its farm animals (find the "fat and sassy flock of chickens") and its historic touches—there's a secret hiding place that was used for the Underground Railroad.

RENTAL SCENE

You can rent whatever space you need out here, from country cottages, forest hideaways, and river houses on the banks of the Potomac.

// Downtown Leesburg

☰ *Plan Around*

Summer and early fall is when the wineries see their biggest crowds. Also, keep in mind that many of these vineyards double as wedding venues, so weekends during wedding season can be busy.

Weekends to Plan For (or Avoid):

- **Wine Harvest (September–October):** Some wineries let you actually stomp the grapes when it comes time for crush.
- **Virginia Wine Month (October):** Many vineyards and wine clusters do special events throughout the month.

GOOD TO KNOW

- Virginia is the fifth largest wine producer in the United States (after California, Washington, New York, and Oregon).
- The region's most popular types of wine are Viognier (considered the signature wine of Virginia), Cabernet Franc, Chardonnay, and Norton.

BEEN HERE, DONE THAT?

- Head down the road to Middleburg's wine alley—the route of vineyards along Highway 50 (Chapter 15).
- Not trying to play favorites here, but some of Virginia's most prestigious names in wine are based in the Charlottesville area. If you're a serious wino, make a trip out of it (Chapter 22).

// Local vines

Discover the Art of Beer

Frederick, MD

This is what happens when a creative, entrepreneurial community develops a taste for beer.

FROM DC: 50 MILES · 1 HOUR, 15 MINUTES | TRIP LENGTH: DAY TRIP

DO	EAT	DRINK	BUY
walk along Carroll Creek	something from Bryan Voltaggio	all the beers	something vintage

Get ready: Frederick will surprise you. The historic city has a cool creative side, which comes alive in its crowd-sourced street art, engaged community who all seem to have cool side gigs, and a surprising number of tattoo parlors (five, count 'em).

All of this is epitomized in its beer scene, which is all about artistry and community. Just look at Flying Dog's body art–inspired logos, or count the number of "competitor" breweries' T-shirts you'll see at any taproom. Frederick's all about making, and lucky for us, many of those makers make damn good beer.

☰ *Getting to Frederick*

At only 50 miles from the Mall, many people treat Frederick as a DC suburb. You'll find people at breweries here in Caps jerseys, griping about politics, or doing a daily commute to the District for work. All this means it's pretty easy to get between the two.

If you're driving, it's a straight shot from the Beltway to I-270, which leads to the Historic downtown district via a quick hop on I-70 and East Street. An Uber or Lyft will cost about $70 one-way.

There's a train station right downtown, but it won't help you as much on weekends. The MARC train runs frequently on weekdays, but on weekends train travel means transferring to a bus at BWI and paying $60 each way. (In other words, it's not worth it; drive.)

>> **Bring the Pup:** Frederick is totally a dog town. Many of the shops, restaurant patios, and breweries in town are dog-friendly.

☰ *Get Your Bearings*

Frederick as a city is pretty expansive, but the downtown's relatively compact and walkable. Anchored by Carroll Creek and its promenade to the south, the main veins of the city are Patrick Street (running along the creek), and North Market Street, which intersects Patrick and runs north–south.

These are your axes for many of the town's trendy restaurants and bars; there are also a few breweries right here. The concentration of beer starts to dilute as you move north, as industrial parks, strip malls, and larger lots become more frequent. Not the most attractive to the eye, but this is a great space for breweries, so you'll find them dispersed throughout.

In terms of getting around, your best bet is to route to downtown, park in one of the downtown garages (only $5 for the whole day on weekends), and then walk or Uber to where you want to go.

☰ *Brewery Hopping 101*

Frederick feels a bit like a college town that's grown up. It still knows how to have a good time, but instead of late-night pizza and cheap pitchers of light beer, the city has graduated to farm-to-table dining and locally crafted adult beverages.

In fact, if Frederick were to earn a graduate degree, it'd be in brewing; the city's become a leader on the Maryland beer scene. Nearly 15 made-in-Frederick breweries, from big names

// Flying Dog Brewery

such as Flying Dog to farm breweries like Milkhouse Brewery @ Stillpoint Farm, are making magic happen with hops.

IF YOU DO ONE BREWERY: FLYING DOG BREWERY

About 4 miles south of Downtown • flyingdogbrewery.com

One of the largest breweries in Maryland, Flying Dog is based in Frederick, a short drive from downtown. With a mantra of "Good beer, no shit" and a tattoo-y aesthetic encouraged by Hunter S. Thompson, they've been pushing boundaries for 30 years.

The brewery is a big place, but the tasting room—and its adjacent outdoor patio—still get really crowded on weekends. You can try around 20 beers on tap (including some brewery-exclusives you won't find anywhere else), take a tour of the production facility, and buy all the swag you'd ever need in the gift shop.

IF YOU NEED A PICK-ME-UP: ATTABOY BEER

1 block east of the train station • www.attaboybeer.com

This cheerful garage-style brewery has a good run of peppy, fruity beers. If the encouraging name (Attaboy, have a beer, you deserve it!) isn't enough, the owners' story is that they met on a blind date that went from meh to amazing, thanks to beer. Cue the awwws.

IF YOU WANT A BIT OF EVERYTHING: SPRINGFIELD MANOR WINERY/BREWERY DISTILLERY

11 miles north of Frederick • www.springfieldmanor.com

This beautiful country estate outside of town does it all. There's a brewery serving a selection of ales. The winery has 12 wines plus sangrias, frosé, and hot mulled wine. The distillery has won awards for its whiskey, rum, and lavender gin. The views, lavender fields, and live music make Springfield Manor a popular place to spend the day on weekends.

IF YOU WANNA GO COUNTRY: FARMHOUSE BREWERIES

Some places name their beers farmhouse brews because . . . well maybe because it sounds cool. But here in Frederick there are actual FARM breweries, like where you'll see cows and the beer is made in a barn and there are hay bales . . . you get the point.

You could say **Milkhouse Brewery @ Stillpoint Farm** (16 miles northeast of Downtown; www.milkhousebrewery.com) invented farm brewing in Maryland; the owner helped get the state's farm brewery law passed. They have five year-round beers made with homegrown hops, plus a rotating list of special releases. Picnics and dogs are welcome and on weekends there's often live music. Meanwhile, **Mad Science Brewing Company at Thanksgiving Farm** (11 miles south of Downtown • www.madsciencebrewing.com) is veteran-run and focuses on American- and English-style ales brewed with hops and fruits grown on the farm.

IF YOU WANT TO CHAT WITH BEER GEEKS: MONOCACY BREWERY

2 miles north of Downtown • monocacybrewing.com

Housed in an old ice cream factory, the tasting room here is small and the staff are well-versed in beer and eager to talk about it. They rarely rebrew anything, and many of their beers never leave the taproom, so odds are if you taste it here, that's going to be the only time and place you'll have it. (With a few exceptions—their Radiance and Brewtus beers are reigning faves.)

IF YOU WANT SOMETHING OUT THERE: OLDE MOTHER BREWING CO.

7 blocks north of Carroll Creek • www.oldemother.com

This place likes to get, uh, creative with their brews. (Ask about their "Tainted Love," the beer they made using an ingredient found in beavers' bottoms.) You'll usually find a nitro of some sort on the list, plus a mix of experimental beers.

Taste Around Town

BREWERY BUS

frederickbrewbus.com

$25 gets you an all-day pass for this shuttle that runs between a handful of Frederick's breweries. You can hop on and hop off as much as you want, and the bus runs 'til 10:30 p.m. (Saturdays only).

KAYAK TOUR

You can actually kayak to some of the breweries around Frederick. **River & Trail Outfitters** (www.rivertrail.com) runs paddle tours along the Monocacy River to Barley and Hops. The trip costs $89 and includes a brewery tour.

≡ *While You're Here*

SHOP ALL DAY

You won't find many chains in downtown Frederick. Instead there are loads of antiques and vintage shops here, from the cavernous **Antiques Emporium** to **Venus on the Half Shell**, a stylish vintage clothing shop that transports you back to another era.

There are also a handful of bespoke boutiques such as the **Treaty General Store**, whose curated collection of homewares smells amazing (thank you soy soaps and candles!), or **Urban Cottage**, a whimsical rustic-chic craft and home goods shop that looks like something straight out of a Pinterest board. At **Retro Metro**, you'll find gifts, quirky decor, and silly knickknacks, like tin lunch boxes themed after your favorite throwback TV shows.

If you *do* want a familiar store, the 90-store Clarksburg Outlets are on your drive home to DC.

WALK CARROLL CREEK LINEAR PARK

The city turned what was essentially a storm drain into a beautiful 1.5-mile-long urban park. Festivals take place here and there's public art on the small pedestrian bridges that cross the creek. The crown jewel of the park is the 1,800-plant water garden, which is full of water lilies and lotus plants. (In summer they all bloom and it's quite the sight.)

CATCH A MINOR LEAGUE BASEBALL GAME

www.milb.com/frederick

The Frederick Keys play a short drive from Downtown, at Harry Grove Stadium. The team is a training ground for the Baltimore Orioles, so you might catch the next big star (or at least a fly ball). Flying Dog and Brewer's Alley both sell beer here (and it's much cheaper than Nats Park).

TAKE A HIKE

About a 20-minute drive north of Downtown is **Cunningham Falls State Park**, where you can hike on an easy 0.5-mile trail (or a tougher 0.75-mile climb) to 75-foot Cunningham Falls. Wear your swimsuit and scramble up the rocks to cool off in the falls, or jump in the manmade Hunting Creek Lake nearby.

Up the road a little ways in Catoctin Mountain Park lie **Wolf Rock** and **Chimney Rock**. It's a 3.2-mile ass-burner of a hike, but the views from the top are worth it.

MONOCACY BATTLEFIELD

www.nps.gov/mono

Only 10 minutes from Downtown, this Civil War battlefield was the site of one of the last Confederate pushes toward Washington. (It's sometimes called the Battle that Saved Washington.)

≡ *Good Eats*

The same craftsmanship you'll find in Frederick's beer scene is found in its culinary offerings. Holiday weekends aside, snagging a seat generally isn't that hard, although of course reservations are recommended if you have your heart set on a time or place.

BREWER'S ALLEY

Downtown • www.brewers-alley.com • $$ • American

This historic brewpub is the heart of the city's drinking and dining scene. Their house-brewed beers typically include a few IPAs, plus a large number of seasonal pours that sometimes coincide with local happenings, like a Frederick Keys pilsner for the season opener. The large space has both indoor and outdoor seating.

VOLT

Downtown • www.voltrestaurant.com • $$$ • Modern American

This restaurant is on many Washington foodies' bucket list. *Top Chef* runner-up and Frederick-native Bryan Voltaggio transformed a 19th-century stone mansion into a culinary mecca, where everything from the beautiful space to the 15-course chef's table is an experience. Its price tag makes Volt good for a special occasion meal, or you can come during restaurant week or Sunday brunch to score good deals.

1 Carroll Creek
2 Attaboy Beer
3 Brewer's Alley

FAMILY MEAL

Downtown • www.voltfamilymeal.com • $$ • American

If Volt's menu prices make you want to cry, head to Chef Voltaggio's other Frederick outpost instead. Family Meal is the casual alternative, which brings Maryland flavors like Old Bay to American dishes and all-day breakfast. Don't miss the fried chicken, which comes in a photogenic chicken bowl. It's a tad outside of the main Downtown core, but it shares a lot with Rockwell Brewery and is across the street from Midnight Run.

WHITE RABBIT GASTROPUB

Downtown • www.whiterabbitgastropub.com • $$ • American

Don't be shy about your beer questions here—most of the staff are certified beer servers, so they know their stuff. The focus at this speakeasy-inspired spot is on craft beer, with 40 rotating taps. The menu's dedicated to locally sourced greens and meat.

AYSE MEZE LOUNGE

Downtown • aysemeze.com • $$ • Eastern Mediterranean

Small plates of Greek, Lebanese, and Turkish classics make this a good place to order a bunch of things and share. The menu has everything from kebabs and pide to soups and salads. A must-order is the tableside flaming cheese.

WAG'S

Downtown • www.eatatwags.com • $ • burgers & bar food

If you were to, *Love Actually*–style, describe an average American bar, it might look something like Wag's. It's a long wood bar with wood stools and some wood tables and nondescript chairs. But the burgers here are consistently rated the best in Frederick. And while they may not be brewing craft ales in the back, happy hour beers cost under a buck.

☰ *Time for a Drink*

The breweries are only part of Frederick's craft beverage scene. Locally made wines and spirits are a big deal, and Maryland's first meadery, cidery, and farmhouse brewery all debuted here.

Craft bevs aside, there are all the usual drinking scene suspects here as well. You've got your Irish pubs, your sports bars, and a lot of the restaurants double as bars.

MCCLINTOCK DISTILLING CO.

www.mcclintockdistilling.com

Just off Carroll Creek, this is the first (and at this writing, only) organic distillery in Maryland. A number of their liquors have won awards, including the Foragers gin—which uses Appalachian botanicals—the Epiphany vodka, and the Maryland white whiskey. Tastings only cost $5.

TENTH WARD DISTILLING COMPANY

www.tenthwarddistilling.com

This woman-owned distillery focuses on rye, brandy, and the first Maryland-made absinthe (*real* absinthe, with wormwood). They pride themselves on sustainability and locally sourced or made-in-the-USA materials. Tastings are $5.

☰ *Stay Over*

While Frederick's easy to get to, if you're going to be beer tasting all day, it's a good idea to just crash here for the night. You can usually find a place pretty last minute, although the main hotels book up more often in spring and fall (thanks to wedding season).

There are plenty of chain options near the highway just outside of downtown.

10 CLARKE

www.10clarke.com • $$

This well-appointed Victorian Inn is a convenient 10-minute walk from downtown shops and breweries. A stay here includes a three-course breakfast, which goes above and beyond with homemade waffles, eggs, and fruit. Some rooms have detached bathrooms.

SPRINGFIELD MANOR

www.springfieldmanor.com • $$

Sleep at a brewery—with their permission, that is. **Springfield Manor**, the brewery-winery-distillery by day, doubles as a country inn by night. You can bring a bottle of your favorite pour to the fire pit to enjoy after hours. A delicious breakfast is also included.

RENTAL SCENE

In addition to the expected apartments or townhouses, you can find some unique rental options around here. Think historic homes, artists' lofts, and even an RV named "Hugo" in someone's yard.

☰ *Plan Around*

Frederick's not a huge festival town. There are a couple big to-dos throughout the year, but even those are fairly easy to join last minute. The biggest "event" scene is actually weddings; in spring and fall you'll see hotel prices spike because everyone wants to come here to get married.

>> **First Saturdays:** Shops stay open late and a street fair takes over Downtown on the first Saturday of every month. Each month there's a theme, usually highlighting something Frederick-y.

Weekends to Plan For (or Avoid):

- **Fire in Ice (February):** Sorry, not a *Game of Thrones* Party. The first Saturday in February brings the crowds out of hibernation for this wildly popular event. Every business in town gets an ice sculpture, and there's a wine ice luge.
- **Restaurant Week (March):** Score specials at some of the city's top foodie spots (including Volt).
- **MD Craft Beer Fest (May):** The biggest beer event in Maryland is held every year along the Carroll Creek Linear Park. Brewers from all over the state set up tasting tents, and tickets sell out quickly. There's also a bus that'll bring you here and back from elsewhere in Maryland.
- **Festival of the Arts (June):** Artists from around the country come to show off their stuff along Carroll Creek.
- **High Wheel Race (August):** There's an annual race of wacky old-school high-wheeled bicycles (a.k.a. penny farthings). It's a big deal here and definitely a sight to see.
- **Oktoberfest (September):** Flying Dog sponsors this annual German heritage festival. There's a big beer hall plus plenty of food.

GOOD TO KNOW

- Francis Scott Key (of Star Spangled Banner–fame) is buried here. The minor league baseball team's name is a nod to him.

- February = FebBREWary in Maryland, so breweries and craft beer bars may have specials or events going on.

BEEN HERE, DONE THAT?

- Head south and add a 'burg to the name, and you'll find yourself in Fredericksburg, another burgeoning beer scene (Chapter 25).

- There seems to be a new brewery opening all the time in Frederick. No harm in making a repeat visit and seeing what's new. You can also pair it with a hike up Sugarloaf Mountain (Chapter 11).

- Beer meets art in a big way up in Lancaster and Harrisburg, PA—many of the breweries in these cities showcase the works of local artists (see Weekend Winter Getaway).

18

Bike the Breweries on the W&OD Trail

Northern Virginia

What do you get when you mix one of the DC area's best rail trails and Loudoun County's exploding beer scene? A 45-mile long bar crawl that's all accessible by bicycle.

FROM DC: 6 MILES · 12 MINUTES BY CAR
TRIP LENGTH: DAY TRIP OR OVERNIGHT

DO	EAT	DRINK	BUY
bike	carbs	beer (and water!)	cans to go

Northern Virginia is craft beer central these days. From hyper local nano-breweries to well-known names like Lost Rhino and Old Ox, more than 30 (and counting) breweries now form the LoCo Ale Trail, a network of beer spots that spans from suburban warehouses to farm-house breweries and experimental garages.

Okay, so beer's booming all around the DMV. But what sets Loudoun's breweries apart is the way you do them. Rather than driving from place to place, you can hit up at least 20 breweries by bike, plus get an awesome workout, just by pedaling along W&OD Bike Trail.

// Beers at Loudoun Brewing Co.

☰ *Getting to the W&OD Trail*

The official Washington & Old Dominion trailhead is in Shirlington, and it ends in Purcellville, but you can pick up the path at numerous entry points throughout its 45 miles. For brewery-hopping, where you start really depends on how far you're looking to pedal and which breweries you're targeting.

If you have a car, breweries like **Beltway Brewing** and **Old Ox** have plenty of parking. Metro is also an option; the Silver Line drops you a few blocks from the trail at the Wiehle-Reston East stop. Pro Tip: don't be *that* person—take the elevator and use the first or last train car if you're Metroing with a bike.

☰ *Get Your Bearings*

The W&OD Trail runs in a pretty straight path northwest from Arlington all the way out to Purcellville in Loudoun County. It basically forms a line connecting Falls Church, Vienna, Reston, and Leesburg along the way.

Biking the Breweries

There are at least 20 breweries within a 10-minute bike ride of the Washington and Old Dominion rail trail. You can hop from spot to spot, hang at one after a long out-and-back ride, or tackle the whole route and many of its breweries over the course of an (aggressive) weekend. (Here's your reminder to pace yourself and not take on more beer—or miles—than you can handle.)

// W&OD Trail

The trail itself is a 45-mile paved two-way route that runs on an old rail line. It's pretty flat, although a few stretches will make your legs burn a bit. In some cases, you'll pass interesting scenery—a golf course, a big quarry, some woods and water. Other parts get very suburban-office park-y. This is a fine tradeoff: this is where many breweries live. Along the way there are stops with stretching posts and water.

For the most part, biking and beering on the W&OD is pretty straightforward: Most stops are on or a short distance from the trail, and most have some sort of bike racks or place to stow.

The main complication here, aside from judging how many beers you can try without wobbling off your bike, is factoring in time. Most breweries on the trail open around 11 a.m. A few open a tad earlier and some, later. On the other end of things, they close between 8 to 10 p.m. on Saturday and 7 to 8 p.m. on Sunday.

That means if you really want to set up your ride for maximum bar-hopping, you've gotta map out your route ahead of time, and keep in mind open-o'clock and last call.

Here are some plans of attack, whether you have one day or two (and keep in mind the list of breweries keeps expanding; there may be more by the time you read this):

One-Day Beer Bike

With one day, a good way to max out your brewery time is to bike out to Leesburg, time your arrival with your first brewery's opening hour, then beer-hop your way back with stops along the way. This lets you tackle the big ride first, and you can get started before the first breweries open, saving more time for tasting on your way back.

Park at Beltway Brewing Co., then start by biking to Leesburg (about 12.5 miles, takes around 1 hour).

LOUDOUN BREWING CO.

0.4 mile from trail • Leesburg • loudounbrewing.com

This little family-run brewery has a cozy cottage-like feel, with two porches plus board games inside. Expect IPAs and a mix of other crafts on tap. On Saturdays, there's often live music and food trucks.

BIKE TRALE BREWING

0.3 mile from trail • Leesburg

You can't bike the beer trail without hitting up this bike-themed brewery. There's a good variety of brews, such as the Road Rash Red, which is way preferable to its cycling counterpart. There are bike racks outside, outdoor seating, and live music on some weekends.

Psst: Reminder to eat! Leesburg is a great place to grab a bite before swinging back toward DC.

DETOUR: LOST RHINO BREWING COMPANY

1.5 miles from trail • Ashburn • www.lostrhino.com

This one is a bit of a hike from the trail (10 minutes or so, by bike), so depending on your timing, it may not work. But if you have the chance to visit, Lost Rhino's one of the most well-known breweries in the area, and their taproom serves all the classics, such as the Rhino Chasers Pilsner and Face Plant IPA, plus there's always something new on tap.

OLD OX BREWERY

On the trail • Ashburn • www.oldoxbrewery.com

This large industrial-style space has ample bike parking. The family-owned spot is always pouring something new, with regular beer releases, seasonal brews, and old favorites such as the Porter and the West Coast IPA. There's indoor tables and an outdoor patio, plus games such as corn hole in the big back room.

// Old Ox Brewery

BELTWAY BREWING CO.

On the trail • Sterling • www.beltwaybrewco.com

It's a contract brewery, which means they mostly make beer for other breweries—both local and farther afield. That means the beers you sip in the warehouse-style tasting room may end up being Crooked Run or Grimm or something custom for a shop.

// Flight at Beltway Brewing Co.

Two Days: The Full Tour

All 20-plus bikeable breweries and 90 miles? That's a heavy order, but you can at least do the whole trail and as many beer stops as you have time to fit in.

To tackle the whole 45-mile trail (so, 90 miles as an out-and-back), split the trip in two parts. On day one, bike west, stopping at the below breweries:

- Kettles & Grains (0.7 mile from trail • Leesburg • www.kettlesandgrains.com)
- Dog Money Restaurant & Brewery (0.7 mile from trail • Leesburg • www.dogmoneyllc .com)
- Loudoun Brewing Co. (0.4 mile from trail • Leesburg • loudounbrewing.com)
- Crooked Run Brewing (0.2 mile from trail • Leesburg • www.crookedrunbrewing.com)
- Bike TrAle Brewing (0.3 mile from trail • Leesburg. Check Facebook)
- Black Walnut Brewery (0.1 mile from trail • Leesburg)
- Black Hoof Brewing Co. (0.2 mile from trail • Leesburg • blackhoofbrewing.com)
- Dragon Hops Brewing (0.3 mile from trail • Purcellville)
- Belly Love Brewing (0.5 mile from trail • Purcellville • www.bellylovebrewing.com)
- Adroit Theory (0.7 mile from trail • Purcellville • www.adroit-theory.com)

Stay in Purcellville, then make your way back and hit up the breweries east of (mile marker 25 on the trail). If you start in Arlington, the full trip will be about 90 miles and pass over 20 breweries.

- Lost Rhino Brewing Company (1.5 miles from trail • Ashburn • www.lostrhino.com)
- Craft of Brewing (1 mile from trail • Ashburn • www.thecraftob.com)
- Old Ox Brewery (on the trail • Ashburn • www.oldoxbrewery.com)
- Rocket Frog Brewing Company (0.5 mile from trail • Sterling • rocketfrogbeer.com)
- Beltway Brewing Co. (on the trail • Sterling • www.beltwaybrewco.com)
- Aslin Beer Co. (0.5 mile from trail • Herndon • www.aslinbeer.com)
- Caboose Brewing Co. (on the trail • Vienna • www.caboosebrewing.com)
- Mad Fox Brewing Company (0.3 mile from trail • Falls Church • madfoxbrewing.com)
- New District Brewing Co. (0.1 mile from trail • Arlington • www.newdistrictbrewing.com)
- Capitol City Brewing Company (0.25 mile from trail • Arlington • www.capcitybrew.com/arlington.php)

Bike Shops & Rentals

If you have a bike you're good to go. If not, there are a few options: First, DON'T do this trail on a capital bikeshare bike. They're not made for long distances like this, plus you'll rack up the fees when you have the bike for longer than 30 minutes.

There are a handful of bike rental companies near the trail—these come with the bonus benefit of trail advice. **The Bike Lane** (www.thebikelane.com) in Reston Town Center is just off the trail, rents bikes, and serves bike-themed beer on tap.

MORE INFO

BIKEABLEBREWS (www.bikeablebrews.com) maintains an interactive guide to breweries and brewpubs along the W&OD trail. The website includes hours, distance from trail, beers on tap, and a helpful map that lays out all the stops along the route.

FRIENDS OF THE WOD TRAIL (www.wodfriends.org), the organization that supports the trail, posts a lot of info about events, historical tidbits, and trail updates.

VISIT LOUDOUN COUNTY has a lot of great beer trail info on its tourism website (locoaletrail.com), including maps and details on the bike route.

☰ *While You're Here*

EARN PRIZES ALONG THE WAY

Pick up an Ale Trail passport at any Loudoun brewery. You can collect stamps as you taste your way along the trail. Stamps = swag; earn enough and you can get a T-shirt.

STOP FOR CHOCOLATE

www.sweetsignatures.com

Break up the beer tasting with some sweets. This trailside chocolate shop has a rich selection of confections, from cookies to truffles to cakes.

GET A MASSAGE

If all that biking takes a hit on your muscles, there are a couple massage places at the end of the trail in Purcellville. **West Trail Wellness and Massage** (www.westtrailmassage.com) is steps from the trail and has discounts for first-time clients.

☰ *Good Eats*

It's pretty easy to find a place to refuel along the trail. Many of the breweries bring in food trucks, so you can grab some food on-site. Reston, Leesburg, and Purcellville have concentrations of restaurants, too.

THE ITALIAN STORE

0.6 mile from trail • Leesburg • www.italianstore.com • $ • Italian

An Arlington favorite, this Italian market and deli makes amazing subs piled high with fresh toppings. They also sell super slices of pizza, and you can browse all the imported Italian grocery goods or sip a wine or beer while you wait for your food.

RESTON TOWN CENTER

This is a central place on the trail to brake for a bite. You may recognize a lot of the restaurants here from their sister outlets in places like Arlington or the Mosaic District.

If you want to keep the beer game going, head to **Crafthouse** (www.crafthouseusa.com • $$), which serves American food and has 250 bottled beers. **Jackson's** (www.greatamerican restaurants.com/jacksons • $$), which is part of the Great American Restaurants chain, has a little bit of everything: burgers, salads, sushi, pasta, seafood . . . you get the picture. For cheap eats, head to **bartaco** (bartaco.com • $), where small tacos are available for under $4.

DELIRIUM CAFÉ USA

0.4 mile from trail • Leesburg • deliriumcafe.us • $$ • Belgian

Yes, *that* Delirium. The famous Belgium brewer opened its debut US location in the heart of downtown Leesburg. The sky blue–accented corner spot is often packed on weekends. There's a full-service restaurant, so this is a good place to fuel up before hitting the trail again.

WHOLE FOODS VIENNA

On the trail • Vienna • www.wholefoodsmarket.com/stores/vienna • $ • market

This supermarket is right on the trail; an easy stop to grab food to go. In addition to groceries, the location has a Brew and Brau with sandwiches and starters like mozzarella sticks. There's bike parking.

VINO9 MARKET

Paeonian Springs • vino9bbq.com • $ • BBQ

Midway between Leesburg and Purcellville, this converted house is part market, part bar. They carry BBQ, sides, and pizza—plus beer and wine—that you can take out for picnicking or eat here on the patio. It's about a block from the bike trail.

MONK'S BBQ

Just off the trail • Purcellville • monksq.com • $ • BBQ

Reward yourself with some of the area's best BBQ when you hit the end of the trail. The beer list here is weighted heavily toward Virginia breweries. There's often live music on weekends.

// Monk's BBQ

≡ *Time for a Drink*

If you're somehow in need of more beer, there are plenty of non-brewery bars along the route. Some are beer destinations in their own right; others are just good ole bars.

WESTOVER MARKET

About 0.5 mile from trail • Arlington • www.westovermarketbeergarden.com

This neighborhood market and beer garden is known for its Great Wall of Beer, which has over 1,000 bottles, plus about 16 draught lines. The market also carries a solid selection of sandwiches.

SPACEBAR

About 0.25 mile from trail • Falls Church • spcbr.com

The drafts at this divey Falls Church bar (and its sister venue Galaxy Hut, in Ballston) change daily, which makes it a favorite among beer geeks. They also "bottle" it to go in mason jars. The grilled cheese is the bomb.

≡ *Stay Over*

While most people treat this as a day trip, the truly dedicated make a weekend out of it (and as a result, can hit up more of the breweries).

COMFORT INN LEESBURG

www.comfortsuitesleesburg.com • $$

This chain all-suites hotel caters a lot to bicyclists. Check out the "Ride and Stay" package, which includes a free shuttle between the hotel and the W&OD. There's also a hot tub, which is everything after a long ride out here.

BIKE B&B

A handful of B&Bs are pretty close to the W&OD Trail. Out near Purcellville, about 1.25 miles from the trail, **Zion Springs Bed & Breakfast** (www.zionsprings.com) is set on a peaceful farm, with a fire pit, walking trails, and a big red barn that's sometimes used for weddings.

RENTAL SCENE

The farther you get from DC's suburban zone (Arlington, Reston, and the like), the more charming home rentals you'll find. Out around Purcellville, you can book farm stays and rooms in cozy country homes and B&Bs.

≡ Plan Around

While you can bike the W&OD breweries any time (they're open all year), the route is most enjoyable in spring or fall or any time the weather's not too extreme.

Weekends to Plan For (or Avoid):

- **Taste of Reston (June):** The area's biggest food festival takes over the Reston Town Center just off the trail.
- **Old Ox Oyster Shellebration (October):** This annual event pairs fresh Chesapeake Bay Oysters (at the start of oyster season) with special beer.
- **Beer Releases (All Year):** Many of these breweries do limited-run beer releases. Check the websites or Facebook before you go to see if anyone's serving something special.

GOOD TO KNOW

- At around 100 feet wide, the Washington and Old Dominion Railroad Regional Park is one of the skinniest parks in Virginia.

BEEN HERE, DONE THAT?

- Take your beer pilgrimage farther afield—Richmond is home to a growing number of breweries, many of which have national followings (Chapter 14).
- Frederick is also a beer haven. While you can't easily bike here *from* DC, you can take a bike or kayak tour of the city's breweries once you're here (Chapter 17).
- Point your bike in the opposite direction of the W&OD. The Mount Vernon Trail runs about 18 miles along the Potomac down to George Washington's historic home. Along the way, especially in Alexandria, there are a handful of brewpubs and bars.

Part Four
Small Town Vibes

19

Arts & Culture in the Shenandoah

Staunton, VA

What do Shakespeare, Harry Potter, and Woodrow Wilson fans have in common? They're all drawn to this charming Shenandoah town.

FROM DC: 158 MILES · 3 HOURS |
TRIP LENGTH: OVERNIGHT OR WEEKEND

DO	EAT	DRINK	BUY
heckle at a Shakespearean play	anything from the Shack	beer along the Beerworks Trail	glass-blown crafts

There's a friendly independence in Staunton—not the "don't tread on me" type, more an artsy "I'm expressing myself" type. In this vein, the town has become a major cultural hub of the Shenandoah, attracting world-class theater and music and a calendar packed with festivals.

Sprinkle in some history and a rockstar of a regional food scene, and you've got yourself a weekend.

☰ *Getting to Staunton*

Amtrak drops you right in town, and the town itself is walkable. A one-way rail-ride from DC costs $37 and takes 4 hours. Check schedules though; the departure times aren't great for a post-work Friday departure (and there's no train on Saturday).

The bus, operated by Virginia Breeze, is longer but cheap—a one-way ride takes about 4 hours and costs $40 (from Union Station), with stops in Northern VA, Front Royal, and Harrisonburg first.

A car isn't necessary in town, but it will let you explore farther afield. The drive from Washington takes about 3 hours. You can either shoot out west on 66 and then take 81 south along the Blue Ridge Mountains/Shenandoah Valley, or cut south sooner and go through Charlottesville. Unless there's a big event, it's pretty easy to find parking on the side streets here, and it's free on weekends.

☰ *Get Your Bearings*

Staunton's made up of five historic districts, although that makes it sound a lot more spread out than it is. The town's very walkable, or if you don't want to stroll, there's also a trolley that runs all over town and costs a quarter.

The main downtown Beverly District is a grid, with the main commercial drag, Beverly Street, bisecting it east–west.

Just south of the main drag is the Wharf District, an industrial hood that's heavy on the red-brick warehouses. Gospel Hill lies to the east and has stately homes in a range of architectural styles. Newtown is to the west; there are more historic homes and Trinity Church here. North of the town's center is Stuart Addition; Mary Baldwin University is up here too.

On Saturdays from May to October, there are free walking tours that last about 2 hours and give you a good overview of both the town layout and its architecture and sites. Tours leave from the **R.R. Smith Center for History and Art** (www.historicstaunton.com).

☰ *What's Cool in Staunton*

First things first, it's pronounced "Stanton." (Named after Lady Rebecca Staunton, wife of the Royal Lt. Governor, no one really knows why the "u" was dropped.)

History runs deep here; the compact downtown packs over 100 mom-and-pop/locally owned restaurants, shops, breweries, and galleries into beautifully preserved 18th-century buildings.

But the town doesn't feel like it's stuck in the past. There's too much going on, from free sunset concerts to chefs pushing culinary boundaries. Maybe this is why Staunton has been named one of the best small towns in America.

>> **Gamified Staunton:** Download the Traipse app, which combines exploring with trivia . . . it's like travel HQ Trivia. You can use it any time for the curated mobile app tour, or join organized "treasure hunts" to win prizes around town. It's free in the App store/GooglePlay at traipsestaunton.com.

SHOUT OUT TO SHAKESPEARE: BLACKFRIARS PLAYHOUSE

Downtown • americanshakespearecenter.com • $20 and up

The American Shakespeare Center celebrates the Bard and his work, putting on plays in an authentic recreation of the playhouse that originally aired Shakespeare's performances in London. But this isn't stuffy theater. The show goes full-Elizabethan, meaning the audience jeers at the actors and throws stuff at the stage.

Unlike other regional theaters, Blackfriars' season has multiple different performances every day. They're not even all Shakespeare—you can see adaptations of Jane Austen, Charles Dickens, and more. It's also a beautiful space; it's the only theater of its type in the world and is worth poking your head in, even if you don't make it to a show. It's one of the top spots in town though, so plan a few weeks out to ensure you can get tickets.

WORLD WAR HISTORY: WOODROW WILSON PRESIDENTIAL LIBRARY & MUSEUM

Downtown • www.woodrowwilson.org • $14

Woodrow Wilson, the country's 28th president (who led the United States during World War I), was born in Staunton. His dad was the minister at the Presbyterian church, and Wilson lived in the Manse of the church until he was two years old.

Now, guided tours showcase the house as it would've looked in Wilson's time. Next door, Wilson's presidential library and museum include artifacts from his life, including a restored Pierce Arrow car that Wilson used to drive around DC. There's also a good amount of World War I history here, including a life-size trench exhibit.

// Woodrow Wilson museum

TAKE A WALK THROUGH FRONTIER HISTORY: FRONTIER CULTURE MUSEUM

3 miles from Downtown • www.frontiermuseum.org • $12

Part nature walk, part history lesson, this outdoor museum showcases a "before and after" of Frontier life in Appalachia.

There's a 2-mile walking trail that takes you past recreated villages that explain life in places that sent immigrants to this area—West Africa, Ireland, England, and Germany. The path then moves from the Old World to "America," where a series of homes shows the evolution of frontier life. You can travel from a 1700s Ganatastwi village to simple wood cottages to homes that look like the beginnings of what you might find in the suburbs today.

The museum also hosts a variety of festivals, like Oktoberfest and wine/jazz fests, plus weddings and events. If your budget's tight, keep an eye out for "pay what you can" days.

≡ *While You're Here*

GLASS BLOWING DEMOS

www.sunspots.com

Pop into the back of the large glass showcase/studio at **Sunspots Studios**, where you can see live glassblowing demos every day until 4 p.m. Watch the master heat the molten glass, then blow and work it into votives, glasses, and the like. The glass you see made eventually finds its way to the showroom floor.

SHENANDOAH BEERWERKS TRAIL

beerwerkstrail.com

Drink hyper-local "Valley brewed" beers along this network of about 12 breweries strung down 81. Pick up a passport at any of the beer stops or the Staunton Visitor Center—you need six stamps to get a prize (a pretty cool T-Shirt, at this writing).

In Staunton, there are three stops: **Redbeard**, which hosts events like Sunday Funday karaoke, **Shenandoah Valley Brewing Co.** on the main drag which focuses on ales and lagers, and **Queen City Brewing**, a 5-minute drive from Downtown which has more than 30 beers on tap.

CAMERA HERITAGE MUSEUM

www.cameraheritagemuseum.com

A must for any shutterbug, this place feels like a camera shop-turned museum. It's FULL of cameras, but not just Nikons and Canons—we're talking spy cams, early sports cams, Pearl Harbor bomber cams, and the like. You pay $5 for a "self-guided tour" although the museum managers will gladly show you around the featured highlights.

ROAD TRIP

Staunton is about 20 minutes from Rockfish Gap, the terminus of both the Blue Ridge Parkway and Skyline Drive. Skyline Drive is part of Shenandoah National Park, so there's a fee to drive it; the Blue Ridge Parkway is free to drive (although it'll take you the opposite direction from DC). For more info, see Chapters 7 and 8.

FARMERS' MARKET

On Saturdays between April and Thanksgiving, there's a huge farmers' market in the Wharf District. We're talking live music, freshly roasted coffee, and breakfast bites to munch on while perusing the wares. Everything sold here is required to be grown or made within 75 miles of Staunton, and the people selling it must be involved in the production.

1 Historic home
2 Summer concert
3 Downtown Staunton

☰ *Good Eats*

You will eat well in Staunton. The city's artsy vein runs through the culinary scene too, with big-name Virginia chefs drawing praise (and diners) from around the mid-Atlantic.

Plus, the Shenandoah Valley supplies a quarter of Virginia's farm products. Expect fresh produce and locally raised meats, and you won't be disappointed.

Outside of major event weekends, you'll be fine at most places without a reservation, although it's best to prebook a table at The Shack and Zynodoa.

THE SHACK

Beverly District • www.theshackva.com • $$ • American

A few years ago, *Esquire* magazine called this an "incredible restaurant in the middle of nowhere that nobody knows about." Well, five years later, people know about it, but the review holds up. The name refers to the restaurant's humble digs—the 26-seat eatery is in an unassuming red shack on the edge of Downtown. Don't judge a shack by its shackiness though: chef Ian Boden has racked up James Beard recognitions and this is one of the best meals in the mid-Atlantic, certainly one worth traveling for.

ZYNODOA

Beverly District • www.zynodoa.com • $$ • Southern

This is the "it" eatery in Staunton. Virginia-sourced fare is the star of the menu, which lists the farms that supplied many of its items, like the Autumn Olive Farm Slow-Roasted Pork and the Wayside Produce Southern Fried Okra. (The wine list also has a strong VA representation.) Countering the hyper-local menu is a metropolitan-sleek design that'll make you feel more like you're in New York than Virginia.

BYERS STREET BISTRO

Wharf District • www.byersstreetbistro.com • $$ • Southern comfort food

"The Bistro," as it's known locally, serves Southern comfort food with modern twists. Faves are the fried green tomato and watermelon salad, Korean steak bowl, and chicken & waffles. After dinner, it morphs into a popular bar with live music and fantastic fresh cocktails.

CRANBERRY'S

Beverly District • gocranberrys.com • $ • health food

Housed in a 1758 building (possibly the oldest in Staunton), Cranberry's is part health food store, part cafe. A menu of made-to-order smoothies, sandwiches, and salads delivers on its mission to make customers "healthier with organic, natural, and delicious foods." Anything you don't eat is composted and turned into mulch via a partnership with a local farm.

THE SPLIT BANANA

Downtown • thesplitbanana.com • $ • gelato

The old-school storefronts on the main drag scream, "This town needs an ice cream parlor." The Split Banana delivers on all fronts: a fun retro interior and damn good ice cream . . . well, gelato actually, but no complaints.

REUNION BAKERY AND ESPRESSO

Downtown • www.reunionbakery.com • $ • coffee shop

The emphasis here is more on the bakery side than cafe; food is limited to baked goods such as croissants, muffins, and merengue. But the coffee is good, and it opens earlier than most places on Sundays. There's local art on display, and the mosaic floor is great Instagram material.

≡ Time for a Drink

For a small-ish town, there's a decent after-hours scene here. It's mostly restaurants that turn into a bar scene after dinner, but there's often live music and dancing on the weekends.

OX EYE VINEYARDS

www.oxeyevineyards.com

You can taste a selection of local wines at this in-town tasting room, set in a historic Wharf District building. Sometimes local artists come in for events like Watercolor & Wine. The winery itself is 8 miles away in the Valley.

POMPEI LOUNGE

Up above Emilio's Italian restaurant, this is a popular after-hours spot. There are multiple levels here, including a cozy outdoor patio and lounge, which feels like you're in someone's sitting room, but with live bands and a bouncer.

SHENANDOAH HOPS

www.shenandoahhops.com

Mix and match your six-packs at this store and tasting room. There are hundreds of beers available, from all over the world. They also have a growler station, which can be filled with local and craft beer on tap, and free tastings on Friday nights.

☰ *Stay Over*

A few hotels anchor downtown Staunton, plus there's a sizeable lineup of little B&Bs. There's also a Howard Johnson near Mary Baldwin University, plus some no-frills motels near the exit to 81.

BLACKBURN INN

www.blackburn-inn.com • $$$

A Thomas Jefferson protege, Thomas Blackburn, designed the beautiful building and its 80-acre grounds. Originally used as a sanatorium, everything here was intended for R&R in a beautiful setting (so its reincarnation as a boutique hotel is fitting). The hotel is very social—they do a happy-hour–style BBQ on summer weekends with corn hole, drinks, and food.

STONEWALL JACKSON HOTEL

www.stonewalljacksonhotel.com • $$

Staunton's iconic hotel (and its giant rooftop neon sign) sits right in the middle of town and dates back to 1924. It has all the amenities of a major modern hotel, including an indoor pool, hot tub, and conference space.

RENTAL SCENE

There's a healthy selection of over 100 rentals on the Airbnb market here. Most of them are rooms or apartments in historic Victorian homes or full home or cottage rentals.

☰ *Plan Around*

Summer is one big music festival in Staunton, with everything from classical to a new "beach music" fest. A wide range of other cultural events line the calendar throughout the year.

>> **Heifetz Hootenannies:** Join the fun every Saturday in July, with great brews, bites, and surprise performances by guest musicians. Tickets cost $10.

Weekends to Plan For (or Avoid):

- **Shenandoah Valley Blues & Virginia Brews Festival (June):** Just what it sounds like—this event brings in blues performances, local beers, and BBQ.
- **Heifetz Institute's Festival of Concerts (June–August):** Mary Baldwin University's music institute hosts this six-week music-palooza, featuring daily concerts, music (and wine) happy hours, and more.
- **Staunton Music Festival (August):** This world-renowned chamber music fest is the culmination of Staunton's music scene and summer festival lineup.
- **Queen City Mischief and Magic (September):** For two days every fall, Staunton goes full-Harry Potter. Wizards, wands and, of course, butterbeer take over street festival-style. Grab your Nimbus 2000—it's free to attend.
- **Shenandoah Fall Foliage Bike Festival (October):** Many Staunton shops and restaurants offer discounts at this fall cyclist extravaganza. There are 11 foliage bike routes for all skill levels.
- **Veterans Day (November):** There's a big parade over the weekend, which includes a drive by Wilson's Pierce Arrow.

GOOD TO KNOW

- During the Civil War, Staunton was a hospital town, so it was spared a lot of the damage seen elsewhere in the region. As a result, it's an architectural gem.

BEEN HERE, DONE THAT?

- In the other direction from DC, Frederick has a similar penchant for arts and culture. See Chapter 17.
- A little farther down the valley, Lexington shares the historic vibe, but with a more university-town feel.

20

Discover Why Berlin's So Cool

Berlin, MD

From Bathtub Races to a fiddlers' festival, this little town is a fun pitstop on the way to Ocean City or Virginia's Eastern Shore.

FROM DC: 142 MILES · 2 HOURS 45 MINUTES | TRIP LENGTH: STOPOVER

DO	EAT	DRINK	BUY
shop local	peaches	Burley Oak brews	Peach Dumpling at Baked

At first glance Berlin (pronounced BER-lin, emphasis on the first syllable) looks like your classic small-town USA.

But poke around a little more and you'll find something other than the stereotypical ice cream shops and antiques stores (although those are there, too). Berlin has a quirky creative side, with flavor-pushing restaurants, wacky events, and an entrepreneurial bent that's earned it a nod as one of the coolest small towns in the country.

☰ *Getting to Berlin*

If you've ever driven to Ocean City, MD, you've probably passed signs for Berlin. Instead of continuing straight on Route 50 (which goes from DC all the way to the beach), you'll turn south on Highway 113. Berlin is about 20 minutes from Ocean City.

Generally, driving is the best way to get here, but if you're staying in Ocean City, MD, **Shore Transit** (www.shoretransit.org) runs a bus from OC to Berlin, which costs $3 and takes about 25 minutes.

Parking can be tough on weekends, especially if there's an event in town. There are six free lots around town, so keep circling and you'll find a spot eventually.

☰ *Get Your Bearings*

Berlin is in Worcester County, the easternmost part of Maryland, about 20 minutes west of Ocean City.

The small historic downtown area is clumped around a criss-cross of some main streets. Many of the shops and restaurants are on Main Street, although you'll find stuff on Pitts, Bay, Gay, Jefferson, and Broad Streets and they all kind of tangle together, which makes it easy to walk to everything in a short distance.

☰ *Explore Berlin*

Berlin has played the "small town" part well, serving as the backdrop for *Runaway Bride* and *Tuck Everlasting*. There are over 45 buildings on the National Register of Historic Places, but what makes Berlin stand out these days is the cool creativity that's coursing through the local businesses and events.

BATHTUB RACES

berlinchamber.org/events/bathtub-races • Every June

One of the weirdest—and most fun—events in the area. The goal here is to deck out a bathtub, put it on wheels, fill it with water, and have someone push it faster than other people's decked-out bathtubs.

The event happens every year and is open to the public to enter, but even if you don't have a tub in the race, it's worth it just for the spectator fun.

FIDDLER'S CONVENTION

berlinfiddlers.com • Every September

Flatpickers, fiddlers, and bluegrass bands convene on Berlin every fall for this annual festival and competition. Prizes go out for the best musicians in a handful of categories. Everyone wins, though, because you'll get three days of free live bluegrass and more.

FRONTIER TOWN WESTERN THEME PARK

10 minutes from downtown Berlin • westernthemepark.frontiertown.com • late May–Labor Day • $14 and up

Westworld fan? Check out the real-life version, complete with mock jailbreaks, shootouts, and more. Except instead of the hedonistic robots-gone-wild hosts, you'll find a more family-friendly atmosphere, plus a campground, mini golf, and a lazy river.

☰ *While You're Here*

BUY LOCAL

The throwback storefronts of Downtown actually house some pretty hip local brands, and it's all very walkable. At Gilbert's Provisions, gourmet groceries get creative. In addition to cheese, charcuterie, and jams, you'll often see crazy bread mashups, like natty boh sourdough. Steel n Glory (www.steelnglory.com) works metal and wood into rustic decor, furniture, and signs—they'll even work with you to bring your own idea to life.

2ND FRIDAY ART STROLL

As the name suggests, art from local artists is hyped up around town on the second Friday of each month.

HUNT FOR GHOSTS

chesapeakeghostwalks.com/berlin

When there are this many historic buildings, there's bound to be a lingering spirit or two. Join a tour to try and spot them, or at least hear the stories of how various town buildings—including the Atlantic Hotel, where the tour begins—are haunted.

PLAY WITH ALPACAS

Say hello to these goofy-looking poofballs at Ocean Breeze Alpacas. The farm is open to the public the last weekend of the month.

☰ *Good Eats*

The town may look old-fashioned, but the food is anything but. Throughout Berlin's restaurants and cafes you'll find fresh takes on Eastern Shore favorites, with an emphasis on local ingredients.

Most places here are pretty casual; if you're here for a big event, then a reservation could help, but walk-ins are typically fine if you're just passing through on your way to or from the beach.

BLACKSMITH BAR & RESTAURANT

Center of town • blacksmithberlin.com • $$ • Eastern Shore

From the pressed tin ceiling to the reclaimed wood backbar, Blacksmith looks as good as the made-from-scratch food tastes. The dishes are locally sourced, with a focus on Eastern Shore fare (although you'll see Creole or Asian twists on some of it). They're closed Sundays.

// Blacksmith Bar and Restaurant

THE GLOBE

Center of town • www.globetheater.com • $$ • American

Eats meet art at this former movie theater-turned restaurant and bar. There's a gallery full of local art, concerts (free if you're dining here), and they do events like murder mystery dinners and film screenings. Try the crab cake and fried green tomatoes.

BURLEY CAFE

Center of town • burleycafetogo.com • $ • brunch

An outpost from the beer-lovers at Burley Oak Brewing Co. up the road, the menu at this cute little eatery is designed to pair well with craft brews. They do brunch all day and encourage chambonging—seriously, it's on their menu.

BAKED DESSERT CAFE & GALLERY

Center of town • bakeddessertcafe.com • $ • bakery

Good things come together at this eclectic cafe: behold Croclairs, the lovechild of a croissant and eclair. Also, chicken and waffles, peaches and dumplings, and cupcakes and bread pudding. On top of the food, there's the wine gallery, a hybrid wine shop and art gallery.

☰ *Time for a Drink*

Need nightlife? Uber to Ocean City. (Or stay there and make a day trip to Berlin.) But while you're here, many of the restaurants mentioned above have great drinks programs, plus there's a beloved local brewery.

BURLEY OAK BREWING CO.

www.burleyoak.com

This local brewery vibes with Berlin's crafts-y M.O. Brews range from hibiscus wheat ales to IPAs to homemade root beer. Plus the labels and names are fun, too. The taproom is a local hangout spot and doubles as a display space for local artists and bands.

☰ *Stay Over*

Berlin's so close to Ocean City that the lodging options here are a bit more specialized. For major chains, budget lodgings, or a wide range of rentals, look to stay in OC. If you crave some historic charm, this little town has you covered.

THE ATLANTIC HOTEL

atlantichotel.com • $$$

Set in the heart of town, this stately Victorian inn dates back to 1895 and has 18 rooms set up with period decor. Don't expect too many modern amenities, although rooms do have TVs and WiFi.

BERLIN B&BS

For a romantic escape, there are a few historic little B&Bs right in town. **Waystead Inn** (www .waysteadinn.com) has cool antique features in an updated historic home. It puts a big emphasis on the Breakfast part of "B&B."

// Berlin Peach Festival

RENTAL SCENE

If you're here with a group, you'll find a few houses to rent, although there are a lot more options in Ocean City.

≡ *Plan Around*

For a small town, there sure are a lot of festivities here. Aside from the events listed above, Berlin's social calendar is packed with everything from free outdoor movies and concerts to seasonal events and small-town throwdowns.

Weekends to Plan For (or Avoid):

- **Jazz and Blues Bash (May):** An annual one-day music festival with wine and beer tastings, plus family-friendly activities.
- **Cruisers Weekends (May and October):** This classic car show isn't just for auto enthusiasts. There's also a street fair and live music.
- **Peach Festival (August):** Not only are peaches brought in from the farms for sale, but all the restaurants around town get peachy with their menus.
- **Oktoberfest (October):** Say "prost" to German-inspired eats and music, plus beer and games like cornhole.

GOOD TO KNOW

- Racehorses Man O'War and War Admiral (the Triple Crown–winning horse who then lost to Seabiscuit) were owned by Berlin's Glen Riddle Farm.

- The song "We Shall Overcome" stems from a hymn written by Berliner Charles Tindley.

BEEN HERE, DONE THAT?

- Over in the Shenandoah Valley, Staunton has its share of quirk, too, especially in September, when the town transforms into a mini-Harry Potter wonderland for one weekend (Chapter 19).

21

Get Main Street Charmed

Culpeper, VA

Good eats, cute shops, and an old-timey air make Culpeper more than just a stopover.

FROM DC: 73 MILES · 1.5 HOURS | TRIP LENGTH: DAY TRIP

DO	EAT	DRINK	BUY
walk around town	Donut Burger at Grill 309	beer from the town breweries	local wine

Easily accessible by train, Culpeper is emerging as a hotspot on Virginia's small-town scene. The main street looks like it time-traveled from the 1950s, with brick storefronts shaded with awnings and mercantile-style business names scrawled across the facades in faded white paint.

Nowadays, on-trend locally owned businesses have set up shop in these historic buildings. You'll find a farm-to-table restaurant in a Civil War jail-turned hardware shop. A vineyard in a restored 19th-century farmhouse. A reimagined tavern from the pre-Prohibition era. All this blends together into a town that feels both fresh and nostalgic and is wonderfully wanderable.

≡ *Getting to Culpeper*

Taking the train here couldn't be easier; you get on at Union Station and get off in Culpeper in the most central part of town. It only takes about an hour and a half and starts at about $18 each way. Some people do use the train to commute, so book your ticket a few days ahead.

If you do drive, the best route is 66 down to 15. Culpeper is also a great stopping point on a drive down to Charlottesville or the Shenandoah. It's even a slightly out of the way but pleasant detour from Richmond, if 95 is doing traffic horrors.

≡ *Get Your Bearings*

The town's a little over halfway between DC and Charlottesville and is surrounded by rural land. In true small-town style, the main street is Main Street, with shops and restaurants clustered in a four-block zone between Cameron and Stevens Streets.

≡ *Meander Around Town*

One of the big draws of Culpeper is that there's no big draw. It's more a sum of its parts, with interesting home-grown shops and eateries that make it the perfect place to wander without agenda.

MAIN STREET SHOPS

The downtown has a couple blocks of fun shopping options. Many of the shops are housed in historic old-brick buildings along E. Davis Street, just off Main.

The Cameleer (thecameleer.com) started as an Australian Aboriginal art shop but has expanded to include crafts from various cultures around the world. Next door, **The Green Roost** (shopgreenroost.com) has a tempting selection of earth-friendly goods, from soaps and candles to clutches to stylish gifts. If you can't make it to the vineyards in the surrounding

EN ROUTE

Ice Cream Stop: If you're driving, swing by **Moo Thru**, a wildly popular hand-dipped ice cream store that sources all its milk from the owners' nearby dairy farm 3 miles away.

countryside, hit up **Vinosity** (www.vinositywines.com), which does free wine and beer tastings every Friday and Saturday.

HANG AT A BREWERY

The two breweries in town sit just a block away from each other, and from the train station. **Far Gohn Brewing** (www.fargohnbrewing.com) specializes in German styles, though they do a little bit of everything. The cozy tavern often has live music on weekends and the lively crowd often spills out onto the side patio.

Around the corner, **Beer Hound Brewery** (www.beerhoundbrewery.com) names all its beers after famous hounds—like the award-winning Kujo Imperial IPA. (All the beer labels are also dog-themed.) There's even a dog happy hour (with treats) every Friday from 5 to 7 p.m.

A BIT OF HISTORY

The town's historic train depot is home to the small **Museum of Culpeper History** (culpeper museum.com). It's got everything from Civil War stories to Native American weapons to dinosaur tracks that were found nearby. At $5 for entry, it's worth a drive-by.

☰ *Good Eats*

For a small town, Culpeper has a lot going on in the food scene. From inventive menus using local ingredients to cuisine from Latin America, Europe, India, and beyond, there are dishes for days.

GRILL 309

grill309.com • $$ • American

Check your calorie consciousness at the door. This place specializes in the marriage of delicious food, like a donut burger or a cheeseburger made with two bacon and grilled cheese sandwiches as the bun.

FOTI'S

www.fotisrestaurant.com • $$ • eclectic

An inviting dining room with vintage French brasserie–style art. The menu has a mix of American and Mediterranean dishes, with a whole menu dedicated to lighter dishes.

FROST CAFÉ

$ • diner

It's cash only at this old-school corner diner. The breakfasts are good and the portions are big.

FLAVOR ON MAIN

www.flavoronmain.com • $$ • American

Main Street's Art Deco feel carries over into this roaring '20s-themed fine dining hotspot. A horseshoe shaped bar mixes specialty and Prohibition-era cocktails, and the menu includes boldly flavored steaks, chops, pasta, and seafood entrées. They're closed Sunday.

18 GRAMS COFFEE LAB

www.18gramscoffeelab.com • $ • coffee

This stylish coffee counter shares a space with a bike shop and makes their espressos with scientific precision.

≡ *Time for a Drink*

It's a pretty sleepy small town come nighttime, although the breweries and a few restaurants keep things lively after hours.

GRASS ROOTES

www.grassrootesculpeper.com

Listen to live music while you sip on craft cocktails (there's food, too). The rustic-mod warehouse is one of the town's oldest buildings; it's been used for everything from a Civil War jail to a hardware store and is said to be haunted.

BELMONT FARM DISTILLERY

www.belmontfarmdistillery.com

Taste copper pot-distilled whiskey, rum, and moonshine at this distillery about 15 minutes from town. Closed Sundays.

OLD HOUSE VINEYARDS

www.oldhousevineyards.com

Just 15 minutes from town, this farmhouse turned wine tasting room is set on a pretty property full of grape vines and a small lake. There's also a distillery on-site that does tastings.

 # Stay Over

The best bet is to stay in the heart of town, so you can walk to the breweries and restaurants. The options here are a tad more expensive; if you're on a super budget and still want to spend the night, there are a cluster of low-cost chains on the southern edge of town.

SUITES AT 249

suitesat249.com • $$

Steps from the train station, this six-room boutique overlooks the action on Davis Street. Each room has its own style, although there are exposed brick walls and fireplaces in all the rooms. Down the street, 249's Art Deco-inspired sister hotel, Culpeper Center, is larger, with space for events and an on-site restaurant.

RENTAL SCENE

There are dozens of rentals within about 30 minutes of Culpeper, including a tiny log cabin and a treehouse.

Plan Around

There aren't many major festivals that will book up Culpeper, but there are a growing number of fun happenings that you might want to time your visit around.

Weekends to Plan For (or Avoid):

- **Gnarly Hops and Barley Fest (April):** Craft beers, eats from local restaurants, and live music take over downtown Culpeper for this annual brewfest.
- **Restaurant Week (October):** Save on downtown dining.
- **Culpeper Air Fest (October):** The town's biggest event of the year, this air show features vintage planes and aero-acrobatics.

GOOD TO KNOW

- Two Hall of Fame baseball players, Eppa Rixey and Pete Hill, are from here. So is Big Kenny of Big & Rich country music fame.

BEEN HERE, DONE THAT?

- Farther to the north and west, Winchester has a similar historic country town vibe to Culpeper but with even more places to eat and drink.
- Fredericksburg (Chapter 25) is also bigger than Culpeper but has that same old-timey downtown vibe.

Part Five

Important Things Happened Here

22

Peep at Presidential Homes

Charlottesville, VA

Pair the presidential estates of Jefferson, Madison, and Monroe with some of the region's best food, wine, and outdoor endeavors.

FROM DC: 116 MILES · 2 HOURS 45 MINUTES | TRIP LENGTH: WEEKEND

DO	EAT	DRINK	BUY
visit Monticello	bagels at Bodo's	Virginia wine	handmade crafts from City Market

There are a lot of reasons to visit Charlottesville. The wine country here may be the best in the state. The music scene's legit too. Farms keep the foodies fueled, while the university makes sure there's a place to party. As for outdoorsy stuff—you've got the Blue Ridge Mountains and the James River a quick drive away.

But you can't mention C'ville without giving a nod to history. Three of America's early presidents called this area home: Thomas Jefferson, James Madison, and James Monroe. And you can throw it back to some of the rooms where it happened by touring their presidential homes.

Getting to Charlottesville

You don't need a car to get to Charlottesville. **Amtrak** runs trains here from DC (the ride take about 2 hours and 15 minutes and starts at $36), and **Greyhound** and **Megabus** also have routes (starting at around $13 each way).

Having a car does make it easier to get out to vineyards and historic sites, but Lyft and Uber are prevalent in the city, so you can easily hail rides from downtown if you don't bring a car.

If you're driving, you can check traffic/your GPS to see which route is clear, but people who frequently make the trip between DC and C'ville swear by the 66-to-29 route, which is more scenic and tends to have less traffic than I-95.

Getting around town is easy sans car. There are bike-share docks around town. There's also a free trolley that runs between UVA and the Downtown Mall.

Get Your Bearings

Nestled between the base of the Blue Ridge and the plains of the Piedmont, Charlottesville is a little bit city and a little bit country. Most visitors spend their time in three main parts downtown: the Corner, the Downtown Mall, and Belmont.

The Corner is the college-y neighborhood around UVA. The Downtown Mall is a cute pedestrian shopping/dining street that runs for about eight blocks through the heart of town. (On summer Fridays, they do Fridays After 5, which has live music at the Pavilion that anchors the Mall.) Belmont is a short walk from the east end of Downtown Mall. This is basically the Brooklyn of C'ville, with a more hip/industrial cool vibe and lots of good restaurants.

C'ville: The Presidential Tour

Virginia wins the prize for producing the most presidents—eight of them were born in the state, and three hail from the Charlottesville area. All three of these men's homes, Monticello, Highland, and Montpelier, have been preserved and are open to visitors.

When you're done, some of the area's best vineyards are a quick drive from each President's home.

MONTICELLO: THOMAS JEFFERSON'S HOME

About 4 miles from the Downtown Mall • www.monticello.org • $26 and up

The crown jewel of Virginia, if not American, architecture, Thomas Jefferson's estate presides over 2,500 acres of bucolic woods and farmland. It's the only UNESCO World Heritage–

// Aerial view of Monticello

designated house in the United States, and a visit here combines history with invention, politics, and beautiful vistas.

The Declaration of Independence author designed this home himself and lived here from 1770 to 1826. You can learn all about the various iterations and influences that shaped Jefferson's work in the on-site museum at Monticello. After that, join a timed tour of the home itself (the only way to see it), where guides dish on the house and its inhabitants.

TJ's legacy isn't the only thing covered at Monticello. A robust roster of tours covers other topics, including slavery here and the life of the Hemings family. There's also a *Hamilton*-themed tour and guided garden walks.

Allow 3 hours to do a house tour plus walk the pretty grounds. Book tickets online before you get here. (There are timed house tour slots, so you don't want to show up and have to wait for a while.) Also, it's cheaper if you book online.

JEFFERSON VINEYARDS

About 5 miles from the Downtown Mall • www.jeffersonvineyards.com

Some people consider Jefferson to be the founding father of American wine growing, too. Stop by Jefferson Vineyards, just down the road from Monticello (right near Highland). This is the site on which Jefferson planted his original vines nearly 250 years ago, establishing the first wine company in Virginia. Now, you can do a tasting or grab a glass or bottle and toast Thomas from the pretty garden and lawn.

HIGHLAND: JAMES MONROE'S HOME

About 6.5 miles from the Downtown Mall • highland.org • $19 • Limited hours October through March

Not only were they friends and colleagues, James Monroe and Thomas Jefferson were neighbors. The fifth president's Highland estate is modest compared to Monticello, but there's still plenty to see throughout the house, museum, and gardens.

The best part about a visit to Highland is the hiking. There are about 7 miles of trails around the grounds, including some mountain trails with good views.

BLENHEIM VINEYARDS

About 11 miles from the Downtown Mall • blenheimvineyards.com

The stunning winery is about 10 minutes down the road from Highland and is owned by another famous name: singer Dave Matthews. (Jefferson and his wife Martha also are said to have stayed here when a snowstorm delayed their travel to Monticello.) Tastings here are coupled with gorgeous views of the surrounding countryside.

MONTPELIER: JAMES MADISON'S HOME

About 26 miles from the Downtown Mall • www.montpelier.org • $20

Madison's mansion technically isn't in Charlottesville; it's about 26 miles north in Orange, VA. In the olden days, when Madison came to visit his buddy Jefferson, this trip would've taken the better part of a day; now the drive only takes about 40 minutes.

The house itself has been restored to look the way it did when Madison lived here, with formal gardens and views of the Blue Ridge Mountains. As at Monticello, there are a handful of tour and exhibition topics here, from general estate tours to ones covering women and slavery at Montpelier.

There are also over 8 miles of hiking trails through old-growth forests and meadows here, including one that follows the remains of a Civil War camp.

BARBOURSVILLE VINEYARDS

About 17 miles from the Downtown Mall • www.bbvwine.com • $10 for a tasting

One of the top-rated wineries in the state, Barboursville has played a big role in putting Virginia wine on the map. The property was originally owned by Virginia governor and Jefferson pal James Barbour. You can still see the ruins of the home that Jefferson designed for the Barbours here.

Now, the winery's Octagon, a Merlot and Cabernet Franc blend that's named for a room Jefferson designed for the estate, has earned recognition far and wide. It's not always available to taste, but even without it, the tastings here are generous and the setting is idyllic.

// Charlottesville Downtown Mall

☰ While You're Here

EXPLORE UVA

Spend a few minutes on the grounds of University of Virginia and you'll recognize the same Jeffersonian-style of architecture: Virginian red-brick, white finishes. This is one of the most beautiful universities in the world, thanks in large part to TJ's enlightened idea of creating an "Academical Village."

Head to the Lawn to get a glimpse of the Rotunda—the impressive dome that Jefferson designed to resemble the Pantheon in Rome. While you're here, grab a drink or a bite at the Corner, the cluster of college-y bars and restaurants steps from the Lawn.

HANG OUT ON THE DOWNTOWN MALL

The cool thing about Charlottesville is that, while it's a college town, it doesn't scream "college" from every angle.

Case in point is the downtown pedestrian mall, which runs for about eight blocks through the heart of town. Here, you'll find many of the city's trendy eateries, bars that cater to people who've already earned their diploma, and cultural fixtures such as the Jefferson Theater, the Paramount Theater, and Live Arts Theater.

Every Friday in the summer, the pavilion at one end of the Mall hosts free Fridays After Five concerts.

HIKE HUMPBACK ROCKS

About 35 minutes from C'ville is one of the most popular hikes along the Blue Ridge Parkway. The Humpback Rocks trail is a moderately tough climb that leads to a rocky outcropping with killer views over the Shenandoah Valley.

The hike usually takes about 2 to 3 hours, depending on your route: you can go straight to Humpback Rocks and back (about 2 miles total) or add distance by hopping on the Appalachian Trail and checking out Humpback Mountain.

GET INTO THE MUSIC SCENE

Dave Matthews Band got its start here, and other big-name acts often stop through on their East Coast tours. There's also a great indie music scene, with a good number of live music spots: The Garage, Southern Cafe & Music Hall, and The Jefferson.

☰ *Good Eats*

The "know your farmer" movement's picking up speed here. And while modern Virginian cuisine is prevalent (the city's trying to make the ham biscuit the official dish), you'll also see the farm-to-table concept applied to everything from Italian to Mexican cuisines.

Overall you can pop in most places without reservations, unless it's parents weekend or graduation. Things quiet down on Sundays when a lot of restaurants close.

>> **Pack a Picnic:** Save money at the vineyards by bringing your own snacks. **Tilman's Cheese and Wine** (www.tilmanscheeseandwine.com) will even pack you a picnic.

RED PUMP KITCHEN

Downtown Mall • www.redpumpkitchen.com • $$ • Italian

This trendy Italian place on the Downtown Mall combines farm-fresh ingredients with Mediterranean flavors. Watch as they pluck a sprig from the live herb wall and garnish your craft cocktail with it.

BODO'S BAGELS

Downtown, the Corner, and Route 29 • www.bodosbagels.com • $ • bagels

People swear by this local chain, which is Charlottesville's challenge to New York bagels. There are three locations around town, all serving bagel sandwiches with fresh house-made cream cheese. Don't worry, the line moves quickly.

BRASSERIE SAISON

Downtown Mall • brasseriesaison.net • $$ • Belgian

Occupying a prime outdoor space on the Downtown Mall, this Belgian brasserie brews their own beer. The food, from the small plates to the steamed mussels, is all beer-conscious. (Rainy? There's a charming indoor space as well.)

MAS TAPAS

Belmont • www.mastapas.com • $$ • tapas

Shareable small plates are the star of the menu here, which pulls in fresh local ingredients to flesh out its Spanish and European flavors. This is one of the hottest tables in town and they don't take reservations, so expect a wait.

MARIEBETTE CAFE & BAKERY

Rose Hill • www.mariebette.com • $ • bakery

At this cute French eatery, you can buy freshly baked goods such as breads, cookies, and pastries to go, bakery-style. Or order from the café menu and dine on-site—there's a full breakfast and lunch menu.

BRAZOS TACOS

2nd St. SE • brazostacos.com • $ • tacos

Known for its Texas-style tacos, this shop has over 30 different mashups, from breakfast tacos to veggie tacos. Trouble choosing? Try the "Taco Bot," which will make recommendations.

SANDWICHES

Don't be weirded out if someone tells you what their favorite gas station sandwich is. Some of these fuel stops have upscale country markets inside, and they make stellar sandwiches. Think fresh ingredients, interesting combos, and creative names. Two local favorites are the **Market at Bellair**, at an Exxon station about 10 minutes northwest of Downtown, and **Market at Mill Creek**, about eight minutes south of Downtown.

Time for a Drink

You won't go thirsty in Charlottesville—In fact, UVA students and sports teams are nick-named "Wahoos," after a fish said to be able to drink twice its weight. College bars, wineries, craft breweries, hidden cocktail nooks, a sake distillery . . . you name it, you can drink it here.

WINERIES

The wineries covered above are the tip of the grape bunch. The Charlottesville area is one of the most productive winemaking regions on the East Coast, with over 35 wineries, most of which host tastings.

You don't even *need* a car—Uber and Lyft are used to shuttle people to the wineries.

One of the most popular—and most stunning—vineyards in the area is **Pippin Hill Farm & Vineyards** (www.pippinhillfarm.com). This white-barn tasting space, patio with sweeping mountain views, and food menu full of vineyard-grown ingredients draws people as much as their wine.

THREE NOTCH'D BREWING COMPANY

threenotchdbrewing.com

This brewery, now expanding throughout Virginia, is located a few blocks south of the Downtown Mall in an airy industrial space with a beer-infused food menu and axe throwing.

// Charlottesville vineyards

THE ALLEY LIGHT

alleylight.com

Tucked in an alley off the Downtown Mall, this buzzing Prohibition-style cocktail bar is a bit easy to miss. (Just look down for the doormat and you'll know which door to enter.) This is one of the best mixology spots in town. The bar lead Micah LeMon even wrote a cocktail guide book.

COMMONWEALTH RESTAURANT & SKYBAR

www.commonwealthskybar.com

One of the few rooftop bars in town, Skybar draws a well-dressed crowd and overlooks the Downtown Mall. Downstairs there's a restaurant that serves good upscale Virginian food.

THE WHISKEY JAR

thewhiskeyjarcville.com

On the east end of the Downtown Mall, this laid-back rustic space carries more than 125 whiskies, ryes, bourbons, and the like. There's often a live band playing bluegrass or other tunes.

CARTER MOUNTAIN ORCHARD

This place has it all: wine tasting, cider tasting, a farm store, corn hole, dog friendliness, and a pick-your-own fruits in the orchards. Oh, and it's at the top of a mountain so the views are ridiculous—especially at sunset (although it closes at 7 most nights).

≡ *Stay Over*

For the most convenient digs, stay as close to the Downtown Mall as you can get, or check out Belmont for a hipper vibe. You'll find the usual chains sprinkled along the edges of the Downtown Mall and in suburban clusters a short drive away.

In summer, you'll find it easier to book a last-minute escape. During football season or around the time of key college happenings, you'll want to book as far out as possible. (Graduation weekend books up years in advance, so good luck.)

OAKHURST INN

oakhurstinn.com • $$$

This beautiful inn just off UVA's campus transformed four historic boarding houses into a modern, but homey, boutique inn. Libraries and fireplaces make it feel like you're crashing at a friend's place rather than a hotel. The espresso bar here is a destination even for nonguests.

THE TOWNSMAN

thetownsmanhotel.com • $$

The Townsman bills itself as an "un-hotel." Basically it's Airbnb meets boutique hotel. Things it doesn't have: a concierge desk, elevator, or big lobby. Things it does have: stylish decor, toiletries, and free access to Common House, the local social club and workspace.

THE GRADUATE

www.graduatehotels.com/charlottesville • $$$

If you're a Wahoo hoping to relive the college days, check out this university-themed hotel on the Corner. The decor is academic-preppy, and there's a rooftop bar with views of campus and the Blue Ridge Mountains.

PRESIDENTIAL TIE-INNS

As do many businesses in Charlottesville, many of the hotels in this area have tie-ins to a presidential past.

The luxurious **Boar's Head Resort** (www.boarsheadresort.com), which sits on 600-acre grounds with a golf course, spa, and grown-on-the-grounds restaurant menu, follows the style Jefferson's builders used at UVA (it's owned by the UVA Foundation).

About 10 minutes east of Charlottesville, **The Clifton** (www.the-clifton.com) has debuted as a boutique hotel housed in a 1799 country estate originally built for Thomas Jefferson's daughter. There's also garden-sourced fine dining at the romantic 1799 restaurant on-site, and the hotel can hook you up with local activities, from fly fishing to hot air ballooning.

RENTAL SCENE

Vacation rentals in C'ville are a convenient and cheap alternative to the hotels. There are plenty of options here. Many are clustered in Belmont in well-appointed apartments and town homes.

☰ Plan Around

Don't forget that C'ville's a college town, so weekend craziness ebbs and flows with some key university events. Check the college calendar online to see if there's anything big going on.

Weekends to Plan For (or Avoid):

- **Restaurant Week (January and July):** Eat your heart out for $35 or less at some of the city's hottest restaurants.

- **Foxfield Races (April):** Put on your finest sundress or seersucker suit. Charlottesville's biggest steeplechase of the year draws busloads of spectators, many of them college or post-college kids who are here just as much for the beer as they are for the horses.
- **Tom Tom (April and September):** Twice a year, C'ville's answer to SXSW brings music, ideas, and innovation to town. During the spring festival, local restaurants put a foodie spin on the "city book club"—a menu item is selected, and each eatery serves it with their own special twist.
- **UVA Graduation (May):** Unless you have reason to go, just don't bother—the entire town will be booked and busy.
- **UVA Football Weekends (Fall):** If you're a college football fan, it's definitely worth the trip. If you're not a fan, you'll likely be fine in Downtown or Belmont (a.k.a. away from campus). Bigger games, such as the Commonwealth Cup (UVA vs. Virginia Tech) will be a bigger to-do around town.

GOOD TO KNOW

- Dave Matthews Band got its start here. It's one of the reasons C'ville has a strong music scene and also why Dave owns a vineyard nearby.
- UVA is no stranger to fame—RFK, Woodrow Wilson, Tina Fey, Georgia O'Keefe, and William Faulkner all attended. Dr. Pepper was allegedly named after UVA alumnus Charles T. Pepper, who studied medicine at the university.

BEEN HERE, DONE THAT?

- For more presidential history, head on over to Staunton, where you can tour Woodrow Wilson's childhood home and presidential library (Chapter 19).
- Charlottesville wineries get all the cred, but the boozeries along the Nelson 151 are a chill and scenic way to winery, brewery, and distillery hop.
- If you've visited C'ville in the past, come back and spend more time outdoors. You can float lazy-river style down the James River or tackle more hiking trails around the Blue Ridge Parkway.

23

Bike the Battlefield in Gettysburg

Gettysburg, PA

Four score and seventy years or so ago, the biggest and baddest battle of the Civil War was fought here. Now, you can tour the hallowed grounds by bike.

FROM DC: 86 MILES · 1.5 HOURS | TRIP LENGTH: OVERNIGHT

DO	EAT	DRINK	BUY
visit the battlefield	local apples	local cider or wine	military memorabilia

When it comes to Civil War battlefields, this is the Big One. Gettysburg is much more than the address of one of the most famous presidential speeches in history. It was the bloodiest showdown of the Civil War. The largest battle ever fought in North America. A turning point that saved Washington, DC, from a Confederate assault. If Gettysburg had gone differently, it's possible the United States would look very different today.

Now, it's one of the country's best-preserved military monuments. You can tour the fields where roughly 50,000 men were killed or wounded. While you're at it, you'll discover a historic town with one foot in the past and the other riding more modern trends, like craft food and drink and a focus on locally made goods.

Getting to Gettysburg

Just over the Maryland state line, Gettysburg is closer to DC than it is Philadelphia.

To get here, you'll want to drive. Head north on Highway 270 all the way to Frederick. Here, you'll continue north on Route 15 until you near Gettysburg. There are ten main routes into town (which actually was one of the reasons the armies converged here during the war), so depending on where exactly you're staying, you'll take one of the turnoffs.

The downtown is walkable; it takes about 15 minutes to get from Lincoln Square to Steinwehr. Since it predates cars, the streets are narrow and not really designed for parking; your best bet is to leave the car at your hotel.

The national park runs a free shuttle between the visitor center and downtown. There are a few Ubers and Lyfts, although they're not ubiquitous. You can also cruise around in a **GettyPed** (www.gettypeds.net), which looks a bit like an escaped bumper car on wheels.

Get Your Bearings

The battlefield is massive and essentially surrounds the town of Gettysburg to the north and south. The bulk of the park lies to the south; this is where most of the fighting happened, and is now home to the visitor center and many of the monuments. The northern section of the

// Gettysburg battlefield

park is smaller but is home to some key sights, like the Seminary Ridge Museum and Lee's battle HQ.

Within the town itself, Gettysburg College occupies the northern district. Then the downtown core is dumbbell-shaped, with two main commercial clusters: one around Lincoln Square, a big traffic circle with four main streets radiating off of it. The other is around the intersection of Baltimore and Steinwehr.

≡ *Bike the Battlefield*

In the summer of 1863, Robert E. Lee had been on a winning streak down in Virginia, at Fredericksburg and Chancellorsville (see Chapter 25). He decided to move north, into Union territory, to pressure Washington and give Virginia a breather from the constant warfare.

Lee's army got a head start, but Union cavalry eventually caught up at Gettysburg.

Spoiler alert: Things didn't go well for General Lee. After three horrendous days of fighting, the Confederate army's northern advance was halted here, thanks to a lot of heroic sacrifices, some big-time blunders, and a decent amount of luck.

We won't go into the play-by-play, but the stories to come out of Gettysburg are legendary, which is why taking a guided battlefield tour is so powerful, versus doing it on your own.

GETTYSBURG BIKE TOURS

Rather than the typical driving tour, a bicycle ride around Gettysburg is the fresh-air way to cover a lot of ground. This battlefield is huge—at nearly 18 square miles, it's about the size of 8,591 football fields. That's far too much to walk, but driving loses some of the intimacy of the battle tour experience.

On a bike, you'll get a better sense for the lay of the land and an appreciation for how far the armies marched (if you think pedaling up Little Round Top is hard, imagine charging up it with heavy battle gear). Plus, you'll get a workout while you're at it—a nice bonus if you plan on capping off your battlefield visit with the breweries and wineries that surround Gettysburg.

WHERE TO GET A BIKE

GettysBike (gettysbike.com) will hook you up with gear, including a nice trek bike and a helmet (BYO water.) The operator runs a few different tours led by licensed guides. Most tours are around 3 to 4 hours and cover at least 7 miles. Prices start at $74 per person. GettysBike also offers electric bikes, if you are worried about the heat or your endurance level.

If you'd rather DIY and go without a guide, make sure you download a map or stop by the Visitor Center first. **Gettysburg Bicycle** (gettysburgbicycle.com) rents bikes and gear (no tours, though).

WHAT THE BIKE TOURS COVER

It depends on the type and topic of your tour, but generally the routes will retrace the main battle lines, following national park roads most of the way. Prepare yourself for cannons and statues. Lots of statues. Some tours cut through town, where you can see buildings that still bear bullet holes from the battle.

Major stops include locations of the heaviest fighting and spots with the best viewpoints:

- **Seminary Ridge:** Lee's battle headquarters were here. Nearby is a museum with a cupola overlooking the countryside; Lee used this vantage point during the fighting. Now it's accessible via dedicated tours.
- **Cemetery Ridge:** The Confederates attacked this point, the center of the Union line, during Pickett's Charge on the third day of battle. The spot where they almost broke through is known as the "High Water Mark of the Confederacy."
- **Devil's Den:** Fierce fighting happened here on the second day of battle. Union and Confederate troops fought hand-to-hand around the jagged rocky terrain.
- **Little Round Top:** The pivotal point of the battle. Union troops had left this elevated position on the left (southern) end of their line unoccupied. If the Confederates got the high ground they would be able to fire cannon down the Union line. It was a race to the top, with fierce fighting all around. Ultimately the Union troops held the position. (If you've seen the movie *Gettysburg*, the climax of the film takes place during this fight).
- **Virginia Memorial:** Lee positioned himself here during Pickett's Charge on the third day of battle. From here you can see Union headquarters across the plain and get a sense of the structure of the battlefield.
- **Peach Orchard:** Halfway between the two armies, on the second day of battle, Union forces were caught out of position here by advancing Confederates.

// GettysBikes

OTHER GETTYSBURG TOURS

If biking's not your thing, there are plenty of other ways to explore the battlefield. Bus, car (a guide will actually come drive your car and show you around), Segway, horse, scooter, foot—name a method of transportation and odds are there's a Gettysburg tour that uses it.

☰ *While You're Here*

GET THE REST OF THE GETTYSBURG BATTLEFIELD EXPERIENCE

The battlefield tour is the main act, but there are a lot of other big-time sights to see while you're here.

The **Visitor Center** (www.nps.gov/gett) is a good place to start. If you can make it here before your tour, great, but it's also a nice way to fill in the gaps afterward. For $15, you can visit the excellent museum, watch a film narrated by Morgan Freeman and Sam Waterston, and see the **Cyclorama**, a massive round painting that lights up a narrated account of what happened at Pickett's Charge on the last day of battle.

From the Visitor Center, there's a shuttle to the **Eisenhower House** (the only way you can actually get to that house) and downtown historic Gettysburg.

For a general's eye view of parts of the battlefield, climb up the **Observation Tower** (free) on West Confederate Avenue or the **Cupola** ($30) up at the Seminary Ridge Museum (seminaryridgemuseum.org).

The **Gettysburg National Cemetery** is also here. After the battle, there were so many dead soldiers who needed to be buried that the country created a national cemetery. It was here, at the cemetery's consecration, that Lincoln made his famous Gettysburg Address.

>> **Brush Up on your Battle Hist:** On Netflix, that is. Ken Burns' Civil War documentary has a whole episode dedicated to Gettysburg, which is fun to watch before or after your trip.

>> **Eisenhower's Farm:** Near Seminary Ridge is a white farmhouse that was owned by Dwight D. Eisenhower. Ike first lived near Gettysburg when he was in the army, and he decided to retire here post-presidenting. If you want to visit, you'll have to buy a pass at Gettysburg and take a shuttle over there. You can't just drive up on your own.

HUNT FOR SPIRITS ON A GHOST TOUR

With all the horrors that happened here, it's easy to believe the town is haunted. As a result, there are a lot of ghost tour companies throughout town.

One of the best is **Mark Nesbitt's Ghosts of Gettysburg** (ghostsofgettysburg.com), organized by the guy who literally wrote the book on ghosts here (for real, you can buy it on Amazon).

WALK ACROSS THE SACHS COVERED BRIDGE

The 100-foot long red barn-like bridge spans photogenically across a small river. It was used by troops on both sides at various points of the battle in 1863; now it's said to be haunted and is also a popular engagement photo spot.

FIND FARM GOODIES

On Saturday mornings, the local farmers' market sets up shop in Lincoln Square, although it's not just farm goodies; you'll find fancy soaps and crafts and the like. You can also go right to the source—there are scores of farms in the countryside just outside town.

GET A CAT'S EYE VIEW OF THE BATTLE

Do you learn history better when cats are reenacting it? (Or are you not sure, because that's a concept that never would have crossed your mind?) **Civil War Tails** (civilwartails.com) at the Homestead Diorama Museum is an amazingly quirky, entirely handmade miniature recreation of Civil War history. But instead of people, all the soldiers are tiny cats.

☰ *Good Eats*

Gettysburg's riding the farm to fork wave. Luckily for the town, it's an easy wave to catch, as rich farmland dominates the surrounding countryside. You'll find local produce and meats on many menus.

Most places here aren't fancy, but they can fill up, especially on big weekends like the battle anniversary or college-related events.

THE PUB

Lincoln Square • the-pub.com • $$ • American

Right on Lincoln Square, this lively spot is a lot of things in one. A press-tin ceiling and stained glass-lit bar gets loud and blasts Bon Jovi, while the eight-page menu covers everything from sandwiches to salads to burgers to pasta to "spaghetti grilled cheese," which is just as decadent as it sounds.

TOMMY'S PIZZA

Steinwehr Ave • tommyspizzainc.com • $ • pizza

This locally loved, family-owned pizza joint has casual counter service for pies, slices, and subs. You can choose from specialty pies or pick your own toppings, plus they have about 10 local craft beers on tap. In a rush? There's a drive-through pickup window.

GARRYOWEN IRISH PUB

Just off Lincoln Square • garryowenirishpub.net • $$ • Irish

Authentically Irish, "the Go" has a homey atmosphere and a menu that goes way beyond pub grub, with classics like Shepherds pie and healthy picks such as quinoa salad. There's often live music, featuring everything from Irish traditional to local rock bands.

MR. G'S ICE CREAM

Baltimore Avenue, near Steinwehr • $ • ice cream

There are about four ice cream shops within two blocks of each other, but this is the one to hit up. A locals' favorite, they serve thick creamy ice cream plus slushies and other treats. You can sit outside and hear the live music next door at Reid's.

RAGGED EDGE COFFEE

Just off Lincoln Square • $ • coffee shop

Set in a transformed house, this coffee spot screams "hang out in me." There's a cozy porch with seating out front, while inside you'll find nooks and a selection of books and works by local artists.

GETTYSBURG BAKING CO.

Lincoln Square • gettysburgbakingco.com • $ • bakery

Tucked in a corner of the Lincoln Square, this small bakery sells good coffee and delicious bread and pastries. They also sell a selection of sandwiches, salads, and soups.

≡ Time for a Drink

For a college town, the overall nightlife scene in Gettysburg is pretty low-key. Just outside of town, a new drinks trail connects a growing number of homegrown craft beverage makers.

ADAMS COUNTY POUR TOUR

This relatively new driving trail links about 21 craft breweries, cideries, distilleries, and wineries around Adams County. Pick up a Pour Tour Passport at any of the participating drinkeries and get it stamped at each stop. Collect enough steps and you'll score some swag—from corks to wine bags and glasses.

If you don't want to do all that driving, **Adams County Winery** (www.adamscountywinery .com) and **Reid's Orchard & Winery** (www.reidsorchardwinery.com) have tasting rooms that are walkable from each other Downtown.

MASON DIXON DISTILLERY

masondixondistillery.com

The rums and vodkas at this small-batch distillery are made from grain from the battlefield. Try the cocktail flight—for $5 you can try their liquors in mini cocktails rather than drinking it straight. All the food here is locally sourced or made in-house, and it's all delicious.

THE FARNSWORTH HOUSE INN

www.farnsworthhouseinn.com

There's a leafy little beer garden at this historic house and inn, and live music some nights. Named after Union Brigadier General Elon John Farnsworth, the building was used by Confederate sharpshooters in the battle.

≡ Stay Over

There is a slew of budget hotels along Steinwehr Avenue on the southern side of town and a handful of historic B&Bs and inns closer to the center of Gettysburg.

GETTYSBURG HOTEL

www.hotelgettysburg.com • $$$

It doesn't get more convenient than this stately hotel on Lincoln Square. The building started off as a tavern in 1797 and has hosted presidents like Eisenhower. It's now totally renovated and has all your standard hotel amenities. Bonus: in summer, there's a rooftop pool overlooking the square.

THE LODGES AT GETTYSBURG

www.gettysburgaccommodations.com • $$

A popular wedding location thanks to its bucolic grounds and wooded lake, the Lodges is a relaxing countryside base. It takes less than 15 minutes to drive into town from here, and individual cabins provide plenty of space, plus small kitchens and fireplaces. There's a two-night minimum.

RENTAL SCENE

There are plenty of options, but not a whole lot of variety—or modernity. Most of the rentals here are set in historic homes and buildings around downtown Gettysburg.

≡ *Plan Around*

Gettysburg reenactments are serious business, and the biggest one happens every year around the anniversary of the battle.

Weekends to Plan For (or Avoid):

- **Memorial Day (May):** A parade and ceremony commemorate veterans.
- **Gettysburg Anniversary Reenactments (July):** Get ready for major commemorative events, large crowds, and plenty of battle reenactments on the annual anniversary of the fighting.
- **National Apple Harvest Festival (October):** Adam County's 100-plus types of apples are celebrated at this two-weekend event.

GOOD TO KNOW

- There are about 1,300 memorials and monuments on the battlefield—so don't expect to see them all in one visit.

BEEN HERE, DONE THAT?

- Why do one battlefield when you can do four? Fredericksburg was the precursor to Gettysburg, so you can head down there and see what led to Lee's push into the north (Chapter 25).
- Combine biking with beer tasting along the W&OD Trail in northern Virginia (Chapter 18).

1 Little Round Top at the battlefield
2 Historic building marker
3 Sachs Covered Bridge

24

Drive the Harriet Tubman Scenic Byway

Cambridge, MD, to Wilmington, DE

Take a road trip along the Underground Railroad to pay tribute to one of America's most influential women.

FROM DC: 88 MILES · 1 HOUR 45 MINUTES | DAYS HERE: DAY TRIP

DO	EAT	DRINK	BUY
drive	seafood	RAR Nanticoke Nectar	driving tour map

This 223-mile drive is a journey through history, past landscapes that look much like the way they did when Harriet Tubman was born and when she helped people escape slavery nearly 175 years ago.

   Though Tubman's life is the focal point, it's by no means the only story celebrated here. The route's an homage to the families that worked the land; the churches that united communities; and the waterways, woods, and marshes that carried people to freedom.

Getting to the Harriet Tubman Scenic Byway

To do this trip right, you need a car.

You can take a bus to Cambridge and see a handful of Tubman sites in town. But to reach the Harriet Tubman Underground Railroad Visitor Center and the majority of the sites along the route, you'll want your own wheels, so you can reach the off-the-beaten-path stops.

The route is actually managed by different orgs in each state, so you'll see signage change along the way. In Delaware, follow the white Harriet Tubman signs. In Maryland, you can follow the route on a mobile app, or follow the brown "Harriet Tubman UGRR" signs.

The Maryland portion of the trail is longer, at about 125 miles. Delaware is 98. Keep in mind that it'll take almost 2 hours just to get to the start of the route. You can do part of the Byway as a day trip, but it'll be a lot of driving and you'll have to select a specific stretch of the road to do.

Get Your Bearings

The trail loops its way from Cambridge, on the banks of the Choptank River, south through farmland and fishing villages and the Blackwater National Wildlife Refuge.

Much of the Byway follows the Choptank River up into Maryland before crossing the state line into Delaware. From here, it shoots east to Dover, then winds north into Wilmington, before passing into Pennsylvania, where a heritage train continues to Philadelphia.

Follow in Harriet Tubman's Footsteps

If you need inspiration as to what one person can accomplish, look no further than Harriet Tubman.

At only five feet tall, she was born into slavery around 1822. She couldn't read or write. She was almost killed as a girl, when a man threw a weight into her head.

Yet in spite of all this, she persevered, first to freedom, then as a legend.

She escaped to Philadelphia, where slavery was illegal, in 1849. But instead of staying there she returned south, again and again, helping family members reach freedom as well.

Tubman became a key conductor along the Underground Railroad, the secret network run by enslaved and free African Americans, abolitionists, and activists who helped people escape slavery in the South. She served as a spy and a nurse in the Civil War, and she worked for women's suffrage with Susan B. Anthony. She's even slated to appear on the $20 bill.

Now, a designated driving route connects many of the places in Maryland, Delaware, and Pennsylvania that played a key role in Tubman's life and in the lives of other people escaping slavery via the Underground Railroad.

The trail leads through farm country, small communities, wetlands, and fishing villages. You'll find solitude on the empty backroads in Dorchester County, water views and seafood along the Choptank and Delaware Rivers, and a sense of awe at the courage and fortitude it took for people to fight for freedom.

Before You Go

Take advantage of at-home WiFi and download the free Harriet Tubman Underground Railroad Byway app before you leave (download it at harriettubmanbyway.org). It only covers the Maryland portion of the trail, but it really brings the journey to life. With re-enactors, interviews with biographers, and descriptions of what you're driving past, it's like driving through a Netflix documentary. Plus there's a map with nearby good-to-knows like restaurants and gas stations.

>> **Trail Maps:** The complete 45-stop map and guide is available for $2 at the Dorchester Visitor Center and Harriet Tubman Underground Railroad Visitor Center. PDFs are also online for free, but it's tough to follow on your phone. Spring for the jumbo print-out.

Highlights Along the Trail

DORCHESTER VISITOR CENTER

Cambridge, MD • visitdorchester.org

Just across the Choptank River Bridge in Cambridge, this riverfront visitor center's a great place to start your road trip. Pick up a trail map and ask about any local events happening this weekend.

HARRIET TUBMAN MUSEUM

Cambridge, MD

A small storefront museum on one of Cambridge's main streets has exhibitions highlighting Tubman's life and some of the sites you'll see along the byway. It's staffed by volunteers, some of whom can tell you about their personal connections to Tubman. (If you're looking it up on Google Maps, it may come up as "Harriet Tubman Organization.")

HARRIET TUBMAN UNDERGROUND RAILROAD VISITOR CENTER

Church Creek, MD • www.nps.gov/hatu

Opened in 2017, this state-of-the-art museum combines quotes, movies, and exhibitions that detail Tubman's life and her relationship with this region. There's a film and a gift shop, as well as knowledgeable rangers who can answer questions about the route you're about to drive.

BRODESS FARM

Bucktown, MD

Harriet Tubman was enslaved here with some of her family members. When the farm owner Edward Brodess died, Harriet and her three brothers ran away (but then, fearing the repercussions, they came back). While the buildings from Tubman's time are long gone and the land is private property, there's a marker commemorating Tubman's childhood home.

BUCKTOWN VILLAGE STORE

Bucktown, MD

When Harriet was around 13, she almost died after being hit in the head with a weight in this general store. Today, the store has been restored and is dedicated to telling the story of life here in the 19th century. Call 410-901-9255 to make an appointment to go inside.

WEBB CABIN

Preston, MD

The lines between free and enslaved blacks were often blurred. Here at this 1850s cabin, James Webb lived with his wife and children. Webb was free. His wife was not. You can poke your head in to see what housing was like for African Americans in the early 19th century.

OLD STATE HOUSE MUSEUM

Dover, DE

On Dover's stately capital green, this museum dives into the legal and legislative arguments surrounding freedom and slavery. It was at this courthouse in 1847 that the free black Underground Railroad conductor Samuel Burris was convicted of helping enslaved people escape. (168 years later, in 2015, Burris's charge was pardoned by Delaware's governor.)

1 Harriet Tubman Underground Railroad Visitor Center
2 Bucktown Village Store
3 Country roads along the byway

CORBIT-SHARP HOUSE

Odessa, DE • www.historicodessa.org

This home of Quaker abolitionists was a stop on the Underground Railroad. Make an appointment to tour the house.

TUBMAN-GARRETT RIVERFRONT PARK

Wilmington, DE

Named for Thomas Garrett, "Stationmaster" of the Underground Railroad, who helped Harriet Tubman and other freedom seekers through Wilmington, this park hosts summer concerts and events. Here you'll find a moving sculpture, Unwavering Courage in The Pursuit of Freedom, which features Harriet Tubman and those who helped her lead enslaved African Americans to freedom.

MITCHELL CENTER FOR AFRICAN AMERICAN HERITAGE

Wilmington, DE • dehistory.org/main-visit

Located in the Delaware History Museum, the Mitchell Center presents stories from Delaware's Underground Railroad, both from people seeking freedom and from the conductors and abolitionists who helped them. Elsewhere at the museum, exhibitions examine civil rights in Delaware throughout the state's history.

≡ *While You're Here*

SHOP THE FARM STANDS

Depending on the season, you can pick up fresh corn, fruit, and flowers from roadside markets. Some are tiny unstaffed stands that ask you to pay via the honor system. Others, like **Emily's Produce** (www.emilysproduce.com) and **Farmer's Daughter Market**, have permanent structures and full staffs. You can also load up on eggs, poultry, and lamb from **Pop's Old Place** (popsoldplace.com), a family-run farm dating back to 1901.

DETOUR THROUGH BLACKWATER NATIONAL WILDLIFE REFUGE

When Tubman was little, she used to trap muskrats in this wetland area. The Blackwater is also home to bald eagles, deer, and egrets, and is a stopping point for huge flocks of migratory birds. Pop off the Byway and drive the 4-mile Wildlife Drive loop, or join a kayaking tour.

☰ *Good Eats*

As much of the Byway is very rural, most restaurant options are clustered in Cambridge, Dover, and Wilmington. Outside of these larger hubs, there are a scattering of eateries along the route.

>> **Byway Bucks:** Some of the local businesses along the Delaware portion of the Byway offer "Byway Bucks" discounts. You can get these coupons at visitor center, or online (www.tubman bywaydelaware.org/bywaybucks.html).

SUICIDE BRIDGE RESTAURANT

Hurlock, MD • www.suicide-bridge-restaurant.com • $$ • seafood

This waterfront restaurant is a good mid-drive place for a meal. The menu focuses on seafood (some from the river just outside), with plenty of land-based options as well. You can also hop on a classic riverboat ride or dinner cruise from here.

BRICK WORKS BREWING & EATS

Smyrna, DE • www.brickworksde.com • $$ • brewpub

About 20 minutes past Dover, the little town of Smyrna has a handful of dining options. At Brickworks, the food and beer are made from scratch on-site, using local ingredients. The menu is upscale pub food, like a build-your-own mac and cheese and a lot of things topped with bacon.

CANTWELL'S TAVERN

Odessa, DE • www.cantwells-tavern.com • $$ • American

This restaurant is part of the Historic Odessa Foundation, which also manages the Corbit–Sharp House. It's set in a beautiful brick Federal-style building and is modeled after the 19th-century tavern that used to operate here. Save room for dessert, which includes things such as s'mores cheesecake.

JESSOP'S TAVERN & COLONIAL RESTAURANT

New Castle, DE • www.jessops-tavern.com • $$ • colonial

Go all-in with the history tour at this traditional colonial-style eatery in historic New Castle. The waitstaff dresses in period attire, and the menu features traditional American fare. This is also a huge beer destination, with more than 350 bottles of mostly Belgian brews.

≡ Time for a Drink

As with the restaurants, you'll find most bars and breweries concentrated in the cities and larger towns along the route.

RAR BREWING

rarbrewing.com

One of Maryland's best craft breweries is based in Cambridge. The busy tasting room is set in a garage-style space on Poplar Street, doesn't take itself too seriously with custom Simpson's-inspired artwork, and has about 12 beers on tap.

LAYTON'S CHANCE VINEYARD

www.laytonschance.com

Tucked in the corn fields, this solar-powered winery does a number of fruit wines, made sans grape with watermelon and strawberry. (They also make normal wines.)

SMYRNA

In addition to the above-mentioned **Brick Works Brewing & Eats**, Smyrna has a couple of cool places to grab a drink.

At **Painted Stave Distilling** (paintedstave.com), small-batch whiskeys, vodka, and gin are made in an old movie theater. If you really want to drink "local," try the Scrapple vodka.

Nearby, **Blue Earl Brewing Co.** (blueearlbrewing.com) pairs artisanal beers with a monthly live blues jam sesh. Claiming to be "brew for your soul," the brewery names a lot of its beers after music and gives them album-cover style label art.

≡ Stay Over

If you're going to make a weekend of it and do the full Byway route, Dover makes for a convenient midway stopping point. You can tackle the Maryland route on Day One, rest up in Dover, and then head up the rest of the way to Philly the following day.

≡ *Plan Around*

For an especially meaningful visit, consider doing the drive in late February or early March, as Black History Month transitions into Women's History Month.

Weekends to Plan For (or Avoid):

- **Harriet Tubman Day (March):** March 10th is recognized as Harriet Tubman Day, and stops along the Byway may have special commemorative events.

GOOD TO KNOW

- Harriet Tubman was born Araminta Ross. She took the name "Harriet," which was her mother's name, after she escaped to freedom.
- Tubman's code name along the Underground Railroad was "Moses."
- Before she escaped, Tubman was married to a free black man named John Tubman. He didn't make the trip north with Harriet when she fled, and he married someone else in her absence.

BEEN HERE, DONE THAT?

- If you want to spend more time in this area, Blackwater National Wildlife Refuge is one of the best places to see bald eagles.
- Harriet helped abolitionist John Brown recruit former slaves to help raid Harpers Ferry. (Brown called her "General Tubman.") You can learn more about the ill-fated raid on a walk around Harpers Ferry (Chapter 12).
- While Tubman was a powerful figure on the Underground Railroad, this wasn't the only route to freedom. Culpeper also played a big role in the UGRR, which you can dig into at the town's small history museum (Chapter 21).

25

Pair Battlefields and Breweries

Fredericksburg, VA

Put a fresh spin on the Civil War circuit by combining your battlefield visit with some great local beers.

FROM DC: 52 MILES · 1 HOUR 5 MINUTES | TRIP LENGTH: DAY TRIP

DO	EAT	DRINK	BUY
visit Civil War battlefields	Carl's frozen custard	local beer	vintage goods

Halfway between the Union and Confederate capitals (DC and Richmond), Fredericksburg was a major Civil War–era crossroads. The town changed hands seven times during the Civil War and was the site of multiple bloody conflicts. Today, the four battlefield parks are a major reason to visit. But there's a newcomer on the scene that's causing quite the buzz: beer! More than eight breweries have sprung up in the past few years, each with their own spin on suds.

≡ *Getting to Fredericksburg*

This is a pretty easy car-free getaway—you can do parts of the Fredericksburg battlefield and then either join a brew tour or walk to the downtown breweries.

The train's easy, and cheap, from DC. Both Amtrak and VRE come here from Union Station (Amtrak starts at around $24 and takes about an hour; VRE costs around $12 and takes 1.5 hours). The station is downtown, about a 10-minute walk to shops and breweries as well as the Fredericksburg battlefield and walking tour.

You can also take a Greyhound bus for about $11—that'll take about 1.5 hours.

Having a car will open up more battlefields and breweries in the greater Spotsylvania area around town—it's an easy, though soulless, hour-long drive down I-95 to get here. If you're driving into town, the Visitor Center is a good first stop. They have parking here, too.

≡ *Get Your Bearings*

Fredericksburg is set along the Rappahannock River in Spotsylvania County. The four major battlefields form a T, with Fredericksburg, Chancellorsville, and Wilderness spread east to west along Highway 3, then Spotsylvania to the south. If you were to drive a loop between all four without stopping, it'd take about an hour.

Train travelers will get dropped off on the eastern edge of town. You can either walk northwest about 5 to 10 minutes to hit the historic downtown core or walk west and a little south about 15 minutes to get to the Fredericksburg Battlefield Visitor Center.

≡ *Battlefield & Brewery-Hop*

Fredericksburg, a.k.a. FXBG, is steeped in layers of history: everyone from Pocahontas to George Washington to Robert E. Lee has a slice of the story. With four battlefields in and around the charming historic downtown, FXBG has long been a destination for Civil War buffs.

A Pint of History

Troops fought back and forth all over this region, and there are four main battlefield sites here:

- **Battle of Fredericksburg:** December 1862. This was a big win for the South, when the Confederate army blocked the Union army's advance toward Richmond.
- **Battle of Chancellorsville:** April 1863. The North tried again to push south. Again, the South blocked them, pulling off a win at Chancellorsville (although a loss for Stonewall Jackson, who lost his arm, and then his life, here).

// Battlefield trenches

- **Battle of the Wilderness:** May 1864. After getting shut down at Gettysburg, Robert E. Lee retreated back to the Fredericksburg area. Enter Union General Ulysses S. Grant, who swooped in and made a new run toward Richmond. The 1864 Overland Campaign saw terrible forest fighting at the Wilderness.
- **Battle of Spotsylvania Court House:** May 1864. Shortly after the Wilderness, this 1864 battle was essentially a stalemate. But Grant kept pushing and slowly wore down the Confederates, eventually forcing their surrender in the spring of 1865.

Today, while the battlefields are still prominent here, the town doesn't feel like it's stuck in the past. The historic downtown storefronts are full of locally crafted products.

A big part of that local business is beer. The town is home to at least eight breweries, from small homegrown shops to brands that migrated here from places such as Richmond. Many are clustered near battlefields, which means you can see something old, then taste something new.

Beer and Battle Plan of Attack

In one day, you can do one to two battlefields, plus up to three breweries (depending on whether you want more beer or more history).

In two days, you can really cover the full spectrum. Spend your first day in Fredericksburg town; do the battle sights there and then hit up the breweries in the immediate vicinity. On the second day, make a battlefield loop by car, stopping at more breweries along the way.

>> **More Info:** Battlefield info is available at www.nps.gov/frsp. The Fredericksburg Tourism Bureau has beer blogs and more at www.visitfred.com

Around FXBG

FREDERICKSBURG BATTLEFIELD, PART 1

If you're looking at a map, this one's a bit confusing, as it looks like the battlefield includes half of downtown. That's because the battle itself raged through town, so now some of the sites are strung together on a self-guided walking tour.

The Visitor Center is about 1 mile from the center of town; it's an easy walk, although there's also parking on-site. The battlefield here is known as the "Sunken Road" portion of the park and was where some of the Confederate lines were positioned. Free guided tours by park rangers last 35 minutes and tell the story of the battle. There's also a small gift shop with Civil War items (if you've ever wanted a bugle, here you go).

// Fredericksburg Battlefield

BREWERIES NEAR FREDERICKSBURG BATTLEFIELD VISITOR CENTER

Some of FXBG's most popular breweries are right downtown. Start your day at **Spencer Devon Brewing** (www.spencerdevonbrewing .com), which is just as well known for its brunch as its brews. It's happy hour all day long on Sundays. A few blocks up the street, **Red Dragon Brewery** (www.reddragonbrewery .com) started as a home-brewing endeavor before settling into its permanent downtown digs. Two Saturdays a month, they host free yoga events.

// Beers at Red Dragon Brewery

FREDERICKSBURG BATTLEFIELD, PART 2

To complete the battlefield tour here, drive over to Lee Drive. More fighting took place here, and now a quiet woodsy road passes pullouts where you can stretch your legs on a few trails leading to overlooks (Lee's Hill is a good one—it's where Lee posted up to survey the battle). Along the way you'll see trenches left over from the war (they look like soft mounds or ridges of earth).

BREWERIES NEAR LEE DRIVE

There's a big cluster of breweries in some of the industrial parks to the south of downtown. It's easy to pair these with a trip down Lee Drive (although that road has no outlet, so you'll have to double back and go around to reach the tasting rooms).

Strangeways (strangewaysbrewing.com) is an outpost of the popular Richmond brewer and is known for its unique flavors. There are always over 30 beers on tap, plus a beer garden, arcade, and local art displays.

A little farther south on Highway 17, **Maltese Brewing** (www.maltesebrewing.com) feels like a firehouse-turned-bar, with jackets on the wall and hoses strung above the bar (the two owners and many of the bartenders are active firefighters).

Across the river, a little south of George Washington's Ferry Farm, **Highmark Brewery** (highmarkbrewery.com) is a popular hangout spot. Set in a big garage, there are dog-friendly picnic tables outside.

// Maltese Brewing

Farther Afield

You'll have to drive about 25 minutes west through strip malls and town centers to get here. Suddenly, you'll go from Walmart to War Front. There are two battlefields out here, Chancellorsville and Wilderness. Spotsylvania Court House is about 20 minutes away to the south.

The **Chancellorsville Visitor Center** actually covers three parks (Wilderness and Spotsylvania don't have their own). There are exhibitions here, plus maps and self-guided driving tours of each battlefield.

If you have two days in the area, you could combine all of the parks in a big driving loop. If you just have one day, just pick one—Chancellorsville's a good choice. A driving tour will take about 1 hour, and follows the battle highlights.

One of Virginia's first farmhouse breweries, **1781 Brewing Company** (www.1781brewing .com), is just across the street from Wilderness Battlefield. Many of the brews are made with ingredients grown right here on the farm. If wine's more your thing, Wilderness Run Vineyards is on the same site and does tastings.

BEER TOURS

If you're arriving by train (or just don't feel like driving), there are a few beer tour companies that will shuttle you around town. **FXBG Brewery Tours** (fxbgbrewerytours.com) and **Fred Vegas Brew Tours** (www.fredvegasbrewtours.com) each organize bus tours that hit up three breweries. (They switch up which three are featured.)

☰ *While You're Here*

GEORGE WASHINGTON'S BOYHOOD HOME

Fredericksburg's American history cred goes further back than Civil War battlefields. George Washington grew up here, and you can visit his childhood home at Ferry Farm. That whole "cherry tree can't tell a lie" story supposedly took place around here, and people also come out to try and reenact GW's legendary "silver dollar toss across the Rappahannock."

For more "House Hunters: Historic Fredericksburg," check out nearby **Kenmore** (www .kenmore.org), where George's sister lived.

SHOP FXBG

The compact downtown is full of antiques and vintage shops, plus some newer boutiques with on-trend styles. Some feel a bit fuddy-duddy, but there are some great finds. Try **Pye & Co.** for stylish home decor, jewelry, and clothing. Load up on adorable bath bombs, sugar scrubs and more at **Sugar and Spruce** (sugarandspruce.com). Everything here is so sweet-looking, you'll be tempted to eat it.

// Downtown Fredericksburg

FIRST FRIDAYS

Check out the music, galleries, and restaurants that open up for a block party—like First Friday, on—you guessed it—the first Friday of the month. Trolleys run a loop to all the downtown spots that participate.

HUGH MERCER APOTHECARY SHOP

www.washingtonheritagemuseums.org

Step back in time in this fascinating old-school pharmacy. Jars of Revolutionary War–era remedies like crab claws and leeches show how far medicine has (luckily) come.

RIVERSIDE CENTER FOR THE PERFORMING ARTS

www.riversidedt.com

This local dinner theater draws big acts, specializing in musicals like *Mamma Mia* and *Beauty and the Beast*. The food is usually decent; the on-stage talent is usually fantastic. You can also opt out of the dinner portion and save about $20 on your ticket.

☰ *Good Eats*

Eating in the 'Burg is a mix of classic and cutting edge—sometimes under the same repurposed historic roof. The locavore movement is strong here, so expect to find produce and meats raised just outside of town. There may be lines at some of the dining institutions, but for the most part, you shouldn't need a reservation to eat well.

FOODĒ

Downtown • foodeonline.com • $$ • American

It's pronounced Foodie, and lives up to its name, with co-owner and *Top Chef* contestant Joy Crump helming the kitchen in a converted 1820s bank. Don't miss the pimento toast—these small rounds of gooey warm deliciousness are under $2 a pop.

GOOLRICK'S PHARMACY

Downtown • goolrickspharmacy.com • $ • American

Stop by for a malt, sandwich, or flavored soda at this classic lunch counter. Goolrick's is also a working drugstore, and has been here for over 150 years. It's also the oldest operating soda fountain in the country.

BENNY VITALI'S

Downtown • www.bennysva.com/BennyVitalis • $ • pizza

This is Fredericksburg's answer to Jumbo Slice: One Benny's slice is the equivalent of two to three normal pizza slices. If that doesn't intimidate you, consider signing up for the Benny's Challenge, where you can win $500 for eating an eight-pound, 28-inch sausage-and-pepperoni pizza in 1 hour. There's a good beer selection here, too.

KYBECCA

Downtown • kybecca.com • $$ • New American

At first the menu items sound pretty familiar, but look a little closer and you'll notice artful twists, like the fish and chips made with trout, or the Old Bay kimchi in the shrimp and grits. Everything here is fresh and most of it is locally sourced.

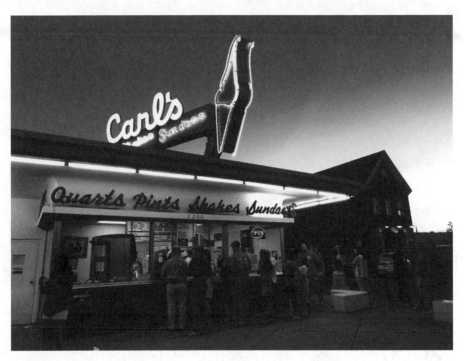

// Carl's frozen custard

THE FALAFEL JOINT

Downtown • $ • Mediterranean

This small eatery next door to the Sugar Shack serves up big flavors in its falafel bowls, shawarma, and tacos (thanks in part to the extensive condiments bar). Try the french fries with garlic mayo, ketchup, and Old Bay seasoning.

CARL'S

North of Downtown, near Old Mill Park • www.carlsfrozencustard.com • $ • custard

This landmark roadside frozen custard window is on the National Register of Historic Places, having served Vanilla, Chocolate, and Strawberry custard here since 1947. Be prepared to wait in line (though it moves quickly), pay in cash, and potentially park a few blocks away. Carl's closes every year between mid-November and mid-February.

≡ Time for a Drink

Aside from the breweries, FXBG's drinking roster is a solid mix of taverns, Irish pubs, beer bars, and sports bars.

>> **Late Night:** FXBG shuts down relatively early—keep an eye out for the flags on business that say "open late." (In some cases that means 8 p.m.)

CAPITAL ALE HOUSE

www.capitalalehouse.com

This large taproom claims to have the biggest beer selection in the area. Cozy up in front of the fire with a pint from one of their nearly 50 taps.

A. SMITH BOWMAN DISTILLERY

www.asmithbowman.com

This family-run microdistillery continuously wins top honors for their single-barrel bourbons. They do free tours but are closed on Sundays.

COLONIAL TAVERN HOME TO THE IRISH BRIGADE

www.irishbrigadetavern.com

This welcoming pub pays tribute to the Irish soldiers who fought in the battle of Fredericksburg. They have a good selection of Irish beers and whiskeys, plus there's live music some nights.

GOOD TO KNOW

- There are two free iPhone apps for touring the battlefields: one for Fredericksburg and one for Chancellorsville.
- Entry at all the battlefields is free.

BEEN HERE, DONE THAT?

- After the battle of Chancellorsville, the armies headed north, where they ultimately had a big showdown at Gettysburg. Today, that battlefield is excellently preserved (Chapter 23).
- Beer and history meet a little ways down the road in Richmond, the site of the Confederate capital, and now, Virginia's brewing capital (Chapter 14).

≡ *Stay Over*

This is a prime day-tripping destination. You can have a full day of history and hops and make it home to DC for dinner. But spending the night will open up more of the area for you to explore, and you can do it all at a more relaxed pace.

There are a couple historic hotels and B&Bs in the town's downtown core—think four-post canopy beds and cozy fireplaces. The vast majority of FXBG's lodging options are budget-conscious chains, which are located in the suburban town centers nearby.

RENTAL SCENE

At this writing, many of the rental listings on sites like Airbnb and VRBO were private rooms in a shared home, and prices were comparable to the budget hotels like Best Western and Quality Inn just outside of town.

≡ *Plan Around*

With so many layers of American history here, there are plenty of patriotic events on the calendar. It's also a college town, so events like graduation and move-in can make things busy up.

Weekends to Plan For (or Avoid):

- **Presidents Day (February):** The town's a bit George Washington–obsessed anyway, so they do it up on this winter weekend with special programming for President Numero Uno.
- **Fredericksburg Brewfest (April):** Brewers from around the region come pour the goods at this one-day fest. There's also wine, whiskey, food, and music.
- **Marine Corps Historic Half (May):** Halfway between DC and Richmond, this popular race is half the distance of its full-marathon cousin in DC.
- **Fourth of July:** FXBG celebrates the Fourth with fireworks, a heritage fest and more.
- **Fredericksburg Agricultural Fair (July–August):** The oldest fair in the country, this country extravaganza has pig races, chainsaw artists, and plenty of food and drink.

Part Six
Destination Stays

26

Do It Up at the Greenbrier

White Sulphur Springs, WV

Treat yourself to a weekend at the grande dame of the Appalachians.

FROM DC: 249 MILES · 3 HOURS 50 MINS | TRIP LENGTH: WEEKEND

DO	EAT	DRINK	BUY
horse-drawn carriage ride	Greenbrier peaches with fresh whipped cream	Mint Julep	*The History of the Greenbrier* book

There's nothing subtle about the Greenbrier. From the palatial front entryway to crystal chandeliered ballrooms and manicured gardens, it's quickly obvious why this place is one of the preeminent resorts in the country.

Set on a sprawling estate in West Virginia's Greenbrier Valley, the Greenbrier has attracted royalty, celebrities, presidents, and international visitors since 1778. There are countless ways to spend the weekend here, from croquet to golf to reading in the sitting rooms . . . but it doesn't come cheap.

// Arrival at the Greenbrier

Getting to the Greenbrier

Amtrak is a super easy and scenic, although longer (like 6 hour long) trip. Trains from Union Station drop you off across the street from the resort. You can snag tickets for as low as $34 each way, but schedules are limited.

Driving's shorter than the train. Once you get past the unexciting interstates (I-66 to I-81), the road turns scenic, winding through the mountainous George Washington National Forest. Parking at the resort is $25 per day to valet, or you can self-park for free.

If you're short on time, there are daily flights from Dulles to Greenbrier Valley Airport (Lewisburg) from spring to fall. The trip takes about an hour and averages around $150 per ticket.

Get Your Bearings

You'll need a map to get around the 11,000-acre estate. Pick one up at the concierge desk. When you're on the sprawling grounds, it's easy to forget the outside world exists.

But the Greenbrier isn't in a bubble; it's situated in eastern West Virginia, less than 15 minutes west of the Virginia border. Half a mile down the road is the town of White Sulphur Springs, which isn't a heavy tourist draw despite the resort being nearby. About 15 minutes farther west is a town with more charm: Lewisburg.

☰ Stay Like Royalty at the Greenbrier

Stepping into the parlors or ballrooms at the Greenbrier feels a bit like you're in *The Crown* meets *Gone with the Wind*.

Enormous crystal chandeliers hang from many ceilings, while every surface, from the carpets to the wallpaper to the curtains, are splashed with brightly colored Dorothy Draper-designed patterns. It looks a bit like a Vera Bradley store exploded here. It's easy to imagine the place looking the exact same in 1948 when John F. Kennedy stayed here, or in 1963 when Princess Grace of Monaco was a guest.

The grounds span 11,000 acres around the property. Paths meander around gardens, cottages, and facilities. Shuttles also run circuits around the resort if you don't feel like walking.

The Greenbrier is truly a place where you can fill every minute with an activity—or fill your time with nothing at all. It checks all the resort boxes: There's an award-winning spa, multiple championship golf courses, plus some only-at-the-Greenbrier features that are worth checking out.

>> More Info: www.greenbrier.com. Price: $$$$

// Greenbrier interiors

Top Things to Do at the Greenbrier

TAKE A BUNKER TOUR: A top-secret bunker was built under the Greenbrier in the 1950s, intended to shelter Congress if the United States came under attack during the Cold War. Now the secret's out, so you can visit the bunker on a guided tour.

RIDE IN A HORSE-DRAWN CARRIAGE: Cruise around the grounds in a carriage. Many of the drivers have been working at the resort for decades (so they know the *real* gossip).

PLAY YOUR BEST GOLF: The five golf courses here have made golf a central part of the Greenbrier experience for over 100 years. Set up a tee time, or if you'd rather see the pros, come here for the Greenbrier Classic, an annual PGA Tour event.

AFTERNOON TEA IN THE LOBBY: Dorothy Draper's bold colors and florals are the perfect setting for an indulgent afternoon tea.

TREAT YOURSELF AT THE SPA: Named for its rich mineral waters, White Sulphur Springs (and the Greenbrier) have been drawing health seekers since the early days of this country. Now the massive spa complex here has everything from sulphur soaks to massages to board-certified plastic surgery. There's also a clinic.

TRY YOUR LUCK AT THE CASINO: The hotel added this entertainment hub a few years ago. (It's underground, so as not to mess with the hotel's external appearance.) Unlike some of the other resort features, only guests have access. There's a mix of classic casino games such as Blackjack and roulette, plus sports betting via FanDuel.

☰ *While You're Here*

EXPLORE SMALL TOWN LEWISBURG

A charming main street, some foodie-forward restaurants and the state's professional theater troupe put this West Virginia hamlet at the top of *Budget Travel's* "Coolest Small Towns in America" list a few years back. If you have a car, it's an easy 15-minute drive from the resort.

GREENBRIER RIVER TRAIL

Hike, bike, or ride a horse along the 78-mile converted railroad trail.

COAL HOUSE

East of town is a wacky structure made of 30 tons of coal. It's been used as a visitor center, tavern, and gift shop with draws such as coal jewelry and a dog-grooming salon.

☰ Good Eats

There are enough restaurants on-site that you could eat every meal somewhere new. (Seriously, there are 20 places to eat.) But get ready to pay for it.

Dress codes vary widely by venue and by time of day. In some cases a jacket and tie is required, especially around dinner time.

Off-campus, you'll find a few small-town restaurants and chains such as Pizza Hut down the street in White Sulphur Springs. The best options for local eats are in Lewisburg, 15 minutes away.

☰ Time for a Drink

From classy craft cocktails to a lively sports bar, the Greenbrier has a pub for every taste. You can also grab a drink to go and find a shady bench on the grounds to enjoy it. A handful of other local spots are a drive away.

>> **The Greenbrier Julep:** Believe it or not, the Greenbrier is said to be the birthplace of the Mint Julep.

SMOOTH AMBLER DISTILLERY

smoothambler.com

A super relaxing local spot where you can hang out at the picnic tables or Adirondack chairs and sip locally made whiskey. One weekend a month, they host "Whiskey in the Park," with a band and a different restaurant coming in with the food.

GREENBRIER VALLEY BREWING CO.

www.gvbeer.com

With a couple of good witbiers, Mothman IPA (named for a sighting of a human-sized bird-like creature in the 1960s that became part of local folklore), and an outstanding barrel-aged stout, this brewer is a local fave.

☰ *Plan Around*

Weekends to Plan For (or Avoid):

- **Concours d'Elegance (May):** Classic car fans converge on the resort for this new international car show.
- **NFL Training Camp (July–August):** The Greenbrier isn't just an ultra-posh resort—it's where the Houston Texans hold their NFL training camp. Tickets to watch the practices are free, and players often sign autographs after the session.
- **The Greenbrier Classic (July):** Every summer the PGA pros arrive for a tournament on the resort's Old White TPC Course.

GOOD TO KNOW

- It's hard to be overdressed at the Greenbrier. Jeans are a no-no in the main dining room (actually, jacket and tie are required in here) and on golf course and tennis courts.
- The chandelier in the lobby bar had a cameo in the 1939 film, *Gone with the Wind*.
- The resort has hosted 26 presidents—you can see mementos from their visits on display around the main building.
- Keep in mind when you're booking that the base rate doesn't include a slew of additional taxes and resort fees, which can add nearly $100 to the daily cost.
- *Bachelorette* fans may recognize the resort from Emily Maynard's season—she flew Joe here for a date.

BEEN HERE, DONE THAT?

- This place is steeped in tradition; in fact many people make it an annual thing and come year after year.
- Head northwest instead from DC, and you'll get to Nemacolin Woodlands Resort (www.nemacolin.com), which is set in the Laurel Highlands, not all that far from Pittsburgh. This spot also has a fantastic spa, casino, and grande resort feel.
- Nearby, the Omni Homestead Resort has an excellent spa, golf, and skiing in winter.

27

Celebrate Something Big at the Inn at Little Washington

Washington, VA

A meal here is one of those once-in-a-lifetime splurge events. And it's totally worth it.

FROM DC: 69 MILES · 1 HOUR AND 30 MINUTES | TRIP LENGTH: OVERNIGHT

DO	EAT	DRINK	BUY
eat	anything on the menu	wine	local farmers' market goods

One Michelin Star is a big deal. Three is the stuff of foodie legend.

The Inn at Little Washington, the ultimate in dining destinations around DC, was elevated to this elite three-star status in 2018, the first time any Washington-area restaurant has held the honor.

// Farm walk at the Inn at Little Washington

Beyond the dining room, the inn is the heart of a charming little village, where Southern charm and elegance meet a countryside hospitality so that people couldn't care less if you're wearing a sport jacket or fleece pullover.

>> **More Info:** theinnatlittlewashington.com. Price: $$$$

☰ Getting to the Inn at Little Washington

You'll want to drive here. There's no easy public transit. The inn can arrange transportation but warns against fake companies offering deals. Play it safe and drive—take 66 west to 29 south, then head down to Warrenton. From here you'll pick up Highway 211 west and take that until you hang a right on Bus-211 straight into Washington.

There's valet parking here (just pull up to the front door), or you can self-park in the lot across the street from the inn. If you're just swinging through, the street parking on Gay Street, one block off Main Street, is free and easy.

// Goat on the farm

≡ *Get Your Bearings*

Washington, Virginia, a.k.a. "Little" Washington is a small well-to-do village with charming historic buildings and a main street actually called Main Street. The inn, its buildings and farm, are in the center of town. Then there are about four blocks of shops and galleries running along Main and Gay Streets.

≡ *The Dining Destination*

You'll dine like royalty (seriously, royals dined here), but a meal at The Inn at Little Washington may not be what you expect. Despite its trophy wall of accolades and country estate character, the inn is warm and welcoming, without a whiff of elitism or stuffiness.

Now, the price tag means you won't be a regular, but for an engagement or milestone birthday-caliber special occasion meal, the Inn at Little Washington lives up to its hype.

Helmed for 40 years by Chef Patrick O'Connell, the kitchen serves three four-course tasting menu options: one that's veggie-centric, one that's seasonal, and one that covers the inn's classics. Or you can mix and match from any of the menus to make your own four courses. Everything skews classic French cuisine, although there's a focus on "cuisine de terroir," or food from this region. Dishes may include pistachio-crusted duck breast, ravioli with mascarpone and chanterelles, and pepper-crusted Virginia bison tenderloin and braised short rib.

Food aside for a second, this is a professional dining experience. The intimate dining room looks like an elegant Wes Anderson set, with colorfully patterned walls, ceilings, and banquettes. The staff is trained in things like course pacing, there's a cheese expert on staff, and the plating presentations are works of art.

So how much will a meal here set you back? Each of the tasting menus costs $238. Then a wine pairing from the 14,000-bottle wine cellar will set you back another $170. And if you really want to treat yo'self, sit chef-side in the kitchen—these tables have a $595 surcharge.

>> Dalmatian Maitre D': Try to spot Luray, the inn's resident Dalmatian.

Free and Almost-Free Things to Do at the Inn

For one of the nicest five-star hotels in the region, there's a refreshing lack of pretentiousness here. The people who work here are warm, welcoming, and eager to point you toward the hotel's attractions that are open to the public—even if you're not a guest and don't plan on eating here.

There are a handful of free things to do around the inn itself:

VILLAGE MARKET: Every Saturday between April and October, an assortment of local merchants set up tents and sell produce, baked goods, BBQ, and herbal products like soaps and oils. Wine tasting and live music add to the festivities.

FARM WALK: The inn takes its farm stuff seriously—there's a farmer in residence. An easy walking path leads to a field of sheep, goats, and llamas. Bring your camera! The path then cuts over to the chicken house—this is where the restaurant gets its eggs—and cuts through the chef's vegetable garden. Along the way there are some big lawn chairs with perfect mountain views.

SHOPS: Across the street from the main building you'll find a mix of gifts for sale, from high-end alpaca clothing to art to wine and food books to cute gifts.

GARDENS AND KOI PONDS: Directly behind the dining room you'll find a small gardenny walkway lined with koi ponds. When the weather's nice they sometimes do cocktail hour out here. Steps beyond that is a small, formal garden—the flowers from here are used throughout the inn.

☰ *While You're Here*

SAY SPAAAA

Walk-ins are welcome at the Little Washington Spa, right on Main Street.

BROWSE THE GALLERIES

There are a handful of galleries and art studios along Main and Gay Streets. Pop in or window-ogle as you walk around town.

PAIR WINE & CHOCOLATE

All good things come together at **Wine Loves Chocolate** (www.wineloveschocolate.com). For $20 you can do a tasting of three wines with three truffles, or you can just buy lots of truffles or lots of wine. The shop is owned by the **Little Washington Winery** (littlewashingtonwinery .com), which is a few miles down the road (and has no affiliation with the inn).

EXPLORE SHENANDOAH NATIONAL PARK

It's only a 20-minute drive from here to the Thornton Gap entrance station of the park. You could cruise down Skyline Drive before sitting down for a meal in Little Washington. (See Chapter 7 for more.)

COOKING LESSONS

For $1,500, you can spend a full day in the kitchen shadowing and cooking with the inn's culinary team through the "Stagiaire" program.

☰ Good Eats

If you're eating at the inn, you're eating well. But while this is the headliner, it's not the only dining show in town.

TULA'S

www.tulasrestaurantandbar.com • $$ • American

A block from the inn, Tula's has a small menu of salads, seafood, and brunch food. There's a flower-potted patio with outdoor seating.

At this writing, there were also rumors that the folks at the inn were going to open a less-fancy, more accessible dining option.

☰ Time for a Drink

The inn's restaurant has about 14,000 bottles of wine in its cellar, including a big selection of local Virginia wines. If you'd rather drink at the source, there are wineries strung along Highway 522, including the aforementioned Little Washington Winery, as well as **Rappahannock Cellars** (www.rappahannockcellars.com).

Nearby in Sperryville, there are two good options for beer fans: **Hopkins Ordinary** (www.hopkinsordinary.com), which has outdoor seating with a fire pit, and **Pen Druid** (www.pendruid.com), which does some fun experimental stuff.

☰ Stay Over

If you're going to pair this much wine and food, you won't want to drive afterwards. The inn has 11 rooms, plus cottages and houses in town. If the rooms plus decadent meal are too much, there are a few other lodging options in and around town.

WHITE MOOSE INN

whitemooseinn.com • $$$$

A country-Scandinavian style permeates this boutique Main Street inn, with all blonde and white decor and minimalistic but homey touches.

AIRBNB

A handful of cottages and private apartments in town and in the surrounding countryside are the most affordable way to stay out here.

≡ *Plan Around*

Fall through the holidays is peak season. If you are coming on a weekend between September and December, reserve at least a month in advance. Late April and May also get busy. Otherwise, you should be able to book a week or less out (and if you're able to swing a week night there are usually tables).

Big holidays, like Valentine's Day, New Year's, and Christmas, are very popular and book up far in advance. On the flip side, you may be able to snag a deal in January or in the summer.

Weekends to Plan For (or Avoid):

- **Innstock (September):** A Woodstock-inspired food and music fest is open to the public (with tickets).
- **New Year's Eve:** The inn knows how to throw a party; on NYE it's usually a themed one.

GOOD TO KNOW

- Cell phone service is barely existent in town. (Except with Sprint; it's decent with Sprint.) Some of the businesses have WiFi, but you might want to make note of the way home in case your map app doesn't load.

- The inn wasn't always this luxurious. It used to be a gas station and auto garage in a little 200-person town until 1978, when the restaurant opened.

- The town's name comes from George Washington, who surveyed the town when he was 17. He actually gave the town streets: Main, Middle, and Gay—the last one being a tribute to Gay Fairfax, a young woman George had a crush on.

BEEN HERE, DONE THAT?

- A few other dining powerhouses dot the Virginia countryside around DC. Check out the **Restaurant at Pawtomack Farm** (www.patowmackfarm.com) overlooking the Potomac, or **Goodstone Inn** (www.goodstone.com) near Middleburg.

- For a less foodie-centric romantic inn escape, check out the waterfront Inn at Perry Cabin over in St. Michaels (Chapter 5).

28

"Getaway" in a Tiny Cabin

Stanardsville, VA

The antidote to an overworked, overstressed life can be found in a tiny house in the woods.

FROM DC: 101 MILES · 2 HOURS | TRIP LENGTH: OVERNIGHT OR
WEEKEND

DO	EAT	DRINK	BUY
explore the woods	s'mores	hot chocolate	a bottle of wine from Early Mountain

Wanna go camping but don't like the idea of bugs, heat, or sleeping on the ground? Give Getaway a try. The tiny houses set you up around a campground in the woods, except there are big fluffy beds and window walls that let the views in but keep the mosquitos out.

But Getaway is more than a place to sleep in the woods. It's an experience designed to take you out of the go-go-go work brain, and give your body and mind a time out with mother nature.

☰ Getting to Getaway

While it's easiest to get here with a car, you don't need one. Take the train to Charlottesville, and from there it's a half-hour taxi ride (the company recommends using iTaxi 434-327-6622 on weekends).

If you're driving, it's a similar route that you'd take to Charlottesville. Take 66 west out of the city and cut south on 29. Once you get to the Getaway site, follow the trail that's been texted to you to the house name that you've been assigned. You can park right at your cabin.

>> **En Route:** If you're driving down after work on Friday, stop for din in Culpeper on the way—it's about halfway along the route. See Chapter 21.

☰ Get Your Bearings

The Getaway grounds look a bit like your average campground, with cabins spread around wooded driveways.

You won't feel alone in the woods here; step outside your cabin and you can usually see a neighbor or two. But the houses are all strategically placed so that the big window wall *inside* the cabin points out at only woodland, so you won't be peering into someone else's cabin.

☰ Make Your Getaway

Leave alarm clocks, email, and mirrors behind (yup, no mirrors in the Getaway) and lean into a weekend of nurturing nature. A stay at a tiny Getaway cabin is camping lite; you'll get all the sights and sounds of the outdoors . . . but with A/C and a private toilet.

Before Your Trip

You won't readily find the Getaway address online (and we'll keep it that way). Part of this is because the point isn't where you are; it's where you're not: the city.

But of course you do actually have to get here, so about a week before your arrival you'll get an email with the deets, plus a lot of handy info about the nearby area and packing tips.

A day before your arrival, you'll receive the name of your house and the code to get in.

What the Cabins Are Like

The cabins themselves are rustic in a modern way—they look like something you'd pine over on *Tiny House Hunters* on HGTV.

// Inside a Getaway cabin

Inside it's all wood, with a big white bed up against the window wall and a small table in the kitchen. Thoughtful touches, like a mini library of woodsy books and wireless speakers, all tie into the rustic-mod Getaway personality. The cabins accommodate either two people or four—basically the four-person ones have bunked queen beds while the duo just has one.

What to Bring

Your pre-arrival emails will outline a few of the things you need to bring: food (there's a camp-fire cooking grate and stove at each unit), booze (plan ahead, there aren't many nearby liquor stores or gas stations), and any personal items. The houses have everything you'd expect from a hotel room (sheets, toiletries, and a little "mini bar" with some snacks [no drinks though]).

On top of that, pack cozy clothes (something you'd want to snuggle up in bed or at a camp-fire in) and something to entertain yourself with. There's no WiFi or TV here, and cell service can be a bit spotty. Since the goal is to unwind, maybe pause on the Netflix downloads; instead how about a good (paper) book and a deck of cards for you and any travel companions.

>> **More Info:** getaway.house. Price: $$

☰ *While You're Here*

FOREST BATHING

The Getaway folks embrace the Japanese concept of Shinrin-yoku . . . a.k.a. "forest bathing." The goal is to take advantage of the array of nature at your tiny doorstep.

It doesn't really count as a full hike, but if you're car-free, there is a walking trail around the campsite. If you're more mobile, there are tons of great hikes in nearby **Shenandoah National Park**. (See Chapter 7 for ideas.)

HIT UP A VINEYARD

There are at least five vineyards within a 20-minute drive from the Getaway site. **Early Mountain Vineyards** (www.earlymountain.com), about 15 minutes away, has won its share of awards, but it's unpretentious and comfortable, with cozy couches to lounge and sip on. It's also a bit of a one-stop-shop: you can try wines from other local vineyards here.

☰ *Good Eats*

What can you cook? That's going to be your closest meal. The restaurant scene is lacking in the immediate vicinity, and besides, the point of escaping to the woods is peace and solitude, right?

The kitchen has a stove, mini-fridge, and pots and pans, and comes stocked with some cabin mini-bar essentials like granola bars, pasta and sauce, and coffee. (Food costs are extra.)

There are also a few markets in the general vicinity where you can stock up: the **Wolftown Mercantile Country Store**, **Payton Grocery** in Stanardsville, and **Yoder's Country Market** (www.yoderscountrymarket.net), which is part grocery, part gift shop, and part petting zoo.

BLUE ELK COFFEE CO.

Elkton • theblueelk.com • $ • coffee

If you don't want to pay for the house coffee, a good caffeine fix is about a 20-minute drive from the Getaway site. This craft coffee shop sometimes hosts live music, like a bluegrass jam band.

1 Campfire cooking
2 Books in the cabin
3 Hiking in Shenandoah National Park

☰ *Time for a Drink*

If you want to enjoy an adult beverage around the campfire, you're going to have to BYO. Check out some of the above local vineyards and bring a bottle or two back to your nest. The nearby groceries also sell wine and beer.

BALD TOP BREWING CO.

baldtopbrewing.com

Rustic and wood-walled (just like your cabin!), this nano-farm brewery has about eight beers on tap and specializes in creative ales. They stay open 'til around 11 p.m. on weekends and usually have live music and food trucks. It's about 15 minutes away.

☰ *Plan Around*

Weekends are obviously Getaway's most popular times; prices can be a bit more expensive during this time. Seasonally, you can stay here all year, but summer and fall will give you the most outdoor bang for your buck.

Weekends to Plan For (or Avoid):

- **Peak Fall Foliage (Usually October):** Wake up with a front-row seat to nature's colorfest. If you're going to do any hiking in Shenandoah National Park, keep in mind the park gets crowded during prime leaf weekends.
- **Fee-Free Days in Shenandoah:** The park waives its entry fee a few days a year. Usually it's MLK Jr. Day and Veterans Day, plus some others. Check the park calendar for specific dates.

GOOD TO KNOW

- The cabin names have a meaning—they're all nods to Getaway staff and guests' grandparents.
- Don't worry, you can drink the water that comes from the kitchen sink.
- Set the mood: The Getaway team will send you some Spotify playlists designed to help you chill out.
- Dogs are welcome! Just don't leave them alone in the house. Many of the hikes and wineries nearby are also dog-friendly, as long as you don't forget the leash.

BEEN HERE, DONE THAT?

- Up your outdoors game and grab a tent. You can camp in nearby Shenandoah National Park (Chapter 7), along the Blue Ridge Parkway (Chapter 8), or with wild ponies on Assateague (Chapter 6).
- Rather than sleeping among the trees, sleep *in* a tree, when you stay in a treehouse. There are some up in Deep Creek Lake (Chapter 9), or down at Primland off the Blue Ridge Parkway near the North Carolina border. Or just browse Airbnb—you'll find plenty of other unique lodging options.

Part Seven
Seasonal Itineraries

Crappy Weather Weekend Getaway

If the weather has you feeling blah, resist Netflixing all weekend! Bad-weather weekends are a perfect excuse to unwind and disconnect while not feeling like a total waste of space on the couch.

A great place to do this is in the Shenandoah Valley. Sure, rain might put a damper on your hiking ambitions, but there are plenty of cozy and covered things to do here, from caverns to wineries and breweries. At the end of the day, relax at Pembroke Springs Retreat, a romantic Japanese-themed B&B about an hour and a half from DC.

This is a trip that's lovely when the weather's nice but equally enjoyable when outside's all doom and gloom.

☰ Friday

Friday Night

Heading west after work can be painful on a sunny day; throw in some weather and it's a test of even the most patient person's sanity. So don't rush to get out of town—wait until at least 7 or so, when the commuters are off the roads, and make your way out toward Pembroke Springs.

The retreat sometimes hosts dinner—check the schedule to see if your dates line up. But if your stomach's rumbling along the way out here, take a quick detour off I-66, onto John Marshall Highway, which passes through the little hamlets of the Plains and Marshall. For small towns, you'll find a lot of dining options—a good bet is the **Front Porch** (frontporchtheplains .com) in the Plains, which serves dinner 'til 9:30 p.m. In Marshall, **Field & Main** (www.fieldand mainrestaurant.com) is a bit splurgey but has a warm, homey vibe and fantastic cooking done on a wood-burning hearth.

When you get to **Pembroke Springs Retreat** (pembrokesprings.com), slippers and a *yukata* (Japanese bathrobe) await. Check in and select your preferred time to use the *ofuros* (baths) the next evening. The B&B has a lot of authentic Japanese elements, like the *tatami* area in each of the five rooms. It's the perfect space for a little pre-snooze meditation.

☰ Saturday

Saturday Morning

Morning begins with a traditional Japanese breakfast. (It's included in your rate.) Usually this means fish, rice, eggs, fruit, miso soup, and more. Just let the hosts know if you're an early riser or late sleeper; they'll accommodate.

After breakfast, if it's not too gross out, take a relaxing nature walk on the trails around the 145-acre property. Overcast days sometimes bring out the best of the forest. Sometimes you can do a morning bath, but traditionally, that's left for the end of the day.

Saturday Afternoon

Lunch isn't served at the property, so you'll want to venture out at some point. Make your way to Front Royal, a charming little town with a mountain backdrop. On bright fall days, this place gets overrun with leaf peepers lining up for Skyline Drive. Other times can be a bit sleepier.

Settle in at **PaveMint** (www.paveminttaphouse.com) or **Front Royal Brewing Co.** (frontroyalbrewing.com) for lunch. Both spots serve good food and brews, and are the types of place you'd want to sit and hang for awhile.

Next, it's time to find a cave! This is one of the best things to do when the weather sucks; it doesn't matter if it's raining or snowing, the weather's always the same inside a cave. **Luray Caverns** (luraycaverns.com) offer one of the most impressive cave systems the eastern United States. Tours here take about 1 hour and lead you through a massive underground world of stalactites, cave lakes, and ceilings that are ten stories high. Luray's about a half-hour drive from Front Royal; for something closer, **Skyline Caverns** (www.skylinecaverns.com) also runs cave tours (it's one of the only places in the world where you can see feathery anthodites crystals), and it's only five minutes away.

Follow up your underground adventure with a stop at one of the Valley's many wineries or breweries. **North Mountain Vineyard & Winery** (www.northmountainvineyard.com) is a welcoming vineyard with $1 tastings that's known for reds such as Chambourcin and Claret. Beer drinkers should head to **Backroom Brewery** (www.backroombreweryva.com), which is set on a farm and includes homegrown herbs like cilantro and basil in its lineup of brews.

Saturday Night

Icky weather calls for comfort food. Winchester's dining scene delivers just that. Winchester is a historic Shenandoah town with a pedestrian mall lined with local shops and boutique restaurants. (It forms a triangle with Front Royal and Pembroke Springs, so you can choose to head straight here or regroup at the inn first.)

Head to **Sweet NOLA's** (www.sweetnolas.com) for generous helpings of Cajun and Creole eats, like chicken and sausage gumbo and po'boys, spiced up by their special Gypsy Sauce. For dessert, four words: Krispy Kreme Bread Pudding.

Retreat back to the B&B for your nightcap: a soak in the authentic Japanese baths. The tradition is intended to release stress and ease muscle pain. The water comes from a local spring and is heated to a wonderful 104 degrees, the perfect temp to lull you into bedtime.

≡ Sunday

Sunday Morning

Take advantage of another delicious breakfast, then just take it easy. You can hang out with the B&B's dog or schedule a massage to squeeze some final R&R into your stay here.

Sunday Afternoon

The route back to DC takes you past one of the region's preeminent vineyards. The price to visit **RdV Vineyards** (www.rdvvineyards.com) is steep: $65 for a tasting and 90-minute tour (and you need to make an appointment). But the vineyard's spectacular, and the wines rival those in California. So if you're out this way, wine not?

If you want the wine tasting without the price tag, detour a little farther north to **Middleburg** (more on that in Chapter 15).

≡ Getting Around

You'll need a car to make this weekend happen.

≡ Lodging Tip

Weekends are a package deal at Pembroke Springs Retreat. You have to book Friday and Saturday nights. If the price ($450ish for two people over two nights) is too steep, there are plenty of places to stay in Winchester and the Shenandoah Valley at all price points.

Winter Weekend Getaway

There are plenty of ways to get out for a big winter adventure near DC. You can ski or snowboard at Snowshoe, Seven Springs, or Wisp (Chapter 9). You can see holiday light boat parades in Solomons Island and Annapolis (Chapter 1). Or you can take your Caps fandom on the road and rock the red in Pittsburgh.

This is not that type of weekend. This itinerary is for those weekends when it's kinda cold, kinda gloomy, and you're feeling a little stir-crazy.

The best antidote for that isn't a big to-do. It's a casual mini-adventure, one that takes in some great local beer, cool art and culture, and a chance to escape the winter woes and warm up in a giant indoor garden. (That's right, a garden visit. In winter.)

This trip takes in all of the above in some of Pennsylvania's burgeoning beer and arts towns: Lancaster, Harrisburg, plus Longwood Gardens.

☰ *Friday*

Friday Night

Honestly, you might want to save the money and skip a Friday night stay. Just drive straight up to Harrisburg on Saturday instead. But if you do make the trip on Friday, head to Lancaster and time your visit for First Fridays on Gallery Row. The town has a huge artistic community, and they all come out to show their stuff at this monthly event—even if it's chilly out.

Next, get your first (but far from last) taste of the local beer scene. **Lancaster Brewing Co.** (www.lancasterbrewing.com) is known for their milk stout, the perfect complement to a winter evening.

☰ *Saturday*

Saturday Morning

If you're up and at 'em in Lancaster, start your day with a coffee at **Passenger Coffee Roasting** (www.passengercoffee.com), a trendy spot right downtown. The minimalist cafe has a selection of teas and pastries, too. If you like what you drink, they run a coffee-by-mail subscription service.

With a warm drink in your belly, hit up a few of downtown's main stops, including **Lancaster Central Market** (centralmarketlancaster.com), which brings over 60 stalls of farm food, crafts, and the area's Amish culture together in a big hall. The market dates back to 1730 — it's one of the oldest farmers' markets in the country—but it closes at 2 p.m. on Saturdays (and isn't open Sunday), so get here early.

Saturday Afternoon & Evening

After perusing the stalls at the market, hit the road for Harrisburg. If Lancaster is the area's arts capital, then Harrisburg gets the beer capital nod. (And the state capital. That too.) At this writing, there were six breweries downtown, largely clustered in Midtown, and more than triple that in the surrounding area.

Tip: If you have a sweet tooth you can peel off en route to **Hershey**. (Yes, the one of chocolate bar fame.) But there's a lot to do there, so a detour could suck up the whole day. If you plan to drink a lot of beer, consider taking the train between Lancaster and Harrisburg, although the last one leaves Harrisburg around 7 p.m.

Start at **Zeroday** (www.zerodaybrewing.com), which is known for its ales and lagers. It's arguably the best brewery in town, and also has strong ties to the local art scene. For something different, try **The Vegetable Hunter** (thevegetablehunter.com), a boutique brewery that doubles as a vegan restaurant. Or post up at **JB Lovedraft's Micropub**, where there are over 40 beers on tap and vintage video game consoles at each table. You can play MarioKart, sip awesome beer, and down a pretty spectacular burger while you're at it.

Actually, most Harrisburg breweries have food, and vice versa, many of the restaurants here have good beer. For dinner, hit up **Sturges Speakeasy** (sturgesspeakeasy.com) for upscale pub fare plus 16 beers on tap. **Millworks** (millworksharrisburg.com) is another good option—the space is all-craft everything; food, beer, art.

Saturday Night

At some point, when you've had your fill of Harrisburg bars, bundle up and hustle out to the car to make your way back to Lancaster. If you have any energy left, you can keep the brewcrawl going and hop over to **Wacker Brewing Co.** (wackerbrewing.com). This place is a Lancaster institution; it originally opened in 1853. It closed for a stretch, but has recently been reopened and now shares an artsy space with local liquor purveyor **Thistle Finch Distillery** (www.thistlefinch.com).

☰ *Sunday*

Sunday Morning

Brunch it at **On Orange** (onorange.wordpress.com), which serves international spins on breakfast, like Swedish pancakes and Indian omelets, in a space that resembles an art studio. Then hit the road about an hour east, to Longwood Gardens.

Sunday Afternoon

Longwood Gardens (longwoodgardens.org) is one of the biggest-deal gardens in the United States. Founded by Pierre S. du Pont (not the same guy as the Dupont Circle namesake, but same family), who bought the land to protect trees from being chopped down, the gardens now draw over 1 million visitors every year.

This isn't just a "stroll through some hedges and rows of flowers" sort of garden. It's a horticultural masterpiece, with heated greenhouses, 20 indoor spaces, and a massive glass conservatory with fountains and 4,600 types of plants. The gardens are open all year, so even if it's frigid out, you can hang indoors and pretend it's summer.

Around Christmas, this place puts on one of the biggest and best holiday displays you'll ever see. Half a million lights and decorations for days draw enormous crowds and are worth a pilgrimage. Even if you're here after the tinsel comes down, this is a "plan ahead" kind of place—you'll want to book a timed ticket before you arrive (and they do sell out).

At some point you're going to have to say bye to the warm, colorful plant world and head back to DC. The drive home takes about 2 hours.

☰ Getting Around

A car's going to be your best bet to do this full weekend, especially if Longwood Gardens sounds up your alley. There aren't any easy public transit options connecting all these dots.

Now you *could* take a Greyhound bus between DC and Harrisburg to check out the beer and art scene there. You could also then train over to Lancaster to either stay there or poke around before heading back to Harrisburg. But overall, try to do this one by car.

☰ Lodging Tips

In keeping with its culture of coolness, Lancaster is home to some artsy boutique hotels. The funky **Lancaster Arts Hotel** (www.lancasterartshotel.com) is covered in art from PA artists in every room. For slightly less per night, you can stay in a converted cork and glass factory, now **The Cork Factory Hotel** (www.corkfactoryhotel.com). The whole space is totally rustic industrial, with exposed brick walls and a cozy lobby fireplace.

Both hotels are easy walks (even in the cold) from restaurants, breweries, and galleries.

Spring Weekend Getaway

There's nothing like that first spring weekend, when you dare go outside without a coat. And while everyone seems to be coming *into* DC this time of year, whether it's cherry blossom watchers or middle schoolers on spring break, this can also be a great time to get OUT of town.

For example, spring means big things for the Eastern Shore. It's not only the mark of shifting weather, with warmer, longer, more boatable days. This is also the change in seafood seasons, with oyster season coming to a close at the end of March, and blue crab season kicking off with April.

So if you're looking to shake off the winter cobwebs and head out of town for a little spring break, make your way to the Bay.

 Friday

Friday Night

Take off for the Eastern Shore after work. The nice thing about heading out this way before prime beach season is that the Bay Bridge may be a little less crowded.

As noted throughout this guide, Kent Island, the first solid land you'll hit after the bridge's main expanse, and nearby Kent Narrows are great places to stop for a bite on your way to this side of the bay.

Keep going all the way to St. Michaels. By the time you get in, there may not be a ton going on, but you can grab a nightcap at **Carpenter Street Saloon** or **Blackthorn Irish Pub**, both of which stay open 'til around 2 a.m.

Saturday

Saturday Morning

Start your day with a coffee at the **Blue Crab Coffee**, a bright lounge-y spot that has a good selection of pastries and breakfast food.

From here, follow Railroad Avenue *away* from the town's main drag. After about a third of a mile, you'll come to the start of the **St. Michaels Nature Trail**, a quiet walking path that runs along the backside of town. You'll pass some parks and waterways, plus a covered bridge. Walk for a mile and you'll be at the other end of town, where the trail intersects Talbot Street.

Legs warmed up, make your way back into the heart of downtown along Talbot Street, which is lined with mom-and-pop shops that range from quirky sea glass art (**Ophiuroidea** is known for this) to shore-style preppy clothing and home decor.

Saturday Afternoon

Grab lunch in town once you've window-shopped your way down Talbot Street. The waterside **Crab Claw** opens for the season in March, and is one of the best places in the region to crack into blue crabs. Or try **Ava's**, the popular pizza joint that crowds up quickly.

Nothing says "see ya winter" like getting out on a cruise around the river or bay. Many of the local boat tour operators start running again around April (see Chapter 5 for boat options). You'll still want some warm clothes early in the season (it gets windy out there), or if you freeze easily, the *Patriot* boat has indoor seating.

Once you're back on solid land, it's time to check out the local drinks "scene." The three local craft beverage companies in St. Michaels check all the boxes: You can taste wine at **St. Michaels Winery**, local beer at **Eastern Shore Brewing Co.**, and homegrown spirits, like rum and gin, at **Lyon Distilling Co.** All three spots are essentially on the same lot, so it's easy to make a micro-tasting tour without going very far. (If you're going to sit and hang out for an extended period, the brewery's your best bet for that.)

Saturday Evening

There's nothing like those start-of-warm-weather-season evenings where you can sit outside and enjoy the fact that you're not wearing seven layers. The place to do this in St. Michaels is at the town's landmark, **Inn at Perry Cabin**, which has a fleet of Adirondack chairs set up on the lawn overlooking the water. (The hotel also has a fleet of ships that returns with fanfare every spring.)

You can bring a drink from the hotel's bar and watch the sky soften as the sun goes down.

For dinner, head back into town and take your pick of some of the foodie faves that line Talbot Street. **Limoncello** stands out with its fresh Italian dishes and impressive wine list—plus it rocks a springtime shade of yellow that's like an instant sunshine kick. For a romantic, more upscale meal, **208 Talbot** serves fine meat and seafood dishes in a cozy historic home.

After dinner, you can return to the above-mentioned pubs, or if it's really nice out, check out **Foxy's Harbor Grille** (www.foxysharborgrille.com), a Caribbean-inspired boater bar with a handful of outdoor tables overlooking the docks.

≡ *Sunday*

Sunday Morning

Today's about taking the slow road back to DC. On your way out of town, stop at the **Rise Up Coffee** trailer on the outskirts of St. Michaels. This is the original location of what's become a beloved and rapidly growing Eastern Shore coffee chain. (You'll see a lot of local restaurants pouring Rise Up, but why not go right to the source.)

From here, it's about an hour-long drive back over the Bay Bridge into Annapolis, St. Michaels' counterpart in the nautical club.

Sunday Afternoon

Extend your getaway with a lovely afternoon in Annapolis. To start, brunch it up at **Iron Rooster**, which serves decadent gourmet all-day breakfasts. From here, take a stroll down to Ego Alley, which is essentially a harbor runway that captains strut (er, expertly steer) their ships through.

Hang out around **City Dock** and watch the boats. There are a handful of bars nearby, or you can shop-hop up Main Street, which will eventually drop you right in front of the impressive Maryland State House and its massive dome.

≡ *Getting Around*

A car's your best bet for this, since it's not even all that easy to get between DC and Annapolis via public transit, let alone St. Michaels.

Another option would be to stay in Annapolis and take a boat over to St. Michaels for the day. This is a good way to get a lot of water time in, but it's expensive (around $80) and doesn't leave you all that much time to hang out in the little town.

≡ *Lodging Tips*

For this weekend trip, it's best to stay in the town of St. Michaels. You can find hotel ideas in Chapter 5. If budget is a concern, consider also the town of Easton, which is about 15 minutes east of St. Michaels. Since Easton's a bigger town, you'll find hotels from many of the major chains.

Summer Weekend Getaway

Let's be honest, all of the ideas in this book really peak come summer. Days are long for hiking, lawns are green for vineyard picnics. Lakes and rivers are perfectly cool and swimmable, and small towns roll out the "come walk down Main Street" welcome mat.

But if you had to choose the greatest summer escape from DC, the answer, hands down, is the beach. (Or "the Shore," but that's up in Jersey. We're talking about the seemingly endless sandy coastline of Delmarva.)

The beach is the perfect response to sluggish over-90-degree days. You've got boardwalks full of ice cream shops, and a giant natural swimming pool (a.k.a. the ocean). It's where you catch up on your tan. Dance to the song of the summer. Read something that doesn't have to do with work or school. Eat all the crabs.

In short, the beach is DC's summer playground, and you'll find a hub town for every personality, from Dewey's party crowd to Fenwick's wide open sand to Bethany's cutesy boardwalk bandstand.

This guide covers a lot of beach escapes in the Beach & Bay section, but for this getaway we're turning to a place we haven't yet covered: Ocean City, Maryland.

Follow this itinerary and you can have your (crab)cake and eat it too. You'll get the food and drink options of the biggest beach city in the area, coupled with unspoiled natural beaches where you won't have to fight for a place to put your towel.

Friday

Friday Night

The only downside of a beach weekend is that seemingly everyone else in town is heading out there for the weekend, too. Either leave really early, leave really late, or load up on podcasts and patience and prepare to wait in traffic.

As you near Ocean City, you'll start to see the beach sprawl. To many people, OC is the OG of Washington-area beaches. It's the most built up, with high-rise buildings and a 2.5-mile boardwalk that has spawned beach classics like **Fisher's Popcorn** and **Thrasher's French Fries**.

Millions of people come here every summer, which has ramped up the dining and night-life scene. Doesn't matter what time you get in on Friday night, you'll find somewhere that's bumping, from dance bars to the nearby 24-hour casino.

Saturday

Saturday Morning

Today's all about beach time, but rather than rolling out onto the crowded Ocean City sand, you can drive about 15 minutes and find yourself on pristine, undeveloped beach.

First, though: food. There are plenty of coffee shops and cafes where you can grab and go. **Uber Bagels** (www.uberbagels.com) puts crab on a bagel (because why not). **Talbot St. Cafe** serves great coffee drinks and smoothies, plus bagels and breakfast sandwiches. **The Fractured Prune** (fracturedprune.com) plays a big donut game, with over 30 different flavored glazes and toppings.

Saturday Afternoon

Now for some sun. Just south of Ocean City is Assateague Island, a long barrier island that is known for two things: beautiful white sand beaches and wild ponies (more on them in Chapter 6).

This part of the island is split between a state park and a national park (well, technically, a national seashore, but it's run by the National Park Service). They're right next to each other, and since the ponies here are wild and don't care what park they're in, you've got a good chance to see them roaming in either place.

So which do you visit? Well, it depends what you're looking for. If you want to be close to a concession stand and bigger bathroom facilities, the state park is a better bet. It's also a little cheaper, depending on the size of your group ($6 per person).

The national park, on the other hand, has a lot more space to work with and is more natural. This means there are usually fewer people per square foot on the beach, but also makeshift bathrooms and no food for sale. It costs $20 per vehicle.

Whichever place you pick to set up your beach chairs, bring lots of water, sunscreen, and bug spray with DEET. The flies here can get very bite-y as the summer goes on.

Saturday Night

When you've hit max sun for the day, head back to Ocean City and prepare for reentry into tourist central.

If you didn't make it to the boardwalk last night, you've gotta pay it a visit now. Built in 1902, the OC boardwalk is the type of place where you can see bachelorette groups in matching T-shirts in the same space as you see little kids with ice cream all over their face. There are amusement park rides, T-shirt shops with ridiculous slogans, and a 100-foot-tall Ferris wheel— you can actually see Assateague from the top.

Grab a bite on the boards—**Wrapper's** (whatsinsideyourpretzel.com) creatively stuffed pretzels are popular because they're easy to walk with. Or, it being summer in Maryland, dig into some blue crabs at one of the many seafood houses here: **The Crab Bag** (thecrabbag.com) and **Phillips Seafood & Crab House** (www.phillipsseafood.com) are faves.

After dinner, it's time for the Ocean City party trifecta: Seacrets, Mackey's, and Fagers. All are on the bay side, not the boardwalk, and by nighttime they all have cover charges, so you'll probably just want to choose one or get here before 5 or 6 p.m. to avoid paying.

Seacrets (seacrets.com) is an Ocean City rite of passage: a wild Jamaican-themed beach bar, with sandy dance floors, frozen drinks, and multiple stages for live music and DJs. It's a hotspot during the day too; the bar actually extends into the water, so you can drink a "Pain in de Ass" frozen cocktail on floaties.

About ten minutes up the road, **Macky's** (mackys.com) is another sandy-floored beach bar that turns into a sweaty dance party around 10 p.m. or so. The daily drink specials go 'til 2 a.m.

Another 10 minutes north, **Fager's Island** (www.fagers.com) does double-duty as a fancy, fine-dining restaurant with a sunset tradition. They play the "1812 Overture" every night as the sun disappears. Then it morphs into a DJ-fueled nightclub (with a dress code) after hours.

☰ *Sunday*

Sunday Morning

If recovery is in order, **Barn 34** (www.barn34oc.com) serves creative and hearty breakfast combos like Captain Crunch French Toast and the Hangover. It's set in a barn-like building, which feels a little confusing at the beach, but the space is cool, so go with it. If that UV index is calling your name, orders come out quickly at **General's Kitchen** (generalskitchenoc.com), an Ocean City classic.

After breakfast you can head back to the beach (just stick to the sand in Ocean City today).

Sunday Afternoon

On your way out of town, make a detour into little Berlin, about 15 minutes west of the beach. This little town has been called one of the coolest in the country. Pop into **Blacksmith** (blacksmithberlin.com) for lunch, or just take a stroll around the fit-for-a-movie-set main streets. (See Chapter 20 for more.)

☰ *Getting Around*

If you're car-free, you can make it to Ocean City via bus, but the Assateague leg of this trip won't be easy. Most people do the whole thing via car. Once you're in OC though, you don't have to drive. There are plenty of cabs, and the city's bus system covers a lot of ground; an all-day bus pass will set you back $3.

☰ *Lodging Tips*

There are thousands of hotel rooms in Ocean City. Most of the major hotel chains have a presence here, plus a slew of local options. High-rise oceanfront condos are clustered from north of 84th street all the way up to the Delaware border, but you'll find rental properties of all sizes around the city.

Fall Weekend Getaway

There's no "best" season in the Washington area—each one has its own . . . wait. Who are we kidding. Fall is the best time of year around DC.

Although its arrival date is a moving target, fall kicks out those muggy summer days of thunderstorms and mobs of mosquitos. It's harvest season, and if you haven't noticed from all the farm-to-table dining in this book, Washington's essentially surrounded by a massive ring of farmland. There's apple picking, pumpkin patches, oyster feasts, wine harvests, and beer fests. The trees suit up, putting on their seasonal finest.

The obvious fall escape is a leaf-peeping road trip down Skyline Drive. It's one of those bucket-list Washington must-dos, but the problem is, everyone wants to do it, which means crowds and traffic and prices flare up when the trees turn. (That's not to say you shouldn't make the trip; just do it smart—see Chapter 7 for tips.)

So instead, for this fall weekend getaway, we're taking the side roads to discover the lesser-known local faves that sit against that kaleidoscopic backdrop of the Blue Ridge Mountains.

Friday

Friday Night

Make your way down to the Charlottesville area after work. If you're able to sneak away a bit early, try get to **Carter Mountain Orchard** (chilesfamilyorchards.com) for some apple cider donuts, pickable orchards, and a sunset view over the color-changing mountains. The hilltop spot closes at 7 p.m. though, and you have to get there earlier than that to pick fruit.

Do dinner in Belmont, a little farther away from the UVA crowds (alternatively, you can go to the Corner and colllleeggggge). **The Local** (www.thelocal-cville.com) serves, yup, *local* ingredients from nearby farms in their seasonal pastas, burgers, and apps. A block away, **Mas Tapas** (www.mastapas.com) is a favorite for small Spanish plates.

Saturday

Saturday Morning

Hit the road early. (If you're staying in C'ville, stop at Bodo's for bagels).

It's a short drive on the Blue Ridge Parkway (Skyline Drive's southern sister road) to **Humpback Rocks**, one of the top hikes in this area. Even though there's a large parking lot at the trailhead, it can fill up on nice fall days (hence the early start).

This hike is an autumnal all-star because once you get to the rocky top of the trail, you're rewarded with colorful views to the west out over the Shenandoah Valley and other peaks. You can do the hike as an up-and-back for about 2.5 miles total (get ready for a steep climb), or do it as a 3.6-mile loop and add in some Appalachian Trail time.

Saturday Afternoon & Evening

The rest of the day is all about taking the slow road. Exit the Blue Ridge Parkway at Waynesboro and head east a short way to pick up Highway 151 south. Commonly called the **Nelson 151** (nelson151.com), this farm-country tasting route connects about three breweries, six wineries, two cideries, and a distillery, plus some farms along the way.

The drive runs along the base of the Blue Ridge, so rather than jostling for space at a Parkway viewpoint, you'll get the ground-level view up at the mountains most of the way.

A good starting point along the Nelson 151 is **Blue Mountain Brewery** (www.bluemountain brewery.com). The large, dog-friendly brewpub has a substantial menu (refuel after that hike), and an outdoor patio with mountain views. Other highlights along the drive include **Afton Mountain Vineyards** (www.aftonmountainvineyards.com) and **Veritas Vineyard & Winery** (www.veritaswines.com) on the north end of the route, and **Bold Rock Hard Cider** (boldrock .com) and **Devils Backbone Brewing Company** (dbbrewingcompany.com/locations/basecamp) on the southern end. None of these places are particularly dressy, but you may want to change out of your hiking gear for the vineyards.

Saturday Night

Crisp fall nights equal campfire weather, and **Devils Backbone Basecamp Brewpub**, at the end of the Nelson 151, has just that. While everything here revolves around the beer (recognize the all-over-DC DB Vienna Lager), this place is more than a brewery. Called "basecamp," it's more like a 100-acre outdoor activities compound, with multiple bars, a large outdoor fire pit, a lodge, and a full menu of soups, salads, BBQ, and shareables.

You can even camp here, or make your way back to wherever you stayed last night (carefully; these roads get dark).

≡ *Sunday*

Sunday Morning

Lazily make your way to the tiny town of Crozet (pronounced kroh-ZAY), about 25 minutes west of Charlottesville. Quaint and neighborhoody **Green House Coffee** (www.greenhouse crozet.com) has good breakfasts, or if you're on the later side of the morning, wait for **Crozet Pizza** (www.crozetpizza.com) to open and eat there. While not everyone agrees with *National Geographic*'s claim that it's the "best pizza in the world," the family-run institution gets rave reviews across the board.

Sunday Afternoon

If it's early fall, head over to **King Family Vineyards** (www.kingfamilyvineyards.com), a gorgeous barn-style winery near Crozet. Every Sunday through mid-October, King Family hosts popular polo matches. Tons of people come out with tailgates and picnics. The weekly matches start at 1 p.m. and are free. (Although if you want a good tailgate spot, get here closer to 10 a.m.)

For a last-ditch fall fun activity, swing through Montpelier (home of James Madison, btw; see Chapter 22) on your way home. A few minutes away is **Liberty Mills Farm** (www.liberty millsfarm.com), which is known for their epic corn mazes every year. (They claim to be the largest corn maze east of the Mississippi.) There's also a farm market and fruit and pumpkin-picking, so you can bring a little bit of the countryside back to the city with you.

Getting Around

Since this trip goes well beyond the Uber-able zones of Charlottesville, you'll need a car to see everything. You can hail a ride from C'ville to some of the nearer places on the route, but finding someone to bring you back could be a bit of a challenge.

Lodging Tips

Many of the stops along the Nelson 151 actually have cottages, so you can do a winery or brewery stay. This time of year, farm stays are also particularly gorgeous. You can find some on Airbnb, but a solid option is **Stay Charlottesville** (www.staycharlottesville.com), a local rental management group. Check out the "Cottages and Retreats" section on their site for stays of all sizes, from couples' cottages to beautiful country homes for groups of eight.

Acknowledgments

Writing a book can be a solitary thing . . . this project was anything but. An enormous shout out goes to all my friends, family, and colleagues who shared ideas, read chapters, gave feedback, and joined me on research trips. You're all the best, and your help and enthusiasm kept me inspired throughout this project.

Thank you, too, to the team at The Countryman Press and W. W. Norton & Company, especially my wonderful editor Róisín, for bringing this book to life.

There are three people without whom this book would not have happened: Mom, Dad, and Torrey. Thank you all for your tireless help with research, driving, photo-stopping, crab picking, coffee tasting, history chasing, fact checking, and so much else. Most importantly, a million thank yous for your unwavering support.

Finally, thank you to all the passionate people who protect, preserve, and promote the parks, bays, beaches, and natural landscapes around DC. Every trip I took left me in awe of the incredible scenery we have in our backyard, and I have immense gratitude for those who are working to try keep these places around to enjoy in future years.

Index

Page numbers in *italics* refer to photographs.